FAST LANE
IN A 97 STREET... POOL HALL

Scars...scabs...and all

Sex, drugs and Rock n' Roll...Lies, lies, lies

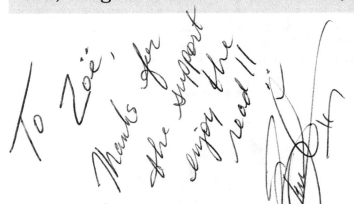

PAUL BLACKBURN

Copyright © 2023 by Paul Blackburn

Paperback: 978-1-961438-85-9
Hardcover: 978-1-961438-87-3
eBook: 978-1-961438-86-6
Library of Congress Control Number: 2023917300

All rights reserved. No part of this publication may be reproduced, distributed, or transmitted in any form or by any electronic or mechanical means, without the prior written permission of the publisher, except in the case of brief quotations embodied in critical reviews and certain other noncommercial uses permitted by copyright law.

This Book is a work of fiction. Names, characters, places, and incidents either are the product of the author's imagination or are used fictitiously. Any resemblance to actual persons, living or dead, events, or locales is entirely coincidental.

Ordering Information:

Prime Seven Media
518 Landmann St.
Tomah City, WI 54660

Printed in the United States of America

Table of Contents

Dedication 1

Introduction... 3

FORWARD...by Klay (the DJ) Tate....................................11

Check...check... check this out...17

Challenge...quarter on the table 31

Rack em up 68

Break...81

The game (eight ball or snooker) 86

Table 22 / Scratch ball 88

Call Shot (one & done)..107

My Music Scene….. 126

List of deaths in rock and roll (1980s) 152

Dirty Deeds Done Dirt Cheap… 168

Scars…scabs…and all 259

Word up… 281

Dedication

For those about to…

Rock, to those who have walked the walk and talked the talk To all of those who gave your heart, mind and soul for all The North side partiers, dreamers and schemers on the loose Whom endured the hardships and never found their way back To those from the Rosslyn in the past, present and future of days and Have lost their battle or still battling addictions and are trying to Find that path to recovery. Fast Lane in a 97th Pool Hall is dedicated to all…

Family, friends & acquaintances

…I salute you,
Your Author & Friend Paul (Blackie) Blackburn

Introduction...

Fast Lane in a 97St Pool Hall…it's been in the making for over forty years actually, I knew one day I would get to writing this book and bring it to fruition, from the time I was that young teenage drug dealer I knew then that would always be the title, just had to get it down on paper and start doing it, you know how delays and procrastination work? Even once you start then there are further delays and other things like life get in the way of what you really like to do. The big halt in progress came on July 12, 2022 coming home from Ft. McMurray I was travelling southbound and just after Boyle, AB I hit a moose on the hi-way, well talk about messing me up, very blessed to be alive, I was driving my sons Audi A4 and once I hit the moose, she flew up and came through the windshield and joined me in the passenger seat, oh, and in her flailing head butted me on the right side of my face before stomping away out of the vehicle, the person that drove up behind me thought I was dead. Believe me I felt like I was too, I was delayed in starting my new job at NWR in Red water AB only by a week, until I could see out of my right eye, I worked fine for two months, then started having stroke like conditions; the inability to perform regular things like walk, write and drive.

I was trying to go to work on the third night of experiencing all of these newly brought on functions, I couldn't get my seat belt on and going to the grocery store my oldest son Calum was asking "Dad are you are having a stroke?" I said "I don't know" upon going to the hospital for observation I ended up needing surgery for a slow brain bleed brought on by the moose two months earlier, the blood was pooling on the left side of the brain shutting down my abilities to do anything with my right side of the body.

There's an old adage that says "Before you judge someone, walk a mile in their moccasin's (boots, shoes or sandals) "there is also a scripture verse in the bible ((John 8) that says something like "whosoever is without sin, let them cast the first stone" Is it in our nature to judge, or to be quick with a negative splash toward somebody? When you say it and speak it into existence, it's like a bitter weed open in the airways, a negative hurtful, harmful or demeaning spite to make one look what, Powerful or better than thou? In my life there's been heartache and pain, just like many others before me and many of those yet to experience it, eventually they too will get their heart broke it's inevitable, whether it's grieving the loss of somebody close to you, a pet or someone that's crushed your heart when you were head over heels for.

Throughout my life's trials and tribulations I have had some terrible times along with the having the best of times, I encourage those who have journeyed the same path or even had it worse than me, and for those that are stuck spinning their tires feeling like you're never going to get unstuck or overcome a certain situation or lifestyle, brighter days lay ahead I can assure you, if you remain positive and begin deleting and purge the negative from your life, you will be victorious!!

The lone shoe on a roadway has always intrigued me as odd and strange, but maybe it's a blessing for the one's that threw it out, out with the old in with the new mentality, there are many thoughts you can think of, just like a picture is worth a thousand words, each time I see an empty sole it's a reminder that a soul owner wore those shoes and made a journey such as it was we don't know nor can we understand it, maybe just maybe say a kind word or a blessing upon the used sole owner. As I embark on my journey full of life's storms and I share within the pages of Fast Lane, it's not to brag or show how much of a god I became (or thought I became) it's a life of ups and downs, struggles and struggles sometimes empty and sometimes full. Whichever the case I'm not trying to sugar coat or glamorize anything, it's in black and white with descriptive verbiage, I bring it out and forward to you the reader and without many glitches in the matrix.

There may have been many stories or even side stories depending on whose telling it, just like how you'd remember something that stood out to you and the same people that make up that memory could have a completely different way of telling the tale, my hope and desire is not to make anyone out to be a bad person nor do I have intent to hurt anybody alive or dead, I'm just simply telling some memories of a life that started out not so good but I have hung on to a life worth living, being in the fast lane is not just being in a pool hall, for many others it could be whatever your fast lane of life is, the go, go, go life style with many different facets in life; job, friendships, relationships, addictions etc., being in synchronicity with something so much you live love and breathe it fully, you can set your watch to it, then one day for whatever reason(s) it's gone, vanished into thin air, your crash test dummy vehicle hit the wall and that thing, those things you wasted so much time on, wasn't important to you at all. The very things that consumed your entire being and soul for, the rainbow you chased for the pot of gold doesn't exist anymore, you wake up and suddenly and that bottle has dried up, those so-called friendships or relationships are over.

Relationships wouldn't last long and the one I was with for four years would end up cheating on me, maybe life was too routine and boring, or I was committed and faithful, I don't know, some like the Hollywood drama…had I known, lol. So she made these entire prenuptial verbal contracts that I had to agree to because she also had a young girl, so I agreed and moved in with her, I'm not going to write to much about it, obviously wasn't meant to be, it certainly re-opened the door to my party lifestyle once again, I was the host DJ at People's Pub on Whyte Ave, and soon after Klay would return to Edmonton, he had a gig going on at Fantasy Night club and called me up to come join him and check it out, People's Pub was soon to expire because an American firm bought the Redford Inn which People's Pub was a part of and they were going to flatten that hotel and build a new one. Klay and I would embark on a new venture called Uncle Charlie's it was for a short duration then the renovations would take place, during this time Klay would leave until we came up with a contract to return as the K & B (Klay & Blackie) road show, we may have not pioneered DJing (yeah we did) but we certainly pioneered the duet

DJ team, keeping the room active (6hours of sweat) from the drop of the needle until the last few slow dances of the night.

Stoking the flame was easy when we were gods, we'd give it our all on the weekends and we'd entertain some of the locals and party goers by showing love and making appearances at house parties or early morning breakfasts, K & B were standing on top of the world, bringing our insanity to Mexico was on another level, the party at a local bar Senor Frogs was crazy and this was the start of our week being here this was in 1992 so still no cell phones, by Tuesday we went on a $20 booze cruise 3 hours of drinking on the water, after landing I poured Klay back into the hotel room and went out with two babes (one from Chicago and the other from Texas) we would go to every night club around but nothing was happening, I passed out around 4am only to awakened to go on a catamaran from 9am-3pm ohh my goodness was I green and a boat ride was making it nauseous, coffee was not working so back to drinking it was, and back to drinking it was for this entire trip.

Upon returning from Mexico, it was really strange in how our friends, party goers, and everyone in the industry had what seemed like a deeper respect or appreciation for us, everywhere we went Cocaine was being offered up freely like; would you like some gum? Here have some blow, no, no I insist c'mon have some, everyone got an overabundance bonus on blow and just sitting on coffee tables like an open candy dish, an afterhours club had it on the little stand up counter like Wile Coyote setting up bird seed for the Road Runner, the flood gates were open and the land of milk and honey added a new party flavor and I was indulging left, right and center, I was all in.

"... Loose wires cause fires
Getting tangled in my desires.
So, screw 'em off and plug 'em in
Then switch it on and start all over again" (lyrics from AC/DC 'Let's Get It Up')

Trying to settle in and adjust to this new lifestyle was something to behold, without even trying to pick up a girl was so easy, you could have five a night easily, for some they wanted to be served the DJ special (not on the menu) banged from behind while spinning head to the other guy of course in the lovely backdrop of the kitchen, hard to imagine the life of rock stars, we were just merely playing their music in an entertaining fashion, I haven't really witnessed an act quite like ours, sure it was ad lib most nights it all depended on the response of the crowd on any given night, we would pack them into that little pub on 34Ave, doing many wrong things that bars were not allowed to do and not looking back to see the path of destruction it has caused, from; Mazola oil on a sheet a plastic covering the dance floor at 2am, beach parties in the dead of winter with a foot of sand throughout the bar and the bachelor auction with fireman and yours truly, who could not forget DJ Klay atop of the booth in a shady Grady rock star hat and red Speedos singing his heart out.

Sadly, like all good things, they come to an end, management wasn't happy, their happiness is based on numbers and most customers wouldn't travel that far south (34Ave) to drink and party, had they made this pub closer to Whyte Ave or downtown they certainly wouldn't have closed down.

The Snow Globe Effect:

A snow globe is an ornament or knick knack that is or was normally shaped like a clear half globe and houses different designs of whatever your favorite objects are like; animals, photos, characters or just about anything now, an isolated little world of a cabin decorated at Christmas time that could also play music and as you give it a gentle shake, it would look as though it was snowing inside the little sphere, mainly a keepsake or collectible piece usually given as a gift for those who would collect them. During one's lifetime within your world (of family and friends) you may find yourself on occasion where you feel like you're inside of your own snow globe, where a situation whether good or bad is being played out, it can be pleasant or a violent experience where i have endured a few different ones, I've made reference to the snow globe effect during some of my stories within these pages, a few times throughout my life they were very pleasant and sometimes you felt like you could reside their and not go back to reality, let's face it...reality sucks most of the time, and those times in a snow globe, it's still reality but separate from normal one that we are trapped in everyday, almost like an alternate route or path along your lifeline.

FORWARD...
by Klay (the DJ) Tate

Ode to Blackie

*I*t was a night like many others, the music was pumpin' and the air was filled with youthful excitement, cigarette smoke and poor life choices. I was 19 years old and the DJ at Club Limelight in downtown Edmonton, AB. But there was something different about this night. This was the night that a tall dude with super long hair stopped by the DJ booth to request a song (probably something by Pat Travers). Not only did I not know who this dude was, I did not know who Pat Travers was either.

"The Dude" introduced himself as Paul, and over the next few weeks, Paul became a regular at club Limelight, and always stopped by the booth for a visit. Eventually I learned his last name was 'Blackburn,' and from that moment on I only called him "Blackie." Blackie was, in one word...cool. He did not say a lot, but he did talk it was either a funny comment about something or someone in the club, or he was laying a little rock education on me. He knew a lot about classic rock, way more than I did. He had a passion for music like no one I had ever met or have met since, and he had a good sense of humor...so it was inevitable that we'd become fast friends.

We spent many a night after work with a mutual group of friends, just hanging out, cracking' jokes and getting kicked out of the occasional all-night diner for being loud and stupid. But man, we were fun!

The owners of club Limelight knew I was getting offers for more money from other clubs, so they gave me a company car to sweeten the deal. It was a brand new IROC-Z Camaro with removable T-roofs. Blackie and I did a lot of cruising in that shiny machine, and like the lunatics we were, and because the car had so much get up and go, we invented something called "Jolt Shots", the passenger would take a 2 Liter bottle of Jolt cola and put it up to his mouth while the driver floored it (stepping on the gas pedal)! More often than not, the cola would go everywhere! And we would laugh ourselves sick, Ahhh, super times, glad that wasn't my car.

About a year into working at club Limelight, the owners opened up a second nightclub called "Rock City", and I migrated over to that venue, Blackie and friends migrated with me. About one year later, I was offered a job at a nightclub in Grand Prairie, AB., it was for a lot more money, and unlike Rock City & Club Limelight, it did not involve working for the Chinese Mafia (true story), as I was mulling it over, there was a gun fight in the parking lot at Rock City, well, that's enough of that! Down the road I went!

After a few months, Blackie and friends paid me a visit in GP, the nightclub I worked for (Roadrunner's Party House) had a promotion "Match the shooters to win a Scooter!" Lol. If you ordered the right pair of shooters that night out of a list of a hundred shooters, you would win a brand-new motorized scooter. It did not take long for this group of seasoned drinkers to achieve their goal. They pooled their resources as a group and had the winning combination before the night was over. The one who claimed the Scooter (we'll call him Scooter – Mc Gee), he was supposed to sell the scooter back in Edmonton and share the proceeds with the group, he did not, he scooted off with all the cash by himself, weasel McGee!

As happens, with time and distance, we all drifted our separate ways for the next few years, by 1992, I was back in Edmonton, and was working for a nightclub on the Southside called "Uncle Charlie's", Blackie and I reconnected, and it was like we never stopped hanging out. He would visit me at the club, and we would hang out with friends after work, and when he wasn't scratching and washing other people's balls at Victoria Golf Course, Blackie and I would hang out during the day on Whyte Avenue and drink our weight in latte's from ridiculously BIG Mugs, while we watched and talked about… everything and anything.

Uncle Charlie's would go through some management changes over the next couple of years, and I rode the wave, in and out and in again. In one chapter of the Uncle Charlie's saga, I somehow talked the management into hiring me & Blackie as a Dynamic duo: "The K & B Roadshow." Basically, I talked on the mic, spun records (yes, we still used records) and Blackie took requests, looked cool and chatted up the guests. But wait, there's more! We also did full costume lip-syncs of AC/DC, Alice Cooper, and others. There was nothing like it in Edmonton. Goose Loonies nightclub did a little bit of lip sync stuff back in the late 80's, but this was different, this was Raw, this was Sweaty, this was Rock and man, it was Fun!

After Uncle Charlie's, Blackie and I went off and did our own thang, and we simply fell out of touch.

Fast forward about 16 years (Facebook is a thing) and we find each-other once again. Now, he is married with children…a lot of children! I am married with children too, but only two. I met him and a few of his boys for coffee in Edmonton, Blackies hair was still legendary, but with a touch of grey. We had both done a lot of living since we last saw each other and had a lot of new stuff to talk about, but we ended up re-living some old stories to entertain his sons. It was like he was saying "look boys, this is the guy I was telling you about. All those stories were real…just listen!" we had a great visit and a lot of laughs.

Since then, Blackie and I have kept in touch via Facebook and a lot of late-night messages as he was working up North, and I was coming home from a wedding of special event. I am still a DJ, but now I wear a tie, and get paid a lot more money to do it. Lol.

Married life with kids and work is busy, very busy. But every once in a while, we will re-connect out of the blue and it is just like we are back at Café Mosaic's on Whyte Ave, talking about…everything and anything. It's like that with real connections.

Unbreakable.

I think that would be a good title for this book, "Unbreakable," because after all Blackie has endured: the loss, the heartbreak, the challenges, the accidents, the changes…he remains, Unbreakable, and cool, very cool.

> I love you my brother from another awesome Mother.
> ~ Klay (The DJ) Tate

Check...check... check this out.

A single wire holds a dome light flickering above a small desk in the middle of a vacant cold concrete room, you paint the picture? On every police, crime, suspense movie, you can usually add this scene to your set. If you're a suspect to a crime, they (the authorities) want to interrogate you, break you, belittle you and make you talk...before proper representation. They ask you a series of typical questions, your whereabouts? Where were you? On the night of such and such? Or what do you know about this that and the other? Were you involved in the crime?

Not so in Canada, up here (Edmonton AB) the detectives (or dicks, whom, look like they've had a six pack of donuts, holding them over until their next coffee break) just make their way into your home; like the uninvited neighbor or relative, that comes and eats your food and over- stays there welcome, (no you're not welcome, now leave your money on the counter and get out!). These law en**force**ment detectives or police usually want to strong arm you to give them something they want!

What they want? Is for you to open your mouth and blah, blah, blah all over the place, that's right, verbal diarrhea, so they can misinterpret what you've said and when the time comes, use it against you in a court of law, this is why you never ever open your mouth to any sort of questions that they fire at you without your lawyer. There was a time when I was fifteen coming home and about to walk into the back door and these plain clothed dicks looked like meter men and they also looked like they were our neighbor's friends (CB'ers), you know? Jean jacket and plaid shirts and jeans, overweight and bald fuckers...anyway, as I was telling them they had the wrong address, they opened up my door and shoved me in, as I hit the wall they said "shut up! Punk!" I was like what the fuck!? It turns out the dicks have been watching our place with a known drug dealer or two living with us and they've had our phones tapped, so a little premature ejaculation on the drug bust (losers) they found some seeds and a little ceramic fucking joint holder hooter, whoop, whoop! Oh, the threats! They dropped some expensive headphones for the stereo that were hanging up, and one of the brothers said, "Take it easy!" 'Those are pricey' there reply was "shut up punk! If you open your mouth again, we'll rip apart this entire house, and leave you to clean it up and pay for it! They were going to try and bust someone, mainly mama Hope who was getting ready for night shift and also had a mutual friend with one of the dicks, her good friend Muriel... like seriously? Fuck off!!

Keep this Picture... (There's a quiz after)

One time a co-worker and myself went up to the clubhouse at Victoria Golf Course to have breakfast, while sitting and waiting we were talking about movies, and the question arose about how and why did Cool Hand Luke (Paul Newman) go to prison? He was arrested for being drunk and disorderly and busting the tops off parking meters, that's pretty much the gist of our conversation, now within the next few days, corporate security (city rent a cop / dicks) came to the golf course to question us.

Firstly, they questioned my co-worker because he was day shift and I was the afternoon guy, so my boss and co-worker knew all about this and waited my arrival at 1400 hours, I'm usually early, and as I walked into the driving range building, these two suits start hammering me with questions about me knowing something about the parking meters downtown getting vandalized! I guess the smirk on my face made me look guilty or suspicious, so these suits took us uptown to a room (not entirely like the one painted above) to get a written report of the know about of the vandalized, damaged (downtown Edmonton) parking meters.

Do you know the feeling when something seems so familiar? But you just cannot pinpoint why? Like I know this conversation was only a few days prior to this questioning, but I must've filed it under "G" for garbage or some other dimension of dementia, it just wasn't clicking or kicking in, my co-worker, said; "you look guilty as fuck!". Then suddenly, as I'm sitting there sweating out trying to realize, what is happening to me? A giant tsunami over floods my brain waves and I start to laugh, realizing then, of our breakfast conversation a few days prior, of Cool Hand Luke and how he wound up in prison, I said "this is so dumb; this is about the movie with Paul Newman in Cool Hand Luke."

So, somebody in the clubhouse at the same moment we were talking and having breakfast overheard our conversation and not chiming in at that moment (it's not a restaurant, in thinking back, there may have been 8-10 tables in the main area) and so easily could have interrupted and said "what are you guys talking about?" or any other way you butt in when its none of your business!, instead of doing the butt in at any time, you took the liberty and the assumption of the now know about of what they thought was a sure thing in solving the case of 'The Parking Meter Bandits', NO you dumb ignorant shitheads, look how much time and money you wasted of taxpayers' money and your budget without the interruption.

I used this reference mainly as the ability to remember, on your feet at a moment's notice, can you remember everything (with time) the order in which you did your routine this morning? How about yesterday? Better yet, can you remember what you did on your last Birthday? Remembering the Who? What? When? Where? And why? Lots of people usually can remember a good amount of what they did, I can, I'm the remember guy, except for the time at the golf course (ha, ha) or is that just with people of authority or you just freeze when you're put on the spotlight.

Sometimes it helps if you can associate the date with mostly a tragedy or an event, then your memory really kicks into gear, as of right now as you read that, those events are popping into your brain now… let's try a few dates in history; November 22, 1963, for some it may or may not register anything, then add the name associated with the date; John F. Kennedy, some of you now know exactly where you were, what you were doing and maybe remember the clothes you were wearing and the smells, smells trigger memory too. As for me, my mom was 7 months pregnant with yours truly, I am named after JFK, and my middle name is Kennedy.

I've been intrigued about his death, not obsessed, I liked to watch the documentaries 'and movies surrounding that event, especially Oliver Stone's directed epic JFK. I did write a poem about JFK as well.

J.F.K

Hypnotic state of emergency

When I coagulate at your dilated eyes

Spiral downward because you were very effective,

your own entourage infused their poison.

While the rest of the world is infected

Americans stuck in the mud,

Spinning their wheels after 40 years.

You're all guilty! Shame ...shame

Who will we blame today?

He did it! No, he did! Over there,

He did it! I think you all did it!

Bring down the vault, bring down the vault!

What are you waiting for?

FBI? C.I.A? Castro? Russians?

I? me? You? And sometimes why?

Because we can...and we did!

The biggest thing about watching the footage and all that surrounds this is the cover ups, the lies, the deceit and how many lives were murdered? Why? Did you ever sit back and ask yourself like what the Fuck? Kevin Costner's line in Oliver Stone's JFK movie- "I'm ashamed to be an American today" I wonder… how many people were not only ashamed that day but scared for their own well-being… Where are we headed as a society? As people that are so corrupted that at any moment in time, you, me, the President, the Pope, Robert Kennedy, Martin Luther king jr., Malcom X, anybody is in the line of fire, these are just to name a few in modern era. What about over time, the senseless murders?

As I quote myself in my poem 'Nineteen Years' "Merry go round… merry go round…When do we all fall? It's a two-fold statement; when do we fall at the hands of some lunatic or when do we get so bombarded, we have ourselves get to have our own falling down day?

Another date: how about, August 16, 1977, I remember like it was yesterday, 13 years old walking into the house and into the kitchen with my mama Hope's back turned (wearing a floral blouse) trying to make dinner, as she turned around, streams of tears rolling down her face, "mom" I said, "what's wrong?" Elvis died today she touted, and I embraced her to comfort her, like it was her close friend that died, many around the globe probably felt that same way, labelled the 'King of Rock n Roll' dead at 42 years old, the thing about it is, you relate to them in some ways; growing up and listening to all of their music, watching the specials on television, going to see them live or maybe you had an opportunity to meet them and talk with them. There's a closeness a familiarity, a bond, almost like they're a friend or a sibling.

What about December 8, 1980? I bet many of you don't even need me to write down the name associated to this day, because its etched into your brain, you may remember it for the one event or both events; firstly John Lennon stalked all day then shot and killed on his doorstep by a crazed fan, I, myself was not a fan of The Beatles or Lennon, but you don't wish that on anybody, I can still remember exactly where I was, I was 16 years old babysitting in an area in Edmonton called Castledowns; late at night all the kids in bed, I was still up listening to music on the radio and they started playing The Beatles / John Lennon, then the broadcast came on the television, then seemed like every radio station was only playing The Beatles songs, the other event on this date was the band Grateful Dead announced its dispersal. Again, not a huge GD fan, but to many fans it probably felt like a dagger to the heart.

Another time on this same date December 8, 2004, a crazed fan or psychopath storms the stage of a rock concert killed guitarist Darrell (Dimebag Darrell) Abbott, formerly of the group Pantera, and also killed four others in the audience before police shot and killed him.

These are only a few dates in the last fifty-five years and they're not even that old, the purpose was not to pick dates in history, but to reflect on your time capsule, your snow globe, the moments in your life that makes or causes you to remember things in great detail. You know those dates on the calendar? Circled and remembered for loved ones that have passed on or special events. It's difficult when the date's co-inside with an event or holiday that everyone else is celebrating.

Could be also the ugliest time in your life, when the dark cloud rolled in and took a loved one that was totally an unexpected death, whereas somebody snatched there life out of existence and you didn't get a chance to even say your goodbyes or even hold them one last time, everyone takes for granted the time we have, yet we don't think or consider anytime, anywhere our life can be gone, taken and deleted. Most times when someone says goodbye there's no hugs, no kisses, they head out the door and our expectations is to see them again, you don't think; oh, a car is going to plough into you, or a crazed person is going to shoot up a schoolyard or whatever it may be, we nonchalantly go about are daily routines until it's a train wreck.

Case in point; the two dates on my calendar; October 31/ November 1, 1975, OMG!!! Talk about a moment in time that haunts your brain, not only because its Halloween and everyone is into it, the stores start decorating and putting out the shit in like mid-August, it's a constant reminder every fucking year, this year (2023) will be the 48th anniversary of my oldest brother Ray Anthony Blackburn was shot and killed outside Kingsway Bar in Edmonton, AB. You cannot help but think about this event, and since his birthday is September 22, 1956, he had just turned 19 years old then the following month was killed on Halloween night into November 1st which is on the catholic calendar 'All Saints Day'. It's automatic, once August rolls around and the stores start setting up displays and the candy hits the shelves, my thoughts are straight away on my brother, some years are harder than others, but mostly my thoughts are webbed in his direction, wondering what he'd be like now. Married? Children? Career?

For almost five decades I have played out this event in my brain, the details of the afternoon and evening leading up to when Ray came over to moms to have a bite to eat, then as I was setting out the candies in the dishes to handout for the kids coming to the door, Ray grabbed a handful of goodies and I slapped the top of his hand as he was heading out that door for the last time, the next morning (Saturday, November 1/75) was strange for me, I woke up early as I normally did on weekends to go outside biking with friends around the neighborhood, mom was up early too (after being at the morgue in the earlier hours) and me not knowing what had gone on through the night just yet, mom didn't want me going outside, she insisted that I stay and wait for our dad (he was on his way over with Aunties and his new girlfriend), which I thought to be strange because I can see when they arrive, I'd be right out front, mom insisted, 'NO', she actually held it together very well, considering what she had gone through already.

All of a sudden as our little house in Dickensfield started to fill up with people (my dad, relatives) and my other siblings waking up, you could hear my mom tell dad "maybe it's time you tell the boys" meaning Robert and I, as RJ got our attention and we were huddled in the living room, he was making reference to his dad (G'pa) and his passing the previous year (1974) then went into the shocking details of our oldest brother was murdered last night, just like that, in an instant, your play book is opened and everything is etched into your memory bank, in a zombie like state of disbelief, you don't believe it to be true, especially at eleven years old, this is little old Edmonton, Canada this doesn't happen up here!

I'm afraid it does, and it did, as I tried to find out the details surrounding what had happened over the next period, information was becoming murky, rumors were clouding the truth of what actually happened at the bar that night. Since I was the youngest of the six boys, the information about that night was not readily available, as years passed on, I found myself really wanting to know what happened that night.

Having this traumatic event play out, and constantly trying to piece together a puzzle of what in the hell happened? walking around going through the motions of the days(daze), in a zombie like state, like never being satisfied with the results, because the rumors you hear and what you know of a person usually never add up, bad form, bad form, from people that make shit up and said they were there that night or lied about what actually went on and wrong. Why? Why do people want to bullshit and cause that kind of interference in my psyche? Like, I don't need a piece of puzzle that doesn't fucking belong!

Then, with time, people become aged or disappeared, others like; Kelly, Ray's good friend and whom apparently Ray had died in his arms, Kelly too had succumbed to his own addictions and passed away in March 1990, like the title of the last Pirates of the Caribbean movie; 'Dead Men Tell No Tales'. No, they do not!

My second oldest brother Vance was to meet up with Ray later that night at the Kingsway bar, Vance was there, looking for Ray in the bar downstairs, Vance couldn't find Ray(no cell; phones in 1975), the one thing about communication back then, was usually your word, you planned ahead; time and place, other than that, it was a pay phone and or pager, anyway Vance figured Ray had left and went somewhere else, so Vance had left to go home, meanwhile… Upstairs in the lobby two criminals out on parole, Oliver L. Patton and William C. Campbell, were handily kicking the shit out of some guy and threw him out of lobby window. Now, you must understand what kind of guy Ray was; he was about fairness, had the fight been one vs one he probably would have left it alone, and also after the guy was thrown out of the window, he maybe had enough at that point!

Because Ray had enough of these two paroles having their way with this guy (never did know who this guy was) Ray stepped in and broke up this so called fight, as he was tending to the guy outside on the ground, Patton leaves that scene of the fight to go to his car and grab his handgun, he returns to the scene of the fight, knowingly that he's intending on using the weapon, walks up to Ray, while Ray is still tending to the injured guy, and Patton pulls the trigger and shoots

Ray point blank in the middle of Rays chest, bullet hole entry (front chest) and Rays back was blown out, no chance of survival! WTF!!

In the early morning hours, the cops found the paroles passed out in the car in a back alley, initially they were charged with second degree murder, I wasn't at the trial, I sure wish I had been, it took them almost a half hour to read Patton's crime sheet, a 27 year old parolee, his entire life was being a criminal, have you got all that? Now, the very interesting part, where this makes no sense at all and is pure nonsense, Patton's lawyer plea bargains for a less charge to manslaughter and is granted by judge Dean Saxx and given a sentence of 2-10 years, guaranteed had I been at the trial and was able to shoot one or both of these paroles I would've received a stiffer sentence has a juvenile, than this premeditated act of murder. MANSLAUGHTER!!! WTF!! Patton serves his ten years, out of jail, he continues with his routine of crime, ends up in prison again in BC, by the early 90's Patton had a heart attack and died in jail. I do not know the whereabouts of Campbell or if he received anything for his involvement with the murder of my brother Ray.

What in the Hell is that kind of a sentence for murder? Do you know what that does to the victim's family? Being unable to appeal the decision because it was a courtroom (back alley, behind closed doors) fucking bullshit deal!! Patton left the scene of the fight, to go to his vehicle and take out a handgun, knowingly going back to that scene of the fight to shoot somebody, I don't care what excuses he had (if any) he was 27 years old out on parole, his crime sheet took a ½ hour for the court to read and understand who and what kind of person he is, Patton is / was a piece of shit living a continuous life of crime, the justice system allowed him back on the streets knowingly that he is a repeat offender and has been his entire life, on a ten year manslaughter charge if you are a good prisoner and you serve your time without any issues you could get out of prison on good behavior serving 2/3rds of 10 years is 6.66 years, Patton couldn't even do that, he served his ten years and was out in 1985 only to continue on his same path and wound up in prison in BC, Patton would no longer have to try and be an outstanding citizen, he had a heart attack and died in prison in the early 90's a dwelling for a waste of life!!

Throughout the next few years afterwards, there was talk and chatter of getting counselling for the entire family, it was talked about with victim's services, they were to provide this service and then through social services programs, and that's all it ever becomes, fucking blah, blah, blah…even the professionals just like to do their due diligence make a phone call or two tell you what they want to tell you and never follow-up on anything, the system fails and people fall through the cracks and end up doing their own self help, mostly at the bottom of many 26's or drugs.

You don't need to be a rocket scientist to see the many problems that exists within families that have lost loved ones and have got little or no help to help them cope with such tragic events, it's the same fucking system that fails when they charge and arrest a person that's criminally responsible and the judicial authorities negotiate a lesser sentence, what about the victim's? The one's that lose their life, those who no longer have a voice!

By the time I turned 30 years old (19year anniversary of Ray's death) I put together a photo collage of Ray on the backdrop of U2's Joshua Tree album with a poem I wrote titled 'Nineteen Years' here it is...

NINETEEN YEARS

Nineteen years, you lived out from the womb.
You grew up way to fad, my childhood hero, you seemed so invincible, where did you go?
I thought you were so grown up; you were still just a lad.
So much life you lost, when you didn't win the coin, they had tossed!

Nineteen years, you've gone, bye. Bye... and
Kingsway Ave. is dripping poison through my veins; injected gunshot hallucinates
'Through our brains. Open wound, gone too soon, chilled skin,
Pressed against a Monet print, so alone, so cold.

Nineteen years frozen framed; look how far we haven't come.
Teaching each generation, the same.
Merry go round...merry go round...when do we all fall?
Sucked out from life, what is it like to be left without the sound?

Nineteen years, we've silently cried.
Shocked faces, stoned look, melting down the hour-glass sand.
Waiting for time to rewind itself and this stain to be removed.
Another, nineteen years...

Challenge...quarter on the table

*C*oming out of the sixties it seemed like life itself was a wonderful and blissful thing aside from the global events that were going on (wrong), young families sprouting up and growing not in age, in vastness, with some deep grounded roots it wasn't uncommon to have maybe twelve, fourteen or more children. You could see why, with many siblings and running acreage or a farm, it seemed that was the way to go, many Catholics also didn't believe in birth control or other methods in stopping the ongoing blood line.

Grandpa Blackburn (Emile) was in the mixture of twelve boys and in turn he himself would only have four kids (2 boys 2 girls) with the eldest boy becoming ill and ended up in the grave, the other boy was the baby (RJ) and ended up being my donor, RJ in turn would end up having six boys, for many cultures having six boys meant you hit the jackpot, the lottery of life, six boys are you kidding me!! Many men in the sixties were very envious especially with others only turning out girls (not that's a totally bad thing) in modern society apparently was a big deal, because the mentality was women stayed home and did the chores and cooking, that was the thinking the logic, women did not go out into the man's world or HIS workforce, that is taboo, if you're wife or woman has to go into the world and work, YOU failed as a man!

RJ was a different breed though, maybe his head got hit a few times growing up, he was a spoiled fucking brat is what he was, his sisters babied him and gave him anything he wanted looking after all his needs and wants, it wrecked him, by the time he had his young family, RJ still expected everything from his bride (Hope), while she was trying to raise her boys, RJ would still want and desire all Hopes attention, to be waited on, looked after or coddled, he was hopeless.

Hope would have to go into the workforce because butt head RJ couldn't or wouldn't hold a job together, if RJ did have a job long enough to get a pay check, he'd blow it, gamble it away like it was his right to do with it what he wanted, no responsibilities nothing, like money grew on trees, it would be dust in the wind, not bringing home sweet fuck all…and food prices were not all that high, you could get a baker's dozen of bread (that's thirteen loaves) for $1 – one fucking dollar, are you kidding me? Like why did you have to blow your entire paycheck? Could you not put $20 in your sock, so you could still buy bread and milk?

The level of toxicity in this relationship had reached the boiling point, with RJ's gambling, drinking and shenanigans also became (or was already) abusive, you can't even feed your family dude! Like wtf!! Your sons are raiding neighborhood gardens to have food on the table, what the fuck does that tells you? That's alright behavior? You taught us to go chop down Christmas trees in the river valley, you taught us that stealing was an alright behavior and yet when we did something out of line you are fucking beat us within an inch of our lives most times…

This lifestyle carried over when Hope and RJ separated and we (Hope with her 6 boys) moved to the North end, street survival and street smarts began and stayed with us…

The early seventies, many times were bleak, living in welfare housing, seemed like a dark and sinister Disney cartoon, the fucking cloud in the snow globe was constantly being shook and raining in our world…nineteen seventy four…the old guy (RJ's dad) past away… nineteen seventy five…oldest bro (Ray Anthony) shot and killed… other neighbors going through this toilet bowl effect, doesn't go away, the toilet keeps backing up…life man, seemed at times like a difficult road to travel, especially for a young single mama in her late 30's with six now five boys, no simple handouts, everything was a fight!

Nothing came easy, fight, fight, fight…you gotta fight for your right to…live, breathe and exist, a lot of times it felt like you were in a concentration camp, digging, kicking, and screaming for help to continue your existence, just keep breathing just keep breathing… It was a challenge, every day…week…month, year after year, we were close with my mom, she wore her heart on her sleeve, with pride and love! I'm sure there must've been a million thoughts or probabilities that mama Hope could've considered, push the 'easy' button, most likely entered her brain more than once, that's what most would've thought or considered.

By the time the eighties came along the bottom fell out of Alberta, being in high school still had some advantages, again very hard times to fight through especially for a single mom with one income and some of the boys unable to find consistent work, myself I had a great babysitting gig with the same family for about nine years, plus odd jobs of ohh you know… selling drugs, paper routes, Klondike days, ice cream vendors just keeping busy all the times making money no matter what.

Life can be like love most of the times, cruel to be kind… (by Nick Lowe)

Oh, I can't take another heartache.
Though you say you're my friend, I'm at my wit's end.
You say your love is bona fide.
But that don't coincide with the things that you do.
And when I ask you to be nice, you say.

[Chorus]
You gotta be.
Cruel to be kind in the right measure.
Cruel to be kind it's a very good sign.
Cruel to be kind means that I love you.
Baby, you gotta be cruel to be kind.

Even love stinks lyrics by J. Geils band…

"Love Stinks"

You love her.
But she loves him.
And he loves somebody else.
You just can't win And so it goes.
'Til the day you die.
This thing they call love.
It's gonna make you cry I've had the blues.
The reds and the pinks One thing for sure

(Love stinks)
Love stinks
Yeah, yeah
(Love stinks)
Love stinks
Yeah, yeah
(Love stinks)
Love stinks
Yeah, yeah
(Love stinks)
Love stinks Yeah, yeah

Two by two and side by side
Love's gonna find you, yes, it is.
You just can't hide.
You'll hear it call.
Your heart will fall.
Then love will fly
It's gone, that's all
I don't care what any Casanova thinks All I can say is.

Life is cold...as it happens people for the most part are not intentionally cold and cruel, just by using their words though, words alone can cut through a person more so than a sword, you're piercing the inner being, the core, each time it happens it destroys and ultimately kills the kindness of that inner soul, for the most part people are genuinely unaware that they even do it, usually it's bad enough even to have those thoughts cross your mind, but it's when put it out there and you air it, speak it into existence, that's when it does the damage that's irreparable!

With street survival instincts, you're not to show any emotion in public or around others, it's a sign of weakness, so stand up and brush yourself off and get back at it, don't get teary eyed or mushy, don't apologize, get up and fight it off or walk away with pride intact. I wrote this poem as a positive influence for those that have been knocked down and discouraged from life, it's very fitting for people in this situation...

'Kisses the Sky'

    Wandering through the streams of life's dreams, it seems...
Like you're in a fantasy, but could this be my destiny?
As I see you strolling down the street, to reach for the stars you thought you'd meet... When you fall to the ground, do you get up?
        A young man who struggles, and stretches, his face grimaces in...
        Oh, the pain, as he falls...again.
        The beads of frustration make puddles in the earth,
            as he stretches forth yet another time.
        Oh, I can't get up, as I'm now...cryin'
            He stretches for a guiding hand.
        Oh, the poor, struggling soul of a man.

       Sighting upward in fear, to reach for the stars
          That you thought were so nearby…
              Just look…in the looking glass mirror!
Crawling to his knees in despair he lifts his head on high.
            Not letting his dreams pass on by.
                  The wind whispers "you're excused."
                With all his might he rises to his feet,
                    Grabs hold, and…
                    "Kisses the Sky"

Life circumstances can also pull you down that endless rabbit hole, to know fault of your own, let alone that of mama Hope's as well, was it entirely her that decided to leave the donor asshole? If divorce was or is so taboo, in the catholic culture, then where the fuck was RJ's commitment to his vows? I don't know and I cannot speak for either of them now, I do know that I was raised by a powerful woman that wouldn't give up on her boys even though we were brought up in the welfare snow globe that wasn't fun.

Even when Hope and good friend Muriel would get harassed or back stabbed, they were still compelled to get food for that entire neighborhood, didn't matter, bygones were bygone and here, come and grab some rotted veggies or fruit, instead of going to the outer limits of local communities where it was obvious people had money and were better off, you had to watch your back, because your own fucking neighbors, the one's also on welfare would come and steal from you too!! Does that make sense now?

The memories of getting caught up in the neighborhood drama my fucking gaud, leave us the fuck alone! Every family had drama, and being on welfare and within the system it just seemed very overwhelming at times, I know we lived among the poor and broken families and at times we didn't need to know all the fucking neighborhood drama and heresy, the gossip was hot n' heavy, and trying to solve all the problems were; Avon lip slicked woman, with washed away stained and faded lips, after a day of chatting it up on the dial up telephones and smoking a package of smokes and drinking some beers or whiskey, my gaud it's bad enough coming home when they've been watching Another World or Days of our Lives, discretion people, why are you filling up with so much soap operas in your life?

The cops wanted to set up a coffee shop at our place, it was joked about many times, the Blackburn's home was the One Stop of knowledge and what was going on in and around the hood, ahhh wrong again fuckers, you can come here as much as you want, but we're not telling you shit!! Whether we knew something or not! Funny story, this one cop that would stop me all the time Ferrone was his name, always looking for scoops or leads, it's like this, I'm not telling you anything…

He was digging for information on some stolen memorabilia from the Commonwealth games that were hosted in Edmonton in 1978, it just so happens that he's looking up at mine and Roberts room, with of course a Commonwealth flag as a curtain hanging in our window, within the conversation, Ferrone wanted to see the receipt for the flag, Robert lied and said its upstairs in the room, great now Ferrone wants to come upstairs and see proof for this flag, Roberts got like a 10" pot plant on his dresser, so as I enter the room with Ferrone, I block his sight from the dresser and guide him to the flag, Robert darts right to the pot plant sticks the entire plant into his mouth and prunes every leaf off of it, when he pulls it out there's a ten inch twig naked and wobbling back and forth, and Robert chewing these leaves like its bubble gum, so hilarious.

This was only one time, it had become a regular daily routine, so routine you could synchronize your wristwatch to it, like Ferrone always said to me "I don't need to get any updates at the station, if I need to know anything going on in the hood, I'll go to the Blackburn's", that was comical because we never ever ratted or gave him any information, he always tried to bait me, but sorry Charlie I'm a smarter fish than you! Another visitation from Ferrone was a time about missing or stolen car batteries, and how we must've known about them, because they were found right next to our place by the parking lot, he was constantly questioning me, I'm like just because there's crime going on it doesn't mean that you butt your nose in anybody's business.

There were always the neighborhood males always in the parking lots repairing their vehicles, changing something adding something else, c'mon man, it's the fucking slums, and people need to work, therefore need their cars.

So, like you think I'm going to butt my nose into these guys that are in the parking lots and check out what everyone is doing…go fuck yourself! I'm a kid on a bicycle hanging out with other kids on bikes,

I don't care if they're doing criminal activity, if it doesn't concern me or my family why pick a fight?

RJ Blackburn and Hope (nee. McFarland/Allen) both stationed overseas with the Canadian Armed Forces, met each other and after a short courtship, married in Metz, France in 1955, it wasn't too long after these love birds started having kiddos, they wound up in Edmonton in 1956 and that is where the first of six boys were born, Ray Anthony, the second and third boys Vance Andrew (1957) and Grant Michael (1958)both born in Quebec, then the Forth son; John Arthur was born back in Edmonton in 1960. A slight break (of being pregnant) then they were transferred to Cold Lake, AB., before having the fifth boy; Robert Mark in 1962 and the last but never the least me; Paul Kennedy born in 1964.

After I was born, RJ and Hope both decided their tenure with the Royal Canadian Forces had come to an end, they both quit and would move in with RJ's parents in the basement suite of a house in Forrest Heights on the Southside of Edmonton (10257-80St) yes indeed, all eight of us crammed into a small 3bedroom basement suite, good thing we were all pretty small and young. So,1966, jobs(career choices) were plentiful, Hope secured her job with the Credit Bureau but also had time to work at Kentucky Fried Chicken, RJ, was trying to adjust and couldn't settle on some of the jobs he was hired for, you could go to one job in the morning and have two or three by the time it was home time the same day.

The problem with RJ, it really didn't matter anyway because any job he lasted at or got a pay check for he blew it, with 6 boys and a wife at home, RJ would gamble his pay check away and lose it all, plus be drunk and wind up fighting the same guys he lost his money to, when he'd come home, he was not coming home with bread and milk, let me tell you that. There was nothing in the fridge except some condiments like; ketchup and mustard, bread was very cheap back then, a baker's dozen (which is 13 loaves) was $1, and we were so poor we didn't have bread most times, when we did have bread it was topped with ketchup or mustard, the older boys usually would go and raid gardens for veggies, it seemed pretty normal to do that rather than buy groceries at a store.

The home of an alcoholic, gambler with added abusive behavior to sprinkle on top, yeah let's cover all the shit up and hope it'll all go away, problem was RJ was jealous of his boys, yeah okay…what?? He could not or would not accept the fact that Hope had to give most of her attention to the boys, in fact he loathed the idea of it, the only thing that made the home a safe dwelling was because of mama Hopes presence, as little boys like to get into mischief, one time I found myself intrigued by this model glue and when you put it on the seats of dinky cars it melted the plastic in them, I was made to believe that when RJ was coming home he was going to whoop my ass! So, the fear factor in place I hid under the bunk beds all afternoon and into the evening, wasn't the first nor was it the last. RJ's house rule was if one of you don't own up to something wrong you did, we all got the belt, stand in line oldest to youngest once you got the belt, you had to knell with your hands in the air no, no not against the wall in the air, then if you got support from the wall, you got smacked again. Fun times!

I was too young to know what their financial commitments were at that time, but I do know it was a stressful strain on the relationship, especially with RJ pissing away his paycheques all the time and leaving the responsibility to mom, in moms later years she said 'RJ went through 25 jobs in one year', that along with RJ's drinking, gambling, abusive behavior and his hate or jealousy towards his six boys, was really taking its toll on the marriage, his outright rage when it was time to discipline, the final straw or the one that sent Hope packing along with her entourage of boys was RJ's out of control abuse, blacking out when you have a belt in your hand and you're trying to discipline your own children is not a good thing, when you lose control and cannot focus on the task at hand (giving your kids stiches for a simple spank is not a good sign) in layman's terms; hold your shit together man! It's time you should seek help RJ (I don't think he ever did get help) RJ certainly needed it, anger issues and being abusive mixed with drinking and gambling was highly toxic especially for this man. In the upcoming years it is very apparent why I think RJ never received council or addiction therapy, it was his constant continuous behavior towards his close family; beating up his Nephew Harvey and dragging him along the picket fence outside because Harvey called Emile (RJ's dad) a 'prick', another time with Uncle Gunther, RJ picked him up and disposed of him into a garbage can, also the story of him picking up his son Ray by the throat for squirting our bird Rocky with a water pistol and threating Ray with his life!

RJ, born Raymond Joseph Blackburn in January 6,1934in Montreal, QB., the youngest of 4 children to Emile and Florence (nee Naubert) 2 boys the oldest one died at a young age and RJ, 2 girls Florence and Claudette, there won't be much discussion or focus on this side of the family considering they weren't a huge part of our lives, especially after mama Hope left RJ with her sons and moved to the North side of Edmonton (14809 -89 St.) Just a note to remember; RJ's sisters both married stable, reliable men that had good jobs, they owned their homes and had good incomes. Also, with Hope separating from RJ meant that side of the family also separated from us, separating and divorcing from a catholic marriage, was taboo during those years, you were committed to stay in it for life, sort it out, work it out, with a suck it up mentality, that's what the vows were for; through thick and thin, sickness and health and the good and bad times.

You'd think that having six healthy strapping boys would be like hitting a 'Jackpot' in RJ's gambling terms, not so, RJ had little or no desire to even put a fight to come and be with us, take us somewhere or do anything with this clan of boys. This one Christmas at Hotel MacDonald where he lived with his second wife Lil, I must've been around 11 or 12 years old, he came and sat next to me on the couch and to see how I was doing, RJ for some strange and sinister reason grabbed the inside of my inner left leg and squeezed it so hard, I started to cry it hurt so bad and when everyone was asking what was wrong, he made up a lie and denied doing anything wrong. The bruise on the inside of my leg was probably eight inches around and black and purple. A few more years would pass before I'd see my sperm donor again, I'm not even sure what influenced this lunch encounter with RJ, anyway, we set up a time for lunch when I was seventeen, i know for certain I was going just for lunch and not to stoop to ask him for a dime, RJ was like old man Potter off It's 'A Wonderful Life', felt powerful and almighty when somebody came crawling begging for his scraps (no thank you).

I was going there with the intention of not asking him for a thing, and with that in mind I was wearing my Sunday best (tongue in cheek) I owned a jean jacket that was naturally worn out, I'm talking my own mom hated that jacket she would be embarrassed when I'd wear it, she'd always mention to throw it away, it was my favorite, it took years of wearing and washing to get it to be so full of holes, you had to weave your arms into the sleeves ever so gently not to create any more unwanted rips. It was settled I'm wearing my jean jacket for lunch, among the pretentious wannabes, the suit wearing so-called business class of Edmonton, smack down in the center of all of them, 109 St and Jasper Ave., a very high end place (in 1981) for business class at every lunch hour, I'm here to have lunch with RJ, upon approaching the table i couldn't tell with his jaw on the floor whether he was happy to see me or in love with my jacket, okay it's settled I will continue to wear it during lunch, I don't think he was very amused by it, I could see his eyes kept scanning over the jacket like he wanted to rip it off my back!

The small talk continued throughout the entire lunch hour, I was holding my own and very content in not asking him for money, in fact, I was going to buy his lunch too, that would've really blown his mind set, as I made my way back from the bathroom, i asked where the bill was? He replied "don't worry it's looked after" I said "I was going to pay" RJ said to "save your money, and also here (hands me a cheque for $200) get yourself a new jean jacket, mmm, well thank you, not sure that I need a new one. Lol

This is the poem I wrote for RJ titled.

'Going…Gone…Bye!'

We didn't see your back as you closed the door on that chapter of your life.
The mirror on the wall fell and it shattered the lives of your six sons! Oh well,
  don't look back, the picture of you left a negative imprint,
   don't worry about the chapters in their lives.
We wrote the book on survival, it was a hard fight; daily, weekly year after year It didn't include leaving your wife after she gave birth to our sons & daughters!
    Who's going to…guide our steps when we dream?
    Who's going to…put a band-aid on it when we bleed?
    Who's going to…tuck us in when we can't sleep?
    Who's going to…coach us when we need a voice?
   Maybe we shivered? Maybe our lives were shattered?
    To you we did not matter!
    You pimped yourself out,
   But for us it's a hard sale, no one's going to buy!

Mama Hope had to make some tough choices, leaving the Credit Bureau to go on welfare and move to the unknown regions of the north side new developments of low-income 4bedroom row-housing with her six boys, I'd just turned 7years old in January of 71' and we moved into this place in the worst snowstorm in February, the ride to the north side during that storm felt like an eternal drive to Northern Alberta, it was very bad conditions.

Think of a time when you had to start a job or something where you have to make a choice, the feeling of being scared or terrified if you're definitely making right choices at all, that's just if it's you, now consider being 37years old, single (separated) mom with 6 boys (ages 15-7) with a beer budget of $380 per month, SAY WHAT? Do the math; rent &utilities were right around $300, what's left? $80, wow, so the remainder for food, clothing, and emergency funds for 7 people for a month is $80? How? There were times sitting with mama Hope at the welfare office and her trying to explain that she needs more money for winter clothing and then getting only vouchers for the store, same with getting extra food during Christmas time, like, OMG how to make people feel worthless, begging for fucking scraps and handouts!!

Like what do you even do? In these earlier years it was very difficult for Hope to make this work, one time she called RJ's sister to borrow $20, she was declined on the fact they were entertaining that weekend! The one- and only-time mama Hope would stoop to ask for money (especially going to the dark side) with RJ's siblings. This would be brought out on face book only a short time ago, I didn't even know that the cousins were on my page, we have never spoke ever! Until i mentioned the facts about RJ and his fucked up way to raise a family and oh yeah i may have mentioned that $20 dollars mom asked for, well fuck me, i did not know i was going to get attacked like that from anybody, it was the only time I've heard from anyone on the dark side since the pretentious plastic wannabes show up at a funeral, she tried to defend her mom and RJ and everyone else on that side, I'm like how would any of you know shit? None of you checked on Mama Hope at all you left her to fend for six boys on her own!! Shame, shame you MOTHER FUCKERS!!!

This event had to happen (to ignite the fire within mama Hope) from the ongoing struggles Hope would get onboard with some neighborhood charity to raise money in 1973 this is where she would meet her good friend Muriel, these two women; Hope & Muriel would become the dynamic duo! Essentially organizing ongoing (weekly) food pick-ups from various stores like; Woodward's, Safeway and sometimes Bakery shops, they would end up receiving boxes of (rotten) left-over veggies, fruit and bread or buns that would be brought to our backyard and neighborhood families would bring their bags, shopping carts or wagons to come pick through these boxes and take whatever they needed to help last through another week. It wasn't prime grade A food, hell, not even B or C most times, the choice; either this or go with-out, after washing it and cutting off the rot mama Hope made it work, she still made meals every night and fed her boys.

Born Hope Allen (McFarland) August 3, 1933 in Vancouver BC., to Wade and Edith, Hope was the oldest and Norman was the youngest, let's just go with this, because it is some crazy shit that went on here, okay first Hope didn't know her dad was this guy Wade, they weren't together growing up, and Edith knew of some guy named Allen, Edith would raise Hope with the last name Allen because she liked the name, maybe the guy too, seemed everyone would like anyone back in the thirties, I thought that's why they were known as the 'Dirty Thirties'. As mama Hope would tell the stories, you'd be horrified listening to them! As it is with just some of the stories that I've heard first-hand from Edith (Hopes mom) at least I think she was mom's mom.

At my brother Johns and newlywed Karen's gift opening in August of 1992, Edith and I sat along the picket fence away from the party but still in everybody's sight line. Edith loved her afternoon Caesar's and even more so when I made them for her, she went on to tell me stories in the 1920's of her Uncles and cousins having their way with all the girls and woman of the house, whether they wanted to or not, didn't matter, a free for all brothel, keeping it all in the family! What? Grandma 'you can't be serious?', 'oh, I'm dead serious', she muttered, at times you could see it in her eyes, the disgusting look of the pigs that she was ashamed to be related to, the years of hate was reflective and evident that the stories could only bring watery eyes, no tears, you could see and feel the hatred that this trail had left in her life now into her 80's with the consumption of alcohol to be brave enough to tell of these times, to her grandson of 28.

This will be confusing to write and read all at the same time, I cannot give an accurate-chronological timeline here with mama Hopes upbringing, why? Because it too is attached to some of this funky junky, WTF!! Is going on, raise your eyebrows stuff, like, how do we even get any sort of who is related to who or whom? With all this inter-relation family wanting to nail the entire woman, chasing them around and having uncontested sex or raping them, all of the time! From my understanding and talking with mom, she related it to me like this; Edith was a McFarland, not married to old man Wade (not sure what his last name is), Wade supposedly is Hopes biological father (not for sure), Edith named Hope with the last name Allen (Hope Allen) not even sure if its legal, but mom used it like that for all of her identification documents and it worked for her with; birth certificate, social insurance card and passport

During mama Hopes early childhood she was raised by the Doukhobors somewhere in Creston BC., not sure for how long because at some point in time she returns to live with Edith and old man Wade,

Tried having his way with Hope, and in turn Hope would then run away at 16/17 years of age to join the Royal Canadian Airforce.OMG, how did people even live and trust each other back then? By the time Hope would join the forces and be stationed overseas, she would meet and be courted by RJ and ultimately get married to him in 1955.

By the time 1974 rolled around it would be my first encounter or introduction of death, RJ's father Emile had a heart attack and died, Emile was 74 years old at the time, very interesting man Emile, loved his beer, the Montreal Canadians' and the New York Yankees, he was the head waiter at the Hotel MacDonald downtown Edmonton,(I heard stories years later from one of the owners at Capital Pizza in the

North end, Nick, he worked under my grandfather at the Hotel, they use to call him the 'Old Guy') he was so sickened by the pretentious, upper echelon, the crusty well to doers. When he arrived home after having to work in that atmosphere all day, he would not only take his hat off, he'd only wear a muscle shirt and boxers while he would eat alone at the kitchen table, Florence would bring his food and you could've just poured it into a trough, that's the way he would eat, like a disgusting barn yard animal, he would not use the utensils, drink straight from the soup bowl and would make all of these grunting and slurping noises and just let it run down his chin and onto his muscle shirt, Robert and I always bear witness to this event because Florence would watch us upstairs, we were just 2 and 3 years old but found this to be very humorous.

Heading into 1975...it started out with Ray being captured for his crimes of break and entering and theft of goods under $1K, Ray and his friends were like Robin Hood and his Merry men, steal from the rich and give to the poor, Ray disliked seeing people go without, especially young single woman with children, in turn, Ray would help out the best way he knew how, may have not been the right way but he had fun doing what he was doing. For the most part Ray and I got along really well, at times of other sibling involvements, Ray would usually have my back and kick their ass, we had some disagreements or instances where I was on the receiving end of a mishap, a war wound that I proudly have from him, when I was 5 years old, we were in the back alley on the Southside using hockey sticks as weapons, and we'd just stated let's use them like an X so I went up with my stick to defend and he came down over top with a two hander and the blade of his stick ripped open my upper lip; like a hot butter knife going through frozen butter, 12 stitches later…another time before picture day at school, wrestling in the living room and his nail carved a chunk out of my cheek, smile!

When I would be coloring or drawing at the kitchen table it wouldn't take too long for Ray to join me, if he had time to doodle or joke with me he would hang out and do art, it wasn't long after High School had finished that Ray was venturing to other places like; Calgary and Vancouver, seeking employment and going to see Led Zeppelin and other shows, Ray was trying to get a job has a long shore fisherman in BC and he had become quite sick, I had sent him a get well card and he replied with a hand written letter back (like always) with his alias name on the envelope because he was still running from the law. When he had gotten better, Ray moved into a place in Calgary AB., where on a hot summer evening, had his front door opened to have a cross breeze in his place, a small child out front on his tricycle was pointing to the policeman and to Rays open door and said, "he's in there, he's in there", doing their due diligence the police officers approached the house, wanted on a Canada wide warrant they made their arrest.

Ray was sentenced to 12 months less a day and 1year probation, he served 7 months in Fort Saskatchewan AB., Penitentiary, and got out early for good behavior, Ray was getting all set to clean up his life, he was registered and enrolled to start school at NAIT in that September of 1975 he would also celebrate his last birthday that month too, as he turned 19 years old on the 22nd, still holding onto the crutches and friends of mis-fortune, after leaving moms place on that Halloween evening, he said 'I'm not going out tonight! 'I'm going home to shower and hangout at home.' Plans changed, along the way and instead of going home to take out his girlfriend's boy for trick or treating, Ray would end up getting harassed by some friends (whom I wish not to name) to go out to the Kingsway Bar, once there, one friend had to leave he was underage, the other so-called friend left Ray to fend off the parolees on his own, and the last friend stuck by Rays side, and Ray would end up dying in his arms.

The process of dealing with a sudden impact death and dealing with the emotions that one experiences during the upcoming days, weeks, months, and years… in no order or specific timeline there is.

- **Denial** – *it's so convincing that you almost believe the events to be untrue, it can't be right, it's the wrong guy in the morgue check again you'll see…* denial can certainly bring you down and beat you up…early comments from friends make you second guess if the event even took place, you start thinking and believing it and contributes to denial a lot
- **Disbelief** – *the inability to accept the events to be true, such long drawnout periods where you think the person is coming back. I beat myself up for years with this, i just could not accept that this could happen up here i little town of Edmonton.*
- **Confusion** – *because you're not accepting the fact that he/she is gone, you start believing your own thought process and causing more confusion, at the first time hearing the news and being*

only eleven years old it's really confusing to separate what in the fuck is happening not only to our family, just in the world too!!

- **Shock** – *the initial 'shock-wave' I still remember standing in that huddle with RJ and Robert, after RJ telling us that our oldest brother was shot and killed, your suddenly, 'did I hear what you just said?' you look at one another like WTF!!! I must've stayed in shock for a long long long time.*

- **Sadness** – *some of the years are harder than others, I remember working for the city in cemeteries and we were doing projects right by where Ray was buried, I was sad for a long period of time, of course it was during the Fall time leading into Halloween, sometimes it's not the time of year that triggers sadness, it can be triggered by a simple thing that nobody else can understand*

- **Yearning** – *the intensity and longing just to be able to see him again, I only got to see him on weekends at Ft Saskatchewan prison, then soon after he was out, he was taken from us again, not even to see him until the open casket.*

- **Anger** – *so many times being so pissed off at God and having hostility inside, it can be very annoying.*

- **Humiliation** – *I remember the humiliation of my friends not believing me when I told them what had happened, like why would you even think that I'd make that up?*

- **Despair** – *everything gets bottled up inside and you end up indulging and hurting yourself by doing excessive amounts of drugs and alcohol, self-medication was always close by*

- **Guilt** – *always asking 'why him?' 'Why did I get to live?'*

- **Zombie State (not listed)** – *so many times during the early years after his death, when you'd be daydreaming and get absorbed in your thoughts, I remember seeing guys that resembled Ray so many times, you start believing he's not dead.*

There are other mixed emotions in the gamut that you go through periodically during the stages of grief, it's crazy, a whirlwind of feelings that some may experience, sometimes so overwhelming you can just start weeping or crying because a memory was so intense, sometimes years later when I would say goodnight to mama Hope she would be bedside in tears, praying for Ray.

This one time there lived this guy close by my good friend's house, it was so uncanny the resemblance he had to Ray, I told mom about him and she said to bring him by onetime, when I did bring him over, mom was so overwhelmed and started crying, he not only left the house, but I never saw him again…ever!

The day of Ray's funeral was very, very sad not only because this should not be happening, i mean like for fucks sake we're all just kids really, the doors were open to South Side Memorial Chapel and there he lay in the casket, looking like he was just having a nap, wake up Ray, Ray WAKE UP!! It's just a fucking dream! Everyone was there like: bikers and his friends he hung out with, the entire neighborhood and schoolmates, relatives on RJ's side (in which case most thought that Ray was the only child, they didn't know about the five remaining that were alive) it all seemed like a bad ending to a movie, Ray played a guardian angel to somebody that didn't even know him, Ray not only saved your ass from that fight, he took a bullet in the chest for you too!! Ray is buried at a Catholic cemetery with his middle name Anthony, meaning 'Priceless One,' it still seems so surreal, this is forty-eight years ago, and the memories of Rays death are so visual and present. The wake along with the open casket was held at Uncle Ernie and Flo's place, the turning point of the night came when RJ announced his engagement to marry his second wife (Lil) and also that RJ's misuse of the funds from victim's services to holiday in Hawaii drop the gloves because now everyone is engaged to fight!! RJ knew the best times when to drop a bomb, this wouldn't be the first time, actually the following time would take place at his own mother's funeral, and RJ would then announce his engagement to his third and final wife (Opal). I'm still not sure why there was so much hatred towards us; we were blacklisted and cut off from his entire side of the family for our entire lifetime!

This was only the start of November 1975, a couple of weeks later was the Grey Cup, Ray's girlfriend at the time wanted the family to come over for a little GC party, unbeknownst to us that some of the 'most unwanted' would be making an appearance, just on a 'oh we were in the neighborhood' thought we'd drop by type of invite, yeah, you weren't invited so maybe kindly show yourselves out! You know the moment? Those guts feeling or bad vibes? When shit is about to go south in a hurry, these 'so called' good friends of Ray's that showed up, started to drop kick and break most of the light scones that were hanging on the walls in the hallways of this apartment complex, within a short period of time Edmonton's finest are showing up and everyone turns into a tough guy, now they want to fight the cops and avoid the arrests, as the smoke would clear, the three older brothers were finally arrested and detained in city cells for the night. I could not imagine what mama Hope was thinking and feeling throughout the night as she rushed to take Robert and I out of this and bring us home. A divorced woman in her early 40's trying to raise six boys alone, the oldest was just murdered in cold blood (a few weeks prior) and the next three all arrested for property damage and resisting arrest charges.

The system totally failed for Mama Hope (and us) when you consider what in the Hell she was going through, certainly she was clinging onto or had hope that everything was going to be alright, with all this shit going on it would've been easy to put the younger two in foster care and walk away, and let the chips fall where they may. What kind of strength did Hope to have? The love for her boys was immeasurable; Hope did everything in her earthly power to provide for us, she rode out many storms, the same storms that would break many others to pieces. Hope would pray all the time by her bedside, many times during her prayers she would be sobbing and crying for nothing less but her boys, that's all she wanted was a strong healthy family, Hope had some kind of wonderful faith (like Job in the Bible).

There was always talk (blah blah bull shit) from these so-called professionals that would maybe just tell Hope what she wanted to hear, they knew that we needed counselling, it was evident, victim services promised us counselling for the family, the social worker also promised Hope we'd get help soon...well, Hope didn't hold her breath for this help, at some point Hope stopped asking for help for her and the five sons. Benjamin Franklin's quote "By failing to plan, you are preparing to fail" so these professionals maybe had a plan to help, they just never put it into action. That's why you have so many dysfunctional people, families or individuals fall through the cracks of life, they end up self-medicating with drugs and alcohol, because it suppresses all of those feelings and washes away the reality, when you're feeling down it's easy to turn that frown upside down or when you want to mope just turn to dope, fastest and easiest way to numb your pain, dope the brain feels no pain!

I've often looked back over my life and questioned if counselling would've really helped? Like for real, they're just channeling another thought pattern or suggestions on what you should do, ultimately you choose the path you're going on...choose, what will you choose red pill or blue pill? Isn't that always a question? The time I chose to be a drug dealer, and after getting arrested and going through all of court system, sentencing and serving time, I still had a choice after the smoke had settled...will I carry on the life of crime and being a drug dealer or will I quit that lifestyle and stay clean and clear of doing any sort of criminal activities? In the end, does the choice matter? Whether you choose to be a good hard working class hero or a criminal and like Bob Dylan sang about "You're going to have to serve somebody" doesn't matter your walk or fate in this life, you could be Royalty or somebody's bitch in prison, you Have to serve somebody, it all boils down to you as an individual and who or what you're going to serve!

Is there any freedom in serving 'The Man' or the 'System'? After getting a criminal record it became so hard even to land a job, the one question on applications was, do you have a criminal record? It doesn't ask what it was for or anything, the best thing to do was to lie and check the no box. We become so enslaved in our employment it cripples us as humans, we become so reliant and dependent on it and end up missing our life, our families life and our children's upbringing, I ended up missing a lot when I finally chased after and got employed in the oil industry, you chase the almighty dollar, it's habitual and addictive, because let's face it, earning that kind of money is almost like being a drug dealer again, only problem now is the Government is taxing the shit out of you, by now (2023) we are so heavily taxed we need an income of over $150K just to get by, to get those jobs means you usually have to work out of town, which by the way is not always the best on any relationship.

This quote by the Dalai Lama is very true...

> "Man sacrifices his health in order to make money Then he sacrifices his money to recuperate his health. And then he is so anxious about the future that he does not enjoy the present.
> The result being that he does not live in the present or the future,
> He lives as if he is never going to die, and then dies having never Really lived."

The one thing about life and growing up is to accept who you are, don't blame others or your parents, take responsibility for you own actions, be a man, step up and grow some balls, it's easy to point the finger and blame others... basically if you can't do anything without accepting responsibility for your own actions then don't do whatever it is...'If you can't do the time, don't do the crime!'

Mama Hope realized that she needed to get some sort of help with the younger siblings and had signed up for the Uncles at Large program, which would help take the unwanted stress off of one parent single or divorced, who couldn't really do anything without the extra help raising a young family, in pursuit for us to get out and learn about life rather than us wasting away and doing nothing, I myself had started smoking at 9 years old and was experimenting (medicating) with weed and alcohol by the time I was 12, getting into some other activities rather than being raised up by the one parent community in which we lived in, one activity in particular was the shop lifting spree that a neighborhood friend and myself went on for the good part of a month, when the smoke had cleared and all the lies that were told we had to fess up and gather all the Hot Wheel toys we stole, our parents meet at Northgate Woodward's to return all of them, not one but two shopping carts full of stolen toys, for punishment my neighbor friend got his head shaved and grounded for a month and me I got to go on a week-long camping trip to Jasper with my Uncle at Large, Len.

Hope had no help of any kind from RJ, welfare didn't go after him like some of the guys I know in recent history, RJ got off so easy, let me just say that he didn't even come and visit his own boys, and we lived in the same city! I'm very certain with my memory ability it was only once a year, at Christmas time, that's it that's all, on a rare very rare occasion (when he'd get hit the head) he would come and see how his sperm donations were living, wasn't that often, I think it was only one time.

No, no there was a second time, I was going camping with my uncles at Large Len, and RJ had shown up to take Robert and me to Long Lake, AB., for a camping day, showing off to his friends how he could be a father, yeah, don't think so their Mr. Donor! This would be the one and only time where we saw my Uncle very upset, Knowing the situation, my Uncle at Large became pretty attached, he bonded very well with this dysfunctional group, for my Uncle he planned ahead and made sure everything would work out, he was an electrician by trade so when he'd book the weekend off to go camping or whatever he'd be missing out on his wage, when RJ just showed up out of the blue, I could see why Uncle was so pissed off!!

Mama Hope finally caught a break and got a really good paying job with the City of Edmonton, her plan was to save for a deposit to finally buy a house for her and her boys, it wasn't long after and somebody informed the low-income housing projects and we had to move out, she couldn't buy a break! After all she did for that community and feeding all the families, someone could not wait for her to save some money to buy a house, shame, shame, dirty motherfuckers!! Hope was able to put together some funds and with some help from her Lebanese connections she was able to get a house on 132ave 118street in the Kensington area, wasn't ideal, just an older 3bedroom house that needed some repairs and a fresh coat of paint. Again, with little and no help, Robert and I were in High School and the older boys would always be getting ripped off from the odd jobs or from the art work they'd be doing, RJ, was still not giving Hope anything to assist in raising the boys, she had to finally take RJ to court to get something, she couldn't do it, so Grant had to represent Hope in court, Grant won, but it was also very little, by this time it was 1980 I was already 16 years of age so RJ only had like two years left to pay, something like $75 each per month for Robert and I alone, no back pay, nothing else for the other boys at all!

We only lasted a year at this house, and we would end up moving into low-income condo units in Londonderry area called Londondale on the southeast corner of 82Street between 144ave and 140ave. Of course this townhouse would have many, many stories....this townhome mom bought only had one bathroom, it was a tiny 3 bedroom for mom, Robert and me, wrong, all the brothers came and lived here along with more borders, friends, free loaders and whomever just so happened to sleep over for a night or a couple of nights okay maybe a few weeks. There were times when I'd get up for school and feel like Sylvester the cat on bugs bunny where he's tiptoeing through the yard with all the sleeping dogs, I had to do that very thing with bodies everywhere on the living room floor and in the basement. I had no idea who a lot of those people were; they weren't there when I went to bed.

There was this occasion which was really rare, when I came home from school, the door was left wide open along with all the windows and the music was loud, almost so loud on the boom box it just sounded like distortion on maximum over drive, I'm calling out 'Hello', 'Helloooo' anybody here? There's no answer...I turned the music off and call out again, set my homework down go into the kitchen where the place is ran sacked, chairs knocked over, table is covered with shit, there's a mirror on the table and a passed out native guy with a full empty 2L of wine beside him, It looked like my brother but also at the same time didn't look like him, I was yelling at him to get up but to no avail, I came to the conclusion it was my brother so I left him, I went about my business and about a half hour passed and he shot up from the floor, started yelling about whatever and not making sense, 'What time is it?' it was like 4:30 by that time, he continued yelling out the door,' I got go party!' He was saying. After he left it was like the only time, I was ever by myself in this place.

Another time Mama Hope went on vacation to BC and said "NO PARTIES" 'I don't want any phone calls' okay, okay you won't get any! So, I was planning on going to the Limelight downtown and our roommate at the time along with Robert were having a few friends over for some drinks and a game of poker, it was going fine no rowdiness or anything bad happening, very innocently our roommate adjusts his kitchen chair and the back leg goes through the floor register and the chair goes down into the hole falling backwards he sticks out his arm to protect his fall, but it goes through the cabinet glass door and cuts his arm badly, like a main artery bad, Mike Burke was there and they wrapped his arm and used an empty beer flat box to contain the blood that was coming out, they jump into Mike's car and speed through red lights and avoid any collisions with four flashers on and horn blaring to get to the hospital. Always some excitement when Hope was away on vacation, crazy times!

It wasn't uncommon for that little dwelling to be a stopover for lunch after church service on Sundays, seemed like every week mom would say there's only a tiny roast or very little whatever it was and each time it fed the multitude of whoever was there, it was a minimum of twenty and one time there was over thirty people having brunch in that tiny shack.

This is my tribute poem to Mama Hope after she passed away on (June 9th, 2016).

Timeline of a Warrior

Eight decades you've overcome the worst.

birthed in the early thirties,

in the forties you were chased by family whores!

Rather than giving in you headed out the door.

To join the Canadian forces

1950's o'er the distant shore, romanced & wed in Metz France

Back in Canada in the mid fifties

Gave birth to six sons, ready to settle in…

Meanwhile the gambler can't even win!

Sacrificed it all, miles apart looking for a fresh start.

Separated and unglued in Seventy- Two

What now? Dear God!!

Oldest son shot down in Seventy-five.

'Nineteen years you've gone by…bye…and

Kingsway Ave is dripping poison through my veins,

Injected gunshot hallucinates through our brains.

Open wound gone to soon.

Chilled skin pressed against a

Monet print, so alone, so cold!

By the late Seventies

Two heroines formed the 'We Care Society.'

Fed neighborhood families & kept the poor alive.

No purple heart, no wallpaper to hang in a frame.

Not even a hand to shake & say a word of thanks.

Enter the 80's.

Alberta's boom hit bottom gloom.

I cannot do much more…into thy hands in Eighty-Four.

Skimmed by and by throughout the Ninety's.

Forced retirement by 96', scraps from the Government table.

Makes me sick.

21st century warfare of a lifetime has come & gone.

Round for round

A deadbeat dad would not lend a hand,

Distant memory of vows that were said…

Echoes of tears that were shed.

Now at the end of your days

Smiling upon your hospital bed where you lay

Ready to take plight and still silenced in your fight.

The toll bell rings, Mr. Barr comes to sing.

My head aching from prayers fallen to a trampled floor.

Your strength shines through an open door

My Hope, my hero

Eight decades you overcame…

Always admired...

My beautiful Mom

... 'The Warrior'

(Throughout the years I would write poems about Ray)

Thirty Years

A lifetime sentenced.

Without you

We held our breath, no answers Just questions?

One is, not knowing.

Where your soul came to rest...

Too young too scared

Took for granted.

The short time we had

The smells, the memories

Dissipating into another

Blood-soaked sunset

Just because...

A parole bluffed his way.

Back into society

When he himself

Should have been served.

The Thirty Years

Brother (R.A.B Sept 22,1956-Nov 1,1975)

So sorry

It had to end this way Maybe you knew…what was best

Taking it right through the chest!

So sorry

That I wasn't any older

We were all caught off guard No one was taught.

That life could be so hard!

So sorry

My big brother

There was no script to 'take cover.'

Maybe that bullet

Was meant for another…

So sorry

You couldn't have just.

Walked away…

"Protecting the underdog" That's what you'd say.

Wasn't even your fight!

Lamenting how

I fuckin' hate this night…

Thinking back those forty plus years…

Choking back many tears

To you again, One like no other

My oldest dear brother

Cheers to you…Ray Anthony

WARRIOR, WATCHMAN…

GUARDIAN over others!

Ray Anthony (1956-75)

Anguished

Shadow Boxer

Through these prison

Walls of my mind

Reliving the scene

Reruns of the same channel

Retracing, replaying.

Embracing my last day

...with you

Darkness of the night

Puddles shined so bright.

Disturbed ripples of black

& white

Echoes of gunfire

Resonates through the years.

Tears stream

Distant screams

Reflections pass within

Stained glass

Rise up

Mighty Phoenix

Out of this

Mire and Ash

Rack em up

The Neighborhood, Dickensfield, wasn't such a bad place to live when they were brand new, for the most part, maybe a step above a modern day 'shanty town', a housing project on the North side of Edmonton (near the perimeter) when the construction phase built them, in the early 70's Okay, not sure whose brainiac idea this was?? Let's build and make 3 phases of low-income dwellings, along with another area with at least a dozen apartments for; single and/or divorced families with children with no social programs or leisure centers in place. What do you think is going to happen? That's correct, off the top of my head, I'll guestimate the total number of kids per household…mmm, average probably 3.5, total number of dwellings around 217, in just the three phases; let's call it 800 kids!! With nothing for these kids in place, let them just hang out and be creative on their own, what do you think is going to happen?

For the most part in the early years like the summers of 1971-74 were pretty fun to play out in the streets, like when your parent actually said 'go play in traffic' because the streets weren't paved yet, it was a mud bowl, much like the Terry Jacks song 'we had joy, we had fun', the neighborhood water fights, bringing the hose through the house from back door to front door, or when a neighbor would go camping or summer vacation, their home would fall victim to being condemned, I mean; they would go all out wrapping the house in toilet paper and newspapers, throw garbage in the yard, paint graffiti over top the paper, egg the windows, dog poop in their mail box, it was definitely a Picasso, an abstract of vandalism, put on display for the humiliation and embarrassment for when the neighbor would return home!

Other times we actually played cowboys vs. Indians with real bow and arrows, pellet / bb guns or rifles, you had best keep your wits and your sights on full alert during these times, only once one kid had to go to the hospital getting shot in the mouth with a pellet gun. The couple of native warriors with the arrows came close many times, but never stuck anyone, good thing! Our one neighbor directly behind us slaughtered a moose in the living room, that's right a full-on Bullwinkle right on the fucking living room floor, little kids playing around the open guts with blood everywhere along with diapers and fly's buzzing everywhere, what a site to behold, welcome to the hood! At times it seemed as though you were bitter rivals with the neighborhood, opposing each other like siblings butting heads constantly, always trying to get the better of the other or one up them in many ways.

The earliest memory of going to what was supposed to be a birthday party in 1976, with Robert and Darrell, we go into this row house up across the street from the junior school (144 Ave., 88 St.) there's absolutely no furniture in the home, nothing, looked they moved out and forgot the kids, the kids at this party are dispersed 3 or 4 per room, with empty toilet paper rolls and a rag on the end of the roll, spraying cooking Pam spray through the rag and toking or breathing in the fumes (as an inhalant), A big-time cheap thrill high event that became really popular, some were dying from this shit! Next up and became a neighborhood hot item was model glue, empty the contents of a tube in a baggie and walk around the hood like a zombie, carrying an empty bread bag with a few tubes was the popular way to go, you needed a note from your parent to purchase modelling glue at the local stores, that's how bad it got!

Growing up in this display of abused and fucked up families, at times when you think that you've got it bad, until you go to a friend's place and witness the outright jaw dropping shit they have to live with, having the mailman over and being fuckin so drunk wasted by 11am, drinking straight from the bottles of Vodka, usually on the second or third bottle by that time, just another normal ho-hum day, or the physical abuse that was just outright in the open with many of these kids, not only by the parents, many of them had siblings kicking the shit out of them too!

Not only with their fists and kicking the shit out of them, you sometimes had to be on guard and watch for the flying debris most times, items that could do some ultimate damage, oh like maybe a cast iron frying pan with some hot bacon grease in the pan to boot, or how about this steak knife coming your way…most times it was over something dumb, maybe taking some smokes without asking. One time a few odd friends (not my normal friends) and me just checking out this motorized dune buggy car, pretty cool toy for early seventies shit, the way it could operate on rough terrain was very impressive,

Will wanted to have a look at it and picked up and a piece broke off the buggy, it wasn't even an important part, and just like that, Mike is on top of Will throwing the fuckin bombs at his face…like, wtf?

Much like all the brothers in my family, didn't matter how much you fought with each other, you could be at each other's throat, fist fighting, pulling hair or biting, if you crossed the line and were not blood, oh, I would have to wish you well, some of them had the shortest fuses and you'd better be ready to go at it! Our neighbors and neighborhood was very much like that, there were times we had our disagreements with some of the neighbors, where we could be at odds with them, but soon enough be having a beer and a smoke on our front step days later, case in point; brother Grant had some friends over (around 1977) for beers in the backyard (these friends are let say from the other side of the tracks; well-to-doers, rich or wealthier than us), they had felt because we lived in the ghetto or the slums lets treat it as such and start smashing the empty bottles on the concrete patio, the fight was on, Grant told them to leave and they were throwing more bottles and fighting with Grant now, by the time I called up John and Robert from the basement and they came out pretty fast, all the neighborhood lights came on and the neighbors came out to assist and help Grant. By the time we came out to the parking lot (which was just beyond our fenced yard), the circle of neighbors that were ready to help kick some needed rich ass, was very amazing to witness, Native Bill (shirtless) looks like a very pissed off Eskimo (nicest guy though), Simon, who would teach me how to use the Nunchakus came out swinging them like he was a scene of kung fu, and many others that were finding their way to our parking lot! I had never seen three guys trying to get on their motorcycles and escape the beating that was about to be bestowed upon them and get the hell out of dodge!!

The closeness of the Neighborhood really started coming together after Ray was killed, what it actually seemed like, was the plague of death (meet Joe Black) had been invited (and never left) into our community and ripping throughout everyone's home; shortly after Ray, a little beautiful neighbor girl (Tara Collins)dies of cancer, another friend from school across the field (Brendan) on a seasonal job delivering mail; on the last trip, his last delivery before going home, the delivery van rolls back and crushes him, next door neighbor with a gorgeous teen aged daughter (Dorothy, may have just turned 18) coming back from an out of town road trip, had her tire blew and she rolled and died. These are just some of the ones that had their life end early into 1976, and the door of death was opened and continued thereafter. By the time of Cindy McClure's (Grant's 1st wife) untimely death at the end of December 1985(Cindy went into a coma) and died around her birthday in January 1986, I had (lost track) of the number of young people's funerals I had attended, I would have to guesstimate around twenty-four by the time in turned 22 in 1986, (is this normal?).

Back in June of 2021, it was requested from our childhood neighbors if I wouldn't mind writing a poem dedicated to her nephew Dylan Kobelka, I was honored, even though I never met him; in remembrance of Dylan…

Forever Young

Hush lil baby

With that runny nose

Somebody left out the garden hose.

    Skinned little knees.

Looked out for you.

    Did what I pleased?

I wasn't embarrassed.

    Or ashamed

I'm an artist by name.

    Dylan Kobelka

Need my time and space.

    No time to be erased.

Energy flows when the wind it blows.

    Up

In all directions

    Create it…write it…rap it.

Like a gift? Hell no!

    My words are a hit though.

I'm from the North side.

    Don't play hide and seek.

I kicked the bucket.

    It wasn't on the list.

Time wasn't on my side.

    …this time

I gave it my best shot.

> When I began to rhyme
>
> Ain't nobody here to blame.
>
> > Don't be digging.
>
> That judgment games.
>
> When you haven't walked a mile
>
> In this life we choose
>
> > Sometimes we win…sometimes we lose.
>
> My family tree, bended knee
>
> They prayed the one, for a hand.
>
> > …not out
>
> I have not overcome I this life,
>
> Down but not out, it was the hand.
>
> > I was dealt, I always felt.
>
> I will remain,
>
> > Forever young
> >
> > Yo

Below is the lyric from an Alter Bridge song titled 'In Loving Memory…' a beautiful song and tribute to anyone that's lost their loved ones for any reason?

In Loving Memory

> *Thanks for all You've done.*
> *I've missed you for so long.*
> *I can't believe you're gone.*
> > *You still live.*

In me

I feel you in the wind.

You've got me constantly.

I never knew what it was to be loved.

Thanks for all you've done.

I've missed you for so long.

I can't believe you're gone and

You still live in me.

I feel you in the wind.

You guide me constantly.

I never knew what it was to be alone, no 'Because you were always there for me

You were always home waiting.

But now I come home, and I miss your face.

So, smiling down on me

I close my eyes to see.

And I know you're a part of me.

And it's your song that sets me free.

I sing it while I feel, I can't hold on.

I sing tonight 'because it comforts me.

I carry the things that remind me of you.

In loving memory of the one that was so true

You were as kind as you could be.

And even though you're gone.

You still mean the world to me.

I never knew what it was to be alone, no

'Because you were always there for me.

You were always home waiting.

But now I come home and it's not the same, no
It feels empty and alone.
I just can't believe you're gone.
And I know you're a part of me.
And it's your song that sets me free.
I sing it while I feel, I can't hold on.
I sing tonight 'because it comforts me.
I'm glad it sets you free from sorrow.
But I'll still love you more tomorrow.
And you'll be here with me still.
All you did you did with feeling.
And you always found a meaning.
And you always will
And you always will
And you always will
And I know you're a part of me.
And it's your song that sets me free.
I sing it while I feel, I can't hold on.
I sing tonight 'because it comforts me.

There were gangs within gangs much like any ghetto, some days you'd hang with a different group, for myself I'd end up getting into a lot of mischief when hanging around with the Native gang for too many days in a row, busting the locks off paper boxes was such an easy hit, to score seventy five or hundred dollars, the problem was splitting it with so many of them, other ways was to cash in rolls of slugs from construction sites putting a quarter in each end in case they opened it, then the store would give you ten dollars, it wasn't very good if they busted the roll open on the cash register, you'd have to run and get the hell out of the store.

Our one mode of transportation was our bikes, we went everywhere and did everything on our bikes, until one of the neighborhood Native kids got a hold of a pipe cutter, then they had this idea to cut bikes in half using this cutter, once they cut my bike in half, I made certain none of them or their bikes were safe anymore, dumb fuckers! Now we're all walking again.

They also had this idea, could have been partially an inside job too, one of them knew somebody at the Commonwealth Stadium and had access to leave an outside door ajar and possibly the equipment room.

Darrell (the only other white kid) and I were supposed to be in on this break and entry and were going to steal the Edmonton Eskimos football equipment, we both wanted nothing to do with that, it turned out they did steal some gear mainly Tom Wilkinson's helmet which was a specially made one and the team wouldn't have another one made in time for the Grey Cup, some other stuff along with a bag of footballs was taken. Darrell and I ended up ratting these clowns out that stole the equipment, and the Eskimos were able to recover all that was stolen before the next playoff game, putting our necks on the line for nothing in return, the Eskimos went on to win five Grey Cups in a row, thanks to us!

Darrell and I never even so much got a thank you from the Edmonton Eskimos football club, my mom was so pissed that they couldn't even give us an autographed football, she contacted the Eskimo office and they said "we cannot reward every kid that does a good deed" what the fuck? We recovered your equipment that was necessary for your playoff game, and for Tom Wilkinson, I would approach him years later at a golf tournament at Victoria Golf Course and he still brushed me off like I was that young teenage boy again! Fuck you Tom Wilkinson and Edmonton Eskimos (my favorite team though)

This is a poem I wrote about our front step at this place in Dickensfield where we lived from (1971-1979) ...

The Step

It wasn't fashioned with the latest patio furniture.
It wasn't decorated with columns, vines or flowers.
It wasn't modernized by keeping up with 'the Jones' kind of stuff.
It wasn't desired, wanted or adored.
It was however,
Familiar and similar as all of the others in the neighborhood.
A one-piece molding of cold hard cement, a replica,
Sitting there, waiting to be walked on,
Sat on or looked at.
If only that Lego block of cement could talk.
It would tell stories that.
Have been journeyed by all those who were just passing by
That would end up hanging out for the day.

Sharing stories, laughing, and enjoying each other's company,

Daily, weekly, and monthly

Summer after summer it had become tradition-making memories.

That would last a lifetime,

Eternally etched on the foundation of

The Step

In and around 1976, the year after Ray died, I don't remember finishing grade 7 at St. Phillip's, I know they (the teachers) were saying I should go to St. Francis of Assisi for grade 8, I would go there for two grades before going to High School, this would be my first introduction into pool halls, Fort Road billiards (FRB) was situated just north of Transit Hotel (66 St Fort Road) which was built in 1908, many of the buildings along this corridor still had the original wood floor planks overtop of the gravel and over time would cause the unevenness or character that they had become. You felt like you were in a black and white photograph or a post card, dingy, dirty, and colorless, which is cool from an artist point of view, like an Ansel Adams photo. FRB, was a very dark and gloomy room not for the faint of heart, they ran 40 watt bulbs for lighting, if you wanted to see, it was best to play on the tables by the front of the hall, with the big store front windows with the daylight coming in, everything in and around the area felt very enclosed, Fort road itself wasn't a very wide road itself, cars and trucks that would park on the street would make it very narrow for the vehicles travelling north and south, sometimes banging there side mirrors into each other, cheers!! All in all it wasn't the prettiest of settings, if you weren't from the local neighborhoods on the north side, you would kind of freaked out and tend to have your back against the wall, as for me and my schoolmates and being a north ender it was normal, lol, normal, what the fuck is normal? Is it even a dryer setting anymore?

When you're raised and grow up in a certain way or in neighborhoods that are not much better than shanty towns in third world countries, do you just become a biproduct? Street survival, a desensitized individual with no empathy, someone that's absorbed in the shit and mire, and has no feelings one way or another, could care a less, for the most part you still hold onto a glimmer of hope, dreams and positivity and always thinking... if only...always thinking of ways to get the fuck out of this neighborhood!! As for me, i still had a few years of school left...

Break

*H*ello, my friend, we meet again, it's been a while…where should I begin? (Lyrics from 'My Sacrifice' by Creed) This is my good friend, 97 Street… (more like my Nemesis), since I was 7 years old, this street has been part of my life in some way or another, either way I had to cross it, be on it, or just off of it, 97 Street aka; **'Heroes Boulevard'** a major artery that runs North (to Nameo and turns into highway 28) and South (from the Anthony Henday connector to some major avenues along the way such as; 167ave, 144ave, 137 and 132aves, Yellowhead Trail, 118ave, 111ave and 107ave then into downtown and then into a 'T' intersection onto Jasper Ave in Edmonton) in between 137 and 135aves on the west side of 97Street housed an area called Rosslyn, there was the Rosslyn Hotel with another strip of businesses, all old school stuff; barber shop, shoe repair, vacuum sales and repair, drug store and bowling alley, there is one more major one that I'll get to, just not yet.

It started out innocently enough, being entrepreneurial at 10 years old, I wanted to start making some money, it always seemed I was too young to work anywhere, nobody wanted to hire me, in my infinite wisdom on what I should do…I didn't want to operate a lemon-aid stand or cut lawns they seemed like a lot of work for what people wanted to pay me at that time, in 1974, I learned early on though, once people start drinking they're more generous with giving money, mmm…I acquired a shoe shine box because for some reason at 10 of age what boy doesn't like having his shoes polished? Anyway I embarked on the confines outside the Rosslyn Hotel, it was crazy busy, it didn't take long and I was raking in some pretty cold hard cash, I still remember this one drunk, he said "if you can put on a shine on these shoes, I'll give you all the change in my pocket" I replied "you probably don't have any" he grabbed his pocket from the outside and embraced it with both hands, that pocket was over half full, my eyes lit up, and so did his shoes, I got every bit of change off of him, close to ten dollars which was fine by me! Soon I hired other neighborhood kids to run my shoeshine box, I supplied the goods, they used my shoeshine box, and it was all good for a 60/40 split.

Every picture tells a story…

For the most part the black & white photos were more of a clear photo than the color ones, color pictures usually looked very grainy, anyhow, the businesses on street level at the Hotel, next to the main doors was the barber shop that Mitch owned, then just past if you went straight it had a breezeway with twin bars with separate entrances, the first one was more for the older crowd, and the other for the novice younger rowdy crowd, after a few drinks it didn't matter much everyone mingled and mashed together.

Along the bottom of the snooker shack facing east toward the parking lot (97 St.) were the old shoe repair, Hoover vacuum store, drug store owned by Asians old style convenient store with smokes and junk food, an accountants office for taxes, then the entrance to the snooker shack and then the main doors facing North was the Rosslyn Bowling Lanes, the parking lot was always pretty full, being one of the more active places around, it was situated ideally for the trades guys coming into town from the North and the military bases to the North of the Hotel, Griesbach which ran from (97 St. 137 Ave to 97 St to 167 Ave North /South) then west to 113 St, a giant squared off area for the military, it had all their practice facilities, buildings, mock tower, shooting range, housing and its own prison, around the middle point (144 Ave) was a private property access point, if you were brave enough you could take this short cut through to get to Castledowns on the other side, most times the MP's (military police) would pull you over and give you a ticket for doing so.

This one time I did get pulled over, had the light been green on the West side I would've made it through, but since it was a red light… the MP's pulled me over, it was taking an extraordinarily lengthy time to write me a violation ticket, apparently there was a warrant for my arrest with the City of Edmonton police so the MP's had to hold me and my dog until the cops came to bring me in to their station, I have to back up as to why there was a warrant issued, so back on St. Patrick's Day of 1990 six months earlier, the plan was to go for a night out a Richard's Pub in Castledowns with my girlfriend Patricia and her family, the night went on with no problems, I was the designated driver and did not partake in the festivities, as the night was coming to a close we were getting ready to leave, I went out to start the car and warm it up and wait for the Patti and her family, well Patti and her sister and mom were getting into the car, Patti's brother Bill got into a little altercation with the bouncers at the door and they were having their way with Bill until I ran up there and grabbed him to take him from there clutches, as I was getting Bill into the car a waitress took down my license plate number and reported us. I had this outstanding warrant for my arrest on this misdemeanor and was being charged for something Bill did.

Little did i know i was ultimately preparing myself for the fast lane of pool halls; the Snooker Shack (home base for myself and 35 other drug dealers) the Snooker Shack was situated on the second floor facing east into the same parking lot as the Rosslyn Hotel, known as the 'Rockin "R" 'was a potpourri of everybody from the Airborne to the Rebels, Hells Angel bike gangs and anybody else that was brave enough to have pints of drafts within these walls. It wasn't glamorous by any stretch, Hell, I think I've seen Satan having drinks on occasion, the pool hall itself was around 30-40 stairs to reach the room itself, which housed around 50 snooker and bar sized tables along with foosball tables and some stand up video machines, like every old room back in the day it had a stale odor brought on by everyone smoking in it including myself. This Snooker Shack was the drug store for the common addict and weekend smokers too, shit, everyone purchased everything from there, from your friendly weed to your not so friendly hallucinogens, LSD, cocaine, and mushrooms. There was a car commercial that would say "You want it? You got it...Toyota," that could've easily been the slogan for the drugs there; "You want it? We've got it...come score at the Snooker Shack tonight!

All of the plans for the following day was usually discussed at the day's end of drinking and partying, especially if you were required to be your own pool mule, that was to bring up a pound or your cut up weed or whatever product you were planning on selling the next day, the problem was if you drank to late or stayed up late and you had to run errands, you had little time the next day if you woke up late and did some running around to be at the Snooker Shack before (4 pm, 1600 hrs.) that was when the beat cop started his shift and would be there until midnight, most of the dealers had a pager since there were no cell phones yet, so if you received a page not to come around it meant that the six did a mock drug bust to scare everyone or the beat cop came on shift early, if the beat cop came up into the shack early he usually hung around and chatted to everyone with small talk while he made his rounds and would stick around for about an hour or hour and a half. Not good if you were trying to mule your load off upstairs, timing was everything.

The sub stations or little outlets around the north end also included; the Soccer Shack 92 St 132 Ave, Castledowns Arcade, followed by the others in and around Edmonton like; Kings Billiards, Century Billiards both of which were downtown along with the Metro birthed in the (early 90's), and then the smaller halls in different areas like Beverly pool hall, (pilot or drop off rooms with less heat) at Northgate and Castledowns. Once the heat figured out some of the dummies routines, they would be hanging around at our pick up or drop off places to cause interference, meaning we had to be on top of our game and to do that we had to stop partying and drinking so much, lol, fat chance that wasn't going to happen!

The game (eight ball or snooker) ...

Depending on where you play the rules could vary from house to house or who you play some people have their own version of the rules or variations of them, some will play bar room rules or typically they settle on the house rules if it's in a pool hall, anyway the quick dummies guide in playing 8 ball is usually a call shot game played on a 8' x 4' table with six pockets, one on each corner and two middle pockets (target or resting home for the balls) to start off their is a triangular rack that sets the 15 balls in place at one end of the table, the coin toss determines who will break the balls by using a cue to hit the solid white cue ball to break up these 15 color balls (#1-7 are a solid color and #9-15 are striped) upon breaking the balls if one of each ball is pocketed then that player has choice as per what group of balls will be his to finish pocketing, you can only proceed and continue pocketing your balls if you make your next pocket, once you miss it is the next players turn, it goes back and forth until one player completes and pockets all of his balls then completes the game by legally pocketing the solid black 8 ball, if the cue ball is pocketed after making the 8 ball the other player wins the game by default.

Snooker is a much different game and is played on a much bigger table (12' x 6') all of the balls in the rack are a solid red color then has six other different color balls that have a point value, with each pocketed red ball (1point) you then have option to pocket any other colored ball, yellow ball is 2 pts, green ball 3, brown ball is 4 pts, blue ball is 5, pink ball worth 6 pts and the black ball value is 7 points. So after each pocketed red ball you hit a colored ball after you sink the colored ball it is brought back onto the table into its original position you would proceed in this pattern until all the red balls have been pocketed, then to complete the game you would pocket each of the color balls from lowest points to their highest points or from lightest to darkest in color. It would only matter if the points that have been tallied and it's a close game, if you sunk two red balls and two black balls your points would be 16 for that turn, the game is done when whoever has the most points.

Table 22 / Scratch ball

There is a time when time stood still for me, I was captivated, intrigued, infatuated, D-all of the above, probably the very first time I had feelings like this, where this brunette-haired girl would walk along our street and I had to meet her, I would watch for her daily (after school hours) I wanted, had to, needed to meet her, I asked my brother Robert, who she was? And he told me, a sister of one of my friends whom I didn't know even had any siblings, let alone a gorgeous sister, I finally intercepted her, the union was innocent mixed with subtle flirtations, over the next little while as I would wait for her to walk by, she would be wearing a downfield vested jacket and by the time she would be going home the sun would be a little warmer so she would have it opened more with other layers of shirts underneath, I started venturing and being brave with her and would ask what she had on under those layers, with each article of clothing there was a pssst, it was cute and a little risqué at the same time, we would smile before getting to the under garments, knowing there was hidden connotations in our laughter.

Within a short time, frame as she would continue to walk up the street towards home, I would be yelling to her, "Will you marry me?" Our friendship was a very unique bond, we could sit or walk and even have coffee for hours upon hours at a local restaurant (hang out), soon I'd be walking her home and hanging out drinking pots and pots of tea or going to her place to make cookies or cakes, there appeared to be more to our friendship than just friends, I'd like to say it was friends with benefits, but it wasn't the case. During my high school years, she treated me as though we were dating, maybe I was holding on for that to come into fruition, we were doing everything together and most guys probably would have bailed. After moving from Dickensfield to the house in Kensington, my family thought they finally broke us up, but to no avail, during this year on 132ave, we continued to tie up the phone lines for the longest times, we could talk for hours upon hours, we didn't see much while we lived there, it wasn't until we moved back near the old neighborhood (Londondale),it was then when I would walk in the coldest of temperatures to bring her smokes and a chocolate bar, hang out for a while and drink tea or we would go across the street and babysit together, it was getting crazy with the mixed feelings and messages that were signaled, the flirting, the looks and the comments, add them all together and one would swear that we were in a relationship, when we went to any restaurant we'd order to share the meal, not our own separate food, always shared! Although she never went to high school, she always wanted to help with my homework and most times I could've attached her name to the work.

My feelings were being suppressed, I know I was still somewhat naïve, but I was going through a cyclone cylinder of emotions, I felt as though I was cheating when I would flirt with other girls at school, I know it sounds strange and probably looked that way at times too, we looked like a legitimate couple sometimes would fight like that too.

Give them what they want to hear, many times as Heather and I would walk and have lengthy conversations with a broad scope on everything as we would journey, there would always be smart ass comments or cat calls for one of us or both of us lol., most times the nasty slurs would be; 'sleeping with my leftovers' or 'have you poked her yet?' We decided to chime in and start saying that 'I poked her on the pool table 22 at the Snooker Shack' or we slept together in room 222 of the Rosslyn Hotel, it was fun to see the reactions now because nobody expected us to say anything!

By the time we (mama Hope) moved back by Londonderry Mall I found myself all of a sudden, a drug dealer at 16 years old and Heather had my back, she was the good angels voice on the right shoulder keeping me ah hum on the straight and narrow, you see the thing with selling drugs you can't get too involved or become addicted otherwise you're chasing your own tail like a dog would. A very difficult situation I might add when after a good day selling or even a bad day every one of us loved to party, so we'd end up in the bar at the Rosslyn and all filter our way to The Cellar, from their we would always find a house party, it was chaotic, the parties heading into the summer months were fucking insane, always on the North side, if you weren't at the bar you were at a house party, and after most the homes were wrecked the bush parties were like no other, most times everyone was from the North side, the crazy antics that went on, if these loonies could tear apart house parties I mean the structures, on an eviction party they would have to deem the house unlivable, they looked like a war torn house, bush parties much like the one in the northeast part of Edmonton called giga boo was totally wreck-less out of control party animals much like any animal house party movies, authorities were unable to access any part of the bush party because the amounts of partying taking place, cars were pushed off the embankment and set ablaze and the fire department couldn't come to put it out, there was an article in the Alberta Report magazine about the partiers and the destruction left in its path. It was total Anarchy from the get-go, so many dysfunctional kids growing up that needed a release.

Heather was soon to join in, not with the selling of drugs, but the party lifestyle, it was then and there where we'd have some heated disagreements, almost as though she didn't want me to see her in the drunken or stoned state, Heather fed off of rejecting me, I liked it too, a little too much, maybe that's where she got her enjoyment, it was frustrating to say the least, on two separate occasions, the first, at this apartment in the ghetto we were gathered drinking gin, mostly the younger drug dealers probably around a dozen of us, with mixing different alcohols you certainly get a different buzz going on, with different fermentations and processes, some drinks can affect you differently (same end result) and with drinking many gin drinks could get certain people in a feisty mood, which was the case at this little afternoon fiesta, sometimes you don't need to say anything, minding my own business getting a good glow on and just a little glance over from Emily with a nod and a smile sets off the fireworks like the 4th of July, and the more I sat there, smug like a bug, was not a good situation not even friendly fire, she was coming at me like a raging bull. Do you know those times when its best just to leave, not say a word…just leave it alone!

This other time Heather finally was single living on her own and there were some passed out bodies on the floor and couch, this is one of those moments if you were to look at a photo would be images of Sepia color just certain splashes of the brighter colors in the room everything else was black & white, it was a time when you could hear the clock on the wall tick, nothing was moving, it was in fact after a funeral, time when people self-isolate and get absorbed into their own thoughts, I was drinking some whiskey straight out from the 26oz bottle holding it gingerly with my left hand (there was maybe 1/3 left in the bottle) and had a lit smoke in my other, sunglasses half way down my nose and my tie on my suit was undone a little and same with my dress shirt the top few buttons were unbuttoned, if I could time travel or even draw this scene for a live stage I can visualize this entire scene and how sexy it was, again after the fact Heather told me she could've or wanted to have sex with me, but again she stated "my arrogance and my attitude" disrupt or get in the way of her doing the actual act.

Remember when...

Being brave and having attitude
Enough to drop by with a bottle of poison and a
smoke in the other hand, talk was cheap.
Being cool, left me in the cold.
Stepping over passed out bodies.
Maybe I should've called 9.1.1
No one on the planet mattered.

I found, it held the interest and thus made me to keep coming back, (like a dog returns to his vomit), but like anyone with Kaunas you get a build up with blue balls and need a release, this one night at a friend's hall party at the Slovinski dome, Heather is wearing a loin cloth skin colored mini skirt with matching top and no underwear, talk about being turned on, she was sitting on the end of the table the other problem she wanted me between her legs and stand there with her all night, not next to her, like actually between her legs and she would wrap one or both of her legs around me so that I couldn't leave, I could go to the bar and the bathroom that was all, otherwise stand here and be teased all night long, Heather knew exactly what she was doing and loved watching me squirm inside my own skin, she knew I could see her flower and the more I squirmed the more she liked it, this was an all-night long party, usually lasting 6-8 hours. I was beyond frustrated, and I took Heather to her place and maybe I was anticipating or expecting too much, I didn't think so though considering she had me in she clutches the entire evening, talk about withdrawing her intentions omg!! Where did that leave me, like a dog begging for scraps, having tea and massaging her, then asks me to leave…I'm like what? You treat me like that all night, invite me in, then say go home, I was being nice but dam it I was beyond being nice I wanted some sex!! It's like knowing you have money in your bank and the machine keeps saying insufficient funds or access denied.

I was pissed off and I left, all I said was "lock your door", and slammed the door, I (or we) didn't end up talking about this night until years later, it left a deep wound, I'm not trying to justify my behavior, I wonder which is worse; mixed signals, good intentions or rejection, I don't know, teasing a guy all night is like putting gas on an open flame and saying you didn't know it was going to do that!

The other thing that Heather told me afterwards was she wanted or waited for me to comeback that night, like; I love you, I hate you, come here, go away, she tried and wanted to desperately to try and tell me but each and every time there was a road blockage or barricade that was always in our way, an invisible force field like in the movie Dead pool 2, we could see each other but something was in the way.

We had all the time in the world but like most friends or families that have a dispute, soon you don't realize how much time has lapsed until the dust has settled then you see somehow years got washed away, vanished over something dumb, an argument, fight or just being bull headed and not saying sorry, I was wrong, even if you weren't wrong. The fact is you can't get those years back, we didn't fight or have many disagreements, we were in fact very compatible, the fact was one was always to damn proud to beg or say their true feelings.

We went on vacation this one time to Fernie BC., mama Hope wanted to go see her mom (Edith), Heather and I had a disagreement, and it ruined my entire time being there, just such dumb fighting and miscommunication, leads down a spiral road to nowhere.

After leaving (the night of the hall party), I never returned, I was ashamed of myself for treating her with such disrespect, then again it wasn't too long afterwards that I became a limelight junkie, the party life got injected back into my veins, running away and not facing your giants, monsters or demons, it was easier to push the easy button and not face anything, it seemed like the normal thing to do, become great friends then destroy it by trying to justify how you deserve to have sex with that individual.

Awakened

Two young souls who couldn't grab hold.
Searching for answers they could never be told.
Living in the fast lane of life, wondering...
If she would ever be my wife.
Desperately trying to reach her and yet.
Couldn't find the words to speak to her.
Always wishing, wondering, hoping
When? When will she appear to me, the one?
That's always been so dear to me...
OH, those two young souls,
How did they miss their ship with set sails?
With opportunities had, opportunities failed.
Questions deep within their souls
Things that you've never been told.
That through mistakes one has gone astray.
Yet both were young, wild n' free birds of prey.
Trust was breaking, contact, that's probably all it would have taken.
They had both slipped when you were not.
Awakened

Within the timelines of me leaving Heather's that night and walking away from our friendship was like the Fall of 1983, although I'd see her on occasion, we didn't speak to one another, nothing was said about the hall party night either, we were content in leaving the elephant in the middle of the room and tip toeing around it, you could certainly tell we wanted desperately to talk with each other, for the time being it was hush, hush don't say a word! Being in silence for those couple of years brought on some unfortunate events and relationships that neither one of us ever dreamed about, Heather wound up in abusive relationships with dishonest guys and me…well that's another story all together (to be added)

After I moved back home from my dead end relationship of four years, Heather and I started fresh and began to speak to each another again, during the day while I was at work she'd root through my things in the basement and would write me notes in my journals, we didn't skip a beat and in no time we were talking on the phone for hours at a time, her marriage was a little rocky (I wasn't there to cause interference), we would talk mostly about my relationship gone sour, catch up on her abusive relationships with the few boyfriends she had and discussed the night of the hall party, basically we picked up where good lifelong friends usually do after they get dismantled. The stuff you realize after walking and going through Hell, what's the old adage "Can't see the forest through the trees?" I mean what it is. There was obviously a connection, if you can spend every day, every day, every moment together without skipping your next breath of air, there has to be a solid line, no dial up…right?

Wasn't it the same for Forrest Gump and Jenny? When one person was ready the other person is going or doing something else, their paths cross but never get connected, and when they finally do, life is gone or done for one, they (everybody) say life is short, and it is, time, it really isn't on anyone's side, we prance around thinking we own our destiny, in some way maybe...

Pink Floyds song called 'Time.'

Ticking away the moments that make up a dull day.
Fritter and waste the hours in an offhand way.
Kicking around on a piece of ground in your hometown
Waiting for someone or something to show you the way.
Tired of lying in the sunshine, staying home to watch the rain.
You are young, and life is long, and there is time to kill today.
And then one day you find ten years have got behind you.
No one told you when to run, you missed the starting gun.
And you run, and you run to catch up with the sun but it's sinking.
Racing around to come up behind you again.
The sun is the same in a relative way but you're older.
Shorter of breath and one day closer to death
Every year is getting shorter, never seem to find the time.
Plans that either come to naught or half a page of scribbled lines.
Hanging on in quiet desperation is the English way.
The time is gone, the song is over, thought I'd something more to say.
Home, home again
I like to be here when I can.

And when I come home cold and tired
It's good to warm my bones beside the fire.
Far away across the field
The tolling of the iron bell
Calls the faithful to their knees.
To hear the softly spoken magic spells

Possibly for many that are reading this and taking this in cannot fathom a relationship like this unless you had a similar situation growing up, maybe the storyline was different and maybe you had the 'Happily Ever after' ending, others may feel this is too close to a Jerry Springer script; with deceit, lies, Tom Foolery, flirting and or outright cheating. Whichever the case maybe, I'm not trying to defend myself or say that I was innocent, I was available, single, and fuckin hot n' sexy. Being pursued by your childhood crush or sweetheart was a totally different kind of twist and it would be twisted had it been an affair, but it wasn't, Heather and her husband were separated heading down the pathway to be divorced, that's all I knew and didn't ask questions mainly because I knew the inside story and to write it would be heresy, why would I? There was other weird mixed-up feelings or emotions going on, usually when we'd go to the mall shopping and other woman would flirt with me, Heather would encourage me to do my part and flirt back, get a phone number or go and talk to them, then put on the jealous girlfriend act either at the mall or driving home, it was dramatic and, in another perspective, it was a turn on, some people like 'The Hollywood 'whatever cranks your wheel, it was fun.

There was still no physical contact between us, there was a level of respect, and I couldn't cross that line, it wasn't initiated either, or was it? Our late-night conversations on the phone going well past the midnight hour and making herself available to me and asking many personal questions, my defenses were being weakened, I started explaining my desired fantasies in detail about the girl in the store at the mall, being aroused and exposed, my weakness truth serum, kryptonite, asking me anything, telling it all like a Barry White sexual song, the long pauses on the phone listening to the heavy breathing and the silence, heart beats through the phone lines, I can feel it coming in the air at night...hold on, and I've been waiting for this moment all my life...hold on(lyrics to Phil Collins 'In the Night')

My thoughts I penned about that girl in this store at Londonderry Mall...

Mmmm...

In the cold warfare of my mind,
I stood in the hall of a
North end mall
Window shopping.
You arrested my stare
I was detained.
In a typical statement of self-denial
You are not the first to be defiled.
Over and over
Caressed with thoughts from a
Lustful shopper

As much as we tried to stop the more and more, we wanted it, desired it, anticipated it we created a habit an addiction that was long overdue, a freight train set on a collision course.

Do you know what it's like to quit smoking cold turkey or any other addiction? When you're not entirely set on quitting or focused, the substance absolutely consumes your thoughts, feelings, and emotions, it takes over your entire mental state much like Venom in the movie Spiderman, and there was no stopping it! The one good thing is, we weren't physical, when we'd go for coffee or shopping there was no touching, holding hands or any indication that there was some mischievous misbehaving's hanging out of the closet, lord knows the Christian do gooders (who are themselves without sin) would even have more to talk about or create a story and a rumor weed that they had seen us together, at this point I didn't even care about what rumors the so called 'Faithful' were starting, people believe what they want to believe anyway.

I tried before to defend my name when I first came back after my 'Mushroom trip from Hell' the stories that some Christian brothers came up with (wowzers) and I thought I was the one tripping out on a bad high, and they (the back stabbers) could without blinking an eye, we would-be out for Sunday brunch or any other gathering and this one so-called brother (Peter), never did apologize, and just let the chips remain on the floor or whatever you want to call it, chips or shit its all the same crap. Bipolar mother fucker believed his own lies and still acted like we were best friends.

Maybe I was or am evil (labelled as the most 'Evil Blackburn' of all-time) I just didn't care anymore, like water beads repelling or maybe my alter ego had really taken me over, Blackie was finished in the bar life and the party scene, but was he really done? Many others hadn't seen that side of me; they have noticed I had become a handsome giant that looked like I had indeed arrived from a tour, Mr. Entertainment, social lite, more popular than ever with really nothing to show for it, just confidence and the winner of a few popularity contests. Had I just run away from my reality life to create a fantasy world in the underground nightlife?

I'm going to tell you a story…about a woman I know…this is '**Blackies Visit to Wonderland.**'

'**The Hollywood Version** 'Even I do not know if this story fiction or fantasy, it has some reality to it, in all fairness to the parties involved **don't Read into It!**

'Rain' lyrics by the Cult

Hot sticky scenes, you know what I mean.
Like a desert sun that burns my skin
I've been waiting for her for so long.
Open the sky and let her come down.
Here comes the rain.
Here comes the rain.
Here she comes again.
Here comes the rain.
Hot sticky scenes, you know what I mean.
Like a desert sun that burns my skin
I've been waiting for her for so long.
Open the sky and let her come down Here comes the rain.
Here comes the rain.
Here she comes again.
Here comes the rain I love the rain.

I love the rain.
Here she comes again.
Here comes the rain Hot sticky scenes, you know what I mean.
Like a desert sun that burns my skin
I've been waiting for her for so long.
Open the sky and let her come down.
Here comes the rain.
Here comes the rain.
Here she comes again.
Here comes the rain.
Hot sticky scenes, you know what I mean.
Like a desert sun that burns my skin
I've been waiting for her for so long.
Open the sky and let her come down.
Here comes the rain.
Here comes the rain.
Here she comes again.
Here comes the rain I love the rain.
I love the rain.
Here she comes again.
Here comes the rain.
Oh, rain.
Rain
Rain
Oh, here comes the rain.
I love the rain.
Well, I love the rain.
Here she comes again.
I love the rain Rain.
Rain
Oh, rain.
Rain
Rain
Oh, here comes the rain.
I love the rain.
Well, I love the rain.
Here she comes again.
I love the rain.
Rain

Heather and I made this music video for Ian Astbury of the band The Cult, this was such a steamy erotic sexual scene they couldn't or didn't want to use it, we both got paid very, very well for our parts and never heard any more about it. The scene actually started upon arrival at People's Pub on Whyte Ave., two hungry souls, lost in the music scene in love with each other but, afraid to admit it or connect, just out partying trying to find other mates or get inebriated and doing ecstasy and forget about their lost state in the world (two lost souls swimming in a fish bowl-Pink Floyd) going into the pub and realizing that the scene had changed, it was no longer a Rock n Roll venue, it's now a grunge, Goth or punk bar, not fitting into this new scene and being disappointed they leave the pub and as they're getting into the car it starts to rain, let's go up to the rooftop of the parkade and watch the storm, Heather agrees and we go park and turn out the lights, the film crew has these huge umbrellas and distant lighting it's as though nobody was up there.

She asks me to kneel between her legs of the car, so I do, Heather is wearing a longer summer dress and pulls it up on top of her thighs, she asks "do you like that" as I answer with a "yeah" the music is cued- 'Rain' by The Cult , in the background and the rain starts hitting the car hard, as I undo my pants to fantasize about her underneath me, I ask "can I come in" and while she is saying "yes" crosses her legs behind me and thrusts me inside her, the music and the rain beating hard together in synchronicity, couldn't have written a better script or maybe you could have, the timing and everything was so on cue, I just don't know what they wanted for the video there wasn't much discussion whether it was good or bad, never heard after filming they gave us our money, thanked us and said "we'll be in touch."

This opened Pandora's Box, I was so intoxicated by what was going on, I was a junkie, off in never, never-land, exit life, with no chance on returning, omg…what have I become? Was I really a pirate? An evil scaly wag of the night life, stuck on an vacant island, two became one everywhere we went, we had to re-visit all of the old stomping grounds and mark them as new territory, crazily feeding off the passion of fifteen years that had expired from us, each visitation had familiarity because the years had vanished all that was, not entirely different but familiar in a lot of ways, making love in those places was so exhilarating, so exciting and yet so natural almost like being in the Garden in our sinful lustful desires, another snow globe state where we were enclosed in our own world, a place where you don't have to answer to anyone or their dumb questions. Pointing their righteous finger and exposing your weaknesses to an open stage while their closet is full but unopened. It was like for the most part an escape, or that I have run away with her and never to return, these magical moments feeling as though time had lost track of its own, there was no more time, the frames of our existence were locked in slow motion so intriguing, lost into each other's motivation and fully surrendering unto each one's passion and desire that was always there, just never tapped into before.

Ashamed

The darkness in my shadow looms heavy night and day
Appearing to be thick of sin...larger than imagination
This game of life I seek and hide but am I going to win?
I choose the road less travelled. Alone I drift to play my part
Challenges of black & white I sift or tear apart!
Wisdom, I do gain, each struggle oozing out of my soul
Lurking behind the corners, chimes no longer sing...
What became of the past? This sorrow did I bring?
No longer demeaning others, this pain I've caused for years.
Offered another Kleenex to wipe away their tears.
Putting on my shades and letting my hair locks weave
Blank lines for you to write a lyric of forgiveness.
So, I've walked that hundredth mile just to see that dimple in
Your smile wasn't my attitude nor was it pride.
Someone meets me halfway there's no place left to hide!

These lyrics to Alter Bridge Ghosts of Days Gone By remind me so much of my time growing up its so uncanny, it fits my life like a glove.

"Ghost of Days Gone By"

The misery I know.
Like a friend that won't let go
Is creeping up on me now once again.
So, I sing this song tonight.
To the ghost that will not die
And somehow it seems to haunt me till the end.

Do you feel the same?
For what was remained?
Yesterday is gone, we can't go back again.
Do you ever cry?
For the ghost of days gone by

I remember summer days.
We were young and unafraid.
With innocence we'd glide beneath the stars
It seems so long ago.
Beyond the life that I now know
Before the years would have their way and break my heart

Do you feel the same?
For what was remained?
Yesterday is gone, we can't go back again.
Do you ever cry?
For the ghost of days gone by

And I know it's drawing closer.
With each day I feel the end I... don't wanna die
Don't wanna die, don't wanna die.

I don't wanna die.

Do you feel the same?
For what was remained?
Yesterday is gone, we can't go back again.
Do you ever cry?
For the days gone by
Do they haunt you like a ghost until the end?

Haunt you 'til the end Until the end.

Call Shot (one & done)

A major piece that was at the Rosslyn Hotel (fast lane in a 97 Street pool hall)...on ground level was all the small store businesses, on the second level above these shops was a very large room called 'The Snooker Shack' of course it was a great front to play pool and billiards along with some video arcade games and some foosball tables, but it was also home to mmm, thirty-five drug dealers, that's right, 35, you see...the Snooker Shack was known for pretty much all the drugs you've ever wanted to purchase, anywhere! Before 1979 would finish, I remember walking along that 135ave with Robert and I never wanted to walk on that side of the street with the Snooker Shack, for some reason I knew it was drawing me in. I avoided it as much as possible, and I finally caved, I gave in and surrendered and it took me over and consumed me, by the time 1979 was over, I was selling drugs.

It was a crazy time, it didn't matter how slow the days seemed, be patient you're going to sell all your shit, everyone always did, sometimes the staircase was aligned with all the dealers and when customers came it sounded like an auctioneer selling shit to the highest bidders, we all competed together, then we'd all party, drank and maybe got high, then shared stories just like any other businesses (maybe), there were times we'd get carried away and take our gatherings out into the parking lot out front, the other businesses and their customers didn't like that, the cops would answer those calls to the Rosslyn as if it were a sale on donuts, like fly's to shit, those cops be upon us! Mind you had you not known any of us…objects in mirror may appear scarier than they are. Although many of them were very unattractive, then with the long dirty or greasy hair, wearing jeans and jean jackets or the back woods look with the plaid, some of the nicest group of people, not only would help in time(s) of need, possibly give you the dirty shirt off their back.

We did have our own personal Jesus with us (Bobby), and he did give his shirt and most of all his other belongings too, call him crazy or whatever you want, Jesus was one of the better looking criminal dealers; a native son with a blend of looks between Muhammad Ali (boxer) and Elvis Presley (singer), he'd dance around the parking lot with open beer being chased on foot by the police, this one time even stole one of their police issue rimed hats that they use to wear, very entertaining to say the least, which ultimately would end with them taking Jesus down (not off the cross) and arrested him. Another dealer named Doug, with waist blonde hair and one of the nicest smiles (with dimples) very laid back, if you needed any cash or anything Doug would just give it to you with no expectations of you giving it back. Doug also had an alter ego that was very interesting, he fancied himself as a criminal mastermind, very devious, had some messed up plans, that ultimately would land him in prison doing some hard time, firstly Doug wanted to rob an event held at Commonwealth Stadium called 'Rock Circus' they would host about a dozen rock bands slated to play on stage at different times during like a 12 hour period, Doug and I would have coffee in the diner at the Rosslyn and he would go over this plan of his step by step, there was no way of knowing the whereabouts of the cash unless somebody was situated (hired) deep inside. Doug's other whacked out plan was to kidnap Wayne Gretzky before the playoffs were to begin, not sure if Doug had a hand in on the kidnapping and holding the Pocklington's hostage in April of 1982, other plans Doug discussed with me was the Brink car robberies mostly occurring at Kingsway mall, Doug may have been involved in some of these crimes.

At one point in the summer of 1980, Doug became involved with another drug dealer within our group, Derrick and Doug had this great venture where they were scoring bails of marijuana, it was low-grade skunk weed back then we called it home-grown, these two clowns had the idea to spread out the weed over two huge bingo hall tables that were situated in their house and spray some mixture all over this weed (maybe food coloring and edible gold paint) once they completed this task they'd roll the weed into oversized ¼ ounce baggies, bring it to the snooker shack and start to announce it as; Acapulco gold, people were dialed into this shit and Derrick and Doug were selling it off like hot cakes, because in comparison their bags of weed looked almost like ½ ounce bags, not quite but you get the picture, during the day if these two were up in the shack selling this shit, nobody else was selling any weed, because they'd interfere the sale by butting in and showing off these baggies and in comparison 9 times out of 10 they would take the sale home.

It was a good thing not to just sell one product like, weed, you see to be a good pharmacist you needed to have a good selection: blonde hash, black putty hash, oil or honey oil, acid, mushrooms or cocaine. Like I said, it was the biggest drug store in North America at the time, whatever you wanted you could get it there, if not at that specific time it would be in route to be in your hands within a half hour, and that's with no Skip the Dishes or Uber! Their romance didn't last too long, like I've said before Douglas the nicest guy, until you double crossed him, Doug was pissed off at Derick for not only ripping him off with some of the drugs that were dealt, but all of a sudden, Doug had this crazy gut suspicion that Derick was setting him up to get busted, the six (cops) was on Doug, and he felt very 'Set-up', like a, betrayal.

Doug set this up with an International golden gloves boxer, he pays the boxer $50 to come to the shack and do a warm-up clinic, like on a punching bag on Derrick, the boxer shows up in the middle of the day, looking like Rocky (hoodie up over his head, taped hands, sweat pants),a fucking boxer, runs up the staircase with his head down at the top of the stairs, in text book fashion, Derrick peeks his head around the corner, the rendezvous, Derrick asks 'wanna score?' the boxer says 'you Derrick?'

Without hesitation or anything Derrick chimes into the response and as quickly as he says 'yes' the gloves are upon him, a flurry to the solar plexus and a few upper cuts to the face, in a moment's notice, he's down for the count, it's not over, Derrick realizes he needs to escape, he gets up and runs for his life, rolling down the stairs (around 25-30 steps) and suddenly hits the door at the bottom, gets up, pushes the door open and runs like; the Roadrunner being in the clutches of Wile Coyote about to be devoured! Derrick had a really nice muscle car he was fixing up, apparently had a pricey paint job on it, and the car possibly worth $16k, one thing was Derrick didn't have was fire and theft on his insurance policy, Doug had known this and paid out another $50 for a Molotov cocktail to be served at Derrick's car, it was torched, and to show everyone that you don't mess or double cross Doug, he had the tow truck driver bring it to the Rosslyn parking lot to put on display before taking it to the junk yard. Not sure of the where about of Derrick after this happened, rumors have a way with words!

A poem I wrote about the…Snooker Shack

'Snooker Shack'

Stale smoke consumes the air,
You've been here far too many times before.
Hidden away in this dim lit pool hall,
You light another cig as you think, 'I need to quit, just not yet.'
What else is there? Another potential customer,
As all the sellers beckon their 'daily specials'
The chatter goes on and on
I'll just play it cool today and watch the forty-watt powered lights as they flicker and buzz like a bee on a flower.
Maybe play a bit of snooker as these jokers compete with each other
Trying to sell off their stuff.

> *Quite a few familiar faces today*
> *Everyone's getting ready for another weekend, funny thing it's only Tuesday.*
> *Oh well, sit back, no need to rush the pharmacist, everyone sells out.*
> *Always do, always have…time for a coffee and a bite,*
> *Maybe some good conversation and share a clubhouse & fries with some gravy.*
> *Yeah, that sounds gooooood!*

So, you want to have a party? You want to drink with these cohorts? This would have to be likened to the days of the Vikings, let me say this, this group all together with their girlfriends and friends (in which I have over 55 names of memory) or acquaintances, could drink a bar dry, what was that? This school of fish (the drug dealers of the North side) could school anyone at the art of partying, they never stopped, they could drink and drink, until there's nothing to be drunk, a lot of times you could drink yourself sober a couple of times in a day, some of the guys didn't know there limits and could soil themselves, because they're too drunk to walk, they could pass out sitting up, piss n shit themselves and come to laugh about it and have another drink, our local watering hole, our daily end of the day relaxer (which was every days end),there was a place kitty corner to the Rockin 'R' on the North east corner of 97Street in the basement of North town Mall called 'The Cellar', OMG…what a place that was!!!

John the manager would make provisions for us, along with a couple of waitresses Irene and Juanita we were well looked after and so were they, and if there ever was any problems or issues, John would always side with us, no matter what! This one time in particular, probably close to fifty of us, we all wanted to sit in one area together, rather than disrupt his lounge with us, he made room in the dining lounge, looked like a scene from a Guns n' Roses video possibly the wedding in November Rain song, the drinks never stopped flowing that night and just after midnight the fire alarms were going off and not one of us moved or left as per Johns instructions, the alarms continued... it sounded like the fire alarm off April Wines song 'Oowatanite' and everyone would be rejoicing to the lyrics of that tune as well, until the firemen showed up, they were so pissed off with us, for not responding to the fire alarms, they were told to 'Fuck Off!!' by this group of bandits and John was scrambling to calm them down and calm us down, eventually we won, it was a false alarm anyway, we would continue drinking and party on throughout the night.

There was always, always somebody's house to party at and to spill into and continue the flow of drugs and alcohol, sometimes if it was an eviction celebration these houses wouldn't stand a chance, walls would be kicked in or taken down, one time they hooked up some chains to a 4x4 truck and were pulling out some structural walls!

One could certainly tell which area of the city you were in just with the house parties alone, the north side never stopped, always had a reason to celebrate or party, the 'off sales' were sold on the north side until last call at 2am sometimes you could get them afterwards too, there were many bootleggers to buy from as well. The south side people were quite reserved, many bars on the Southside along with off sales would only be open until midnight, the odd one or two in hotels would remain open.

Who would've known that we were in the market to sell horse tranquilizers? Why would we sell those? There are horses in a pool hall, apparently, we had some chemists in the midst of our operation, wanted to create an 'Ultimate High' pill, made with; Mescaline (hallucinogenic drug), Strychnine (white, odorless, bitter crystalline powder) a strong poison and PCP (Phencyclidine) aka; angel dust. One of these pills could take down an average sized horse between (900-2000 lbs.), let's just say... it'll 'fuck you' every which way and twice on any other day!! The size of the pill was close to the biggest size vitamin pill that you had ever seen, almost 1"long and just over an 1/8" in diameter, one of the younger dealers 'Bear' decides to take a full capsule by himself, had you ever seen a person take on human form of a concrete pillar? That was Bear, sitting on a window ledge at the back of the unlit area of the pool hall, completely just gone, no movement, no talking, just absolute concrete colored and still like a pillar, I approached Bear and tried my best to communicate with him, total unresponsiveness, in this moment I was unaware it was these pills that were circulating that did this to him. Bear did eventually come back down from this cloud but said 'it certainly fucked him up!.' Once you take hallucinogenic drugs, they sure mess with your psyche, reality vs. the shaken snow globe.

We could have great discussions at great lengths about making comparisons from the drugs of my day and for the sake of arguments let's call my day (1969-1999) so basically a generation of the 'Experimental Age' to (2000-present) what should we call this age of drugs? Age of the Opiates, Meth, or the era of one and done. Those would all be fitting titles for this generation of drug users that scored from their dealer and it was such a pure product that they OD after the first use, that would be like playing Russian roulette every time you scored, giving you a one in six chance of survival, a little better than that of ecstasy where 1 in 4 pills you will become a statistic, for myself and the other dealers (I think I can speak on their behalf) we weren't out to harm anybody, when we would stretch out the products we weren't using household cleaning products or shit (killer) filler, most things we did were tricks of the trade, why risk harming or killing off your clients? That baffles my mind, especially in and around 2010 in Vancouver, BC; the dealers on the streets were selling pure un-cut cocaine, what was that? Yeah, pure shit that was killing off their clientele like almost instantaneously, like wholly fuck man!! Why? Yeah, like good question.

This song by Shinedown is very fitting for the Snooker Shack days…

'Save Me'

I've got a candle.
And I've got a spoon.
I live in a hallway with no doors and no rooms.
Under the windowsill they all were found
A touch of concrete within a doorway
Without a sound
Someone saves me if you will.
And take away all these pills.
And please just save me if you can.
From the blasphemy in my wasteland

How did I get here?
And what went wrong?
Couldn't handle forgiveness.
Now I'm far beyond gone.
And I can hardly remember the look of my own eyes.
How could I love this?
My life's so dishonest
It made me compromise.
Someone saves me if you will.
And take away all these pills.
And please just save me if you can.
From the blasphemy in my wasteland
Jump in the water.
Jump in with me
Jump on the altar.
Lay down with me.
My hardest question to answer is why.
Someone saves me if you will.
And take away all these pills.
And please just save me if you can.
From the blasphemy in my wasteland
Someone saves me.
Someone saves me.
Somebody saves me.
Somebody saves me.
Please don't erase me.

Living large and making drug money on what a nice feeling, always having cash on you is such a great feeling, considering you had to work pretty hard in order to make anything, up to this point in time (1980) I had the shoeshine business, babysitting job for one person that was my second home and they looked after me very well from 1974-83 (paid better than min. wage), paper routes, every summertime worked Klondike Days at Northlands from 1976-84, nothing though comes close to the money you made selling drugs, always being able to help out mama Hope with money put a smile on her face and without knowing that it was drug money, because of the front of my other jobs. Top it off by going to high school (or trying to) and I was golden, lol, so I thought, I went to Archbishop O'Leary(87St 132ave) to the west of the school on 92St was another little drug depot called The Soccer Shack, HS started out not bad in grade 10 made around 44 credits looking alright for grade 11, wrong…the drug scene hit me that summertime, it was all in good fun though, right?

Grade eleven, the year was coming to a close, I felt I could breathe, then with two weeks remaining brother Robert came to the HS to visit, he wasn't allowed to be there, (he was kicked out previously) now he's trespassing on private property, at the north end of the school was a big open field with soccer posts and football fields, you could sense something wasn't right and teachers were making their way towards Robert and I, my Spidey senses were tingling and I could see what was about to transpire, as I was trying to usher Robert (who was egging the teachers on to engage into a fight)off the property, they kept pressing and pressing, finally I turned and said 'If you don't stop pursing Robert, I will personally kick your ass!' I may have also grabbed or shoved the teacher in the heat of the moment. There you have it, with two weeks remaining in grade 11, I got expelled! Mama Hope was not happy, so for that summer I got a job with the next-door neighbor (Spike)installing eaves troughs on houses if you're going to remain a criminal (selling drugs) its best to show why you have so many cash in your pocket.

With a new outlook and registering at St. Joe's for grade 12, I lasted a month, it wasn't the same as O'Leary, I quit, tried to get into other public schools but they said if you try back to O'Leary and if they don't take you back then we'll accept you here, I went back to O'Leary and they accepted me back into their culture on some bullshit conditions, Walla back on home turf, but now they also hired a policeman on duty into the school, had to watch myself on high alert, and to be sure that I carried little drugs on me and none in the locker, the school and cop were always searching lockers.

As soon as the school year was rolling along, so was the selling of drugs and going up to the snooker shack at the Rosslyn was getting more and more tense, they installed a 'beat cop' on site at the Rosslyn from 1600-2400 hrs., (everyday)the police along with undercover dicks were on a shake down and they were trying to bust all the dealers and close down the ongoing trafficking problem that existed there, the cops started coming up in waves, see how many they can catch, make some arrests, do their questioning, find out names and thin out drug dealers little by little. Across 97 St., to the east of the Snooker Shack was stood a stand-alone liquor store, where the cops would have ghost cars watching the snooker shack with binoculars, Wave after wave would come(of cops) and I avoided all of them, the cops would make their way in droves, the employee at the shack allowed the druggies to escape out the backdoor fire escape, problem was if he wasn't able to silence the alarm going off before people ran out the back doors it would trip the alarm and the cops knew what was going on.

Early October of 1981, around mid-afternoon, a cop wave hit us hard, everyone ran out the back doors, except for me I decided to stay back and play it cool, I went onto a video game pretending to be a customer, they didn't care, they tilted my game, and wanted my name and purpose for being there, I had nothing on me nor did they, first time getting my name, no criminal record and no priors… nothing, all they said was 'we're watching, always watching.' You must understand the entire picture here, early 80's, cops were eager to beat up on white kids on dope, they hated everything about drugs and felt we were a menace to society, (the cops were usually military buzzed hair and overweight) they loved nothing more than kicking the shit out of drug dealers, especially with long hair. When the cops would stage a raid or answer a call to the Rosslyn, this was top grade shit, this was like answering a bank robbery or a murder, they would think a donut shop was burning down!

Sometimes playing it cool wasn't always the best thing, my thinking was, why fucking run out the back door? They're waiting for you downstairs as well, so what the fuck is the difference?

As I'm waiting patiently and into the evening on this same day, I went into the bar and my up line (dealer) was there, I asked 'where my stash was?', I had previously sold what I had and needed more drugs to sell, they informed me exactly where it was.

They gave me the precise location, go upstairs the fifth pool table along the windows underneath on the ledge of the table is my ounce of hash cut up into chunks in a clear baggie, perfect…my mind was set and focused (like in the movie Karate Kid; the instructor says to the kid "your focus, needs more focus") obviously i was to focused, without hesitation and my eagerness to go get it was all that I could think about, like; being in the game, the zone, I was so zoned it was unbelievable, and I've been in that place (throwing darts at a dartboard or playing pool and running the table, the times playing golf and putting) no matter what, locked in my own snow globe world and nobody or nothing could penetrate, interrupt or knock you off your game, you're that dialed in (the zone). Just like that, a game changer, I go directly to that table, bend down to get my stash, the entire room of dealers and friends were trying to interrupt my game plan, nobody could enter, I was blind and deaf for that moment in time, indescribable, I got up and counted the tables again to be 100% sure, because the amounts of drugs that were on that ledge of the table was totally off the charts! There was every kind of drug imaginable on there, I bent down one more time and grabbed my baggie, I turned and started to head out, when my ears finally popped open and I hear this voice 'drop it, you're under arrest!' I froze, looked out and around the dim lit pool hall, everyone looking at me like wtf! All I can say was fuuuuccccckkkk! the beat cop was on duty and was at the other end of the pool hall along the windows just watching me, he bent me over the pool table and put me in cuffs, brought me into the bowling alley to await my transportation to downtown. I was so lucky that the beat cop didn't look under the table to check what I was looking at, I'd probably still be doing time, lol., as it was the beat cop looked so disappointed almost like he didn't want to arrest me or send me downtown, knowing I was the last of the Blackburn boys that have been arrested.

At the start of January of 1980 the new law was that a 16 year old could be tried as an adult if the crime and the crown felt it was a more serious offense, apparently they had felt my charges; possession for the purpose of trafficking was fitting under that law and I was tried as an adult, as a first offense and still a high school student, I got sentenced to 30 days to be served on weekends from Friday's at 1900hrs –Mondays at 0600hrs it was counted as a 4 day weekend, with the period of Christmas I was able to stay home and continue into the new year of 1982, I finished my weekends the morning of my 18th birthday (the Royal Birthday) the added benefit of being tried as an adult, I didn't have to do probation or any counselling, I was completely finished, only problem now is a criminal record. My period of incarceration was an experience to say the least, my first weekend; I checked in at the front desk of the Remand Center, they say "You're two minutes late" (I didn't think so, but who am I to argue) the guards at the front radio to another guard that a weekender has arrived and is late, I get into the elevator, with a short fucker named Scottie and another guard, Scottie pipes up 'so, you're late you little fucker, and you think it's funny do ya?' 'No sir' as I replied, 'what's with the fuckin' smirk lad? You think this to be a joke?' 'No sir' I said again!

"We'll show you how much of a joke you be in for" he states, puffing out his tiny chest on his 5' frame, "that's fine we have some room up with the Maximum-Security mates, you'll be sure to enjoy your weekend!" I bit my tongue that entire elevator ride, not a very joyous 1st weekend to be stuck with the hardened criminals that Edmonton had locked up, even those very criminals asked me why? a weekender was locked up with them, and telling me I should go to the local radio announcer from 630 CHED named, Eddie Keen on this matter, the 2nd weekend was scheduled for Belmont Correctional Institute (corner of Victoria Trial and 144ave) it was so over populated that there was no room in the general building so they bunked everyone in the heating plant, it looked like a scene from the TV show M*A*S*H, and with such dry heat too, it was pleasant to walk outside to the general building for eating times, because it was winter and nice and cold. The weekends to follow happened to be along the west side perimeter of Belmont, there were seven houses, the main one to the north end close to (144ave) was the check-in house with a counsellor on duty (never checked in the houses my entire time there), and the following six houses located to the south, all in a row, you were assigned a house and once you checked in you were to remain there (wink, wink), the old adage says "it's easier to ask for forgiveness, than permission." A few of the inmates and I would sometimes walk across the avenue to the little strip mall to grab smokes or snacks for the evening, there was also a KFC as well.

The 'Routine,' on the weekends that followed; you went to your assigned house early and ditched your case of beer in the snow bank, you'd walked back to the first house and checked in before 1900hrs, then walked back to your house and brought your beers inside under your cot and proceed to watch hockey games or movies. Simple enough, very easy and low key, once the other boarders (inmates) felt the easiness in being there, they started to party hard and were doing drugs, having their friends drop by and just getting too loose with the liberties. As my time was winding down in finishing my sentence, my partying was becoming less and less, I didn't want to chance getting caught doing stupid shit and have to do more time, it was coming up to my last weekend, the last night, I can sense victory, plus the added bonus it was going to be the morning of my 18th birthday (my Royal birthday on the 18th). Then, all hell was about to break loose in the house, a couple of bikers were getting high on mescaline (a hallucinogenic and intoxicating compound present in mescal buttons from the peyote cactus), woke up another inmate that just so happened to be in the same house as us, turns out this guy they woke up ratted these guys out for whatever crime and now they're all in the same loving confines together. You can't make this shit up, unfortunately I'm not!

Middle of the living room, my bed is the front hall closet with a single cot, they start smacking this dude down, punches thrown and literally kicking the crap out of him, I couldn't and wouldn't help him, it was my last weekend, my last night, I'm three hours away from walking out that door and not returning. Sorry dude, you pick and choose your battles in life, and it was unfortunate and untimely circumstances, and I chose not to engage into that one. Plus, my fun button had been deleted from being busted and going through this whole process, why does anyone want to continue down this road over and over? It's beyond me, and I guess for me, I could not continue to be a criminal! Maybe for others it's like an addiction you get the high from being a criminal, I use to get that; having that satisfaction of bringing your drugs up to the snooker shack, knowing you're being watched, and the beat cop was there most the times and not knowing the element of a surprise bust. Trying to move a pound of cut up marijuana in ¼ ounce baggies in one big brown bag was just such an incredible feeling with your little gerbil racing on your heart wheel.

After my time in jail and high school, it was time to become responsible and get a job, good luck…1982, the bottom fell out from Alberta, many lost their jobs and houses, interest rates soared to over 19% many, many good people lost everything they had vested in. I wanted to be an artist so bad, everywhere you turned though there were road blocks, plus family and friends would knock you down and say there's no money in being an artist, the road blocks were just the same with a criminal record, all jobs were cash jobs under the table, but then trust was a two way street, lots of guys would end up ripping you off, so it was a very tough situation to be in.

I went to John Casablanca's and took make-up artistry, I wanted to go to Rick Bakers school (a special effects school in California), after finishing at JC's but to no avail, it seemed like a door would open, then three would close, I was scrambling, job applications had the criminal record box on them, and nobody was hiring! I was doing many odd jobs and under the table too, also trying to sell artwork or graphics to different places or drinking establishments trying to muster up some business, the thing with graphics back then it took forever to do a layout for a price list or a menu, each letter, number or icon was rubbed onto your page separately, using different fonts and what have you to be creative. Was a sheet called Letraset, almost $10 per sheet!

I must say, I made this beautiful price list for a hairdressing shop at Northwood mall on grey poster board with white advent guard lettering with their logo of a man and woman's hair meshed in between, in the center of the board painted in a bright fuchsia color, it took roughly 12 hours to create not including the meetings and discussion of what they wanted. They would only pay me $75 that's like $6.25 /hr., better than min wage but worth way more than that!

Other jobs were cutting siding for new homes, I'd work the saw, they'd yell out the measurements and you needed to be precise and at 0.10/cut and you were docked for mistakes, lots of pressure.

I was also the maintenance guy at the greenhouse bar & grill, plus it was a way in to do some posters or the menu, I got the job to do the menu there, but again a lot of hours by hand and really no money for the work (no computer's yet).

My Music Scene...

Fortunately, my musical journey began at a very young age, born the youngest of six boys in 1964 (last of the boomers) that did not deter me from my pursuit of happiness; I enjoyed very much everything about the music scene, the record stores and concerts when I was able to go to them. I want to describe the scene back in my day, without trying to be biased or speak negative toward any genre or specific band, group, or artists. Not everybody grew up with just listening to the music influences that I grew up with and depending on the parents they happened to be raised by, they had to listen to what their folks had going on whether it was the Blues, Country or Classical, coming out of the 1930's and 40's they had the Big Bands and Swing music were popularized by the likes of; Glenn Miller, Benny Goodman and Duke Ellington, entering into the 1950's was the start of Rock n Roll era.

I'm not going to give a history lesson on the facts of R n R and who was first and who was second and so forth, you have to dig into it and read or watch some of the pioneers back in the day and the development or evolution of how that scene exploded into the 60's with the British Invasion, there's an abundance of information along with just as many unnecessary deaths, these untimely deaths was for the most part just really, really sad and unfortunate.

Let's talk about deaths...

From leaving the Summer of Love in 1969 and going into the early 70's we were already witnessing some transitions and some pretty key players and front men were dropping dead, crazy times, especially with this 27 Club, a club of whose names on this list are only 27 years of age (which became popularized once Kurt Cobain died from a self-administered gunshot suicide in 1994) have a look at that list its insane,

Identified members.

Because the 27 Club is entirely notional, there is no official membership. The following table lists people described as "members" of the club in **reliable published sources**, in the opinion of their respective authors.

Name	Date of birth	Date of death	Official cause of death	Fame	Age	Sources
Alexandre Levy	November 10, 1864	January 17, 1892	Unknown	Composer, pianist, and conductor	27 years, 68 days	[42]
Louis Chauvin	March 13, 1881	March 26, 1908	Neurosyphilis sclerosis	Ragtime musician	27 years, 13 days	[42]
Rupert Brooke	August 3, 1887	April 23, 1915	Sepsis	Poet	27 years, 263 days	[43]
Robert Johnson	May 8, 1911	August 16, 1938	Unknown	Blues singer and musician	27 years, 100 days	[42][44]
Nat Jaffe	January 1, 1918	August 5, 1945	Complications from high blood pressure	Swing jazz pianist	27 years, 216 days	[42]
Jesse Belvin	December 15, 1932	February 6, 1960	Traffic collision (car)	R&B singer, pianist, and songwriter	27 years, 53 days	[42]
Rudy Lewis	August 23, 1936	May 20, 1964	Drug overdose	Vocalist of the Drifters	27 years, 271 days	[46]
Joe Henderson	April 24, 1937	October 24, 1964	Heart attack	R&B and gospel singer	27 years, 183 days	[46]
Malcolm Hale	May 17, 1941	October 30, 1968	Poisoning (carbon monoxide)	Original member and lead guitarist of Spanky and Our Gang	27 years, 166 days	[42]
Dickie Pride	October 21, 1941	March 26, 1969	Drug overdose (sleeping pills)	Rock and roll singer	27 years, 156 days	[47]
Brian Jones	February 28, 1942	July 3, 1969	Drowned in a swimming pool; coroner's report states "death by misadventure".[48][49]	Rolling Stones founder, guitarist and Mult instrumentalist	27 years, 125 days	[42][50]
Alan "Blind Owl" Wilson	July 4, 1943	September 3, 1970	Drug overdose (barbiturate), possible suicide	Leader, singer, and primary composer of Canned Heat	27 years, 61 days	[42]
Jimi Hendrix	November 27, 1942	September 18, 1970	Asphyxiation[51]	Pioneering electric guitarist, singer and songwriter of the Jimi Hendrix Experience and Band of Gypsys	27 years, 295 days	[42]

Name	Date of birth	Date of death	Official cause of death	Fame	Age	Sources
Janis Joplin	January 19, 1943	October 4, 1970	Drug overdose (probably heroin).[52]	Lead vocalist and songwriter of Big Brother and the Holding Company, the Kozmic Blues Band and Full Tilt Boogie Band	27 years, 258 days	[42][57]
Arlester "Dyke" Christian	June 13, 1943	March 13, 1971	Murdered	Frontman, vocalist and bassist of Dyke and the Blazers	27 years, 273 days	[42]
Jim Morrison	December 8, 1943	July 3, 1971	Heart failure.[54]	Singer, lyricist, and leader of the Doors	27 years, 207 days	[42]
Linda Jones	December 14, 1944	March 14, 1972	Complications from diabetes	Soul singer	27 years, 91 days	[55]
Ron "Pigpen" McKernan	September 8, 1945	March 8, 1973	Gastrointestinal hemorrhage associated with alcoholism	Founding member, keyboardist, and singer of the Grateful Dead	27 years, 181 days	[42]
Roger Lee Durham	February 14, 1946	July 27, 1973	Fell off a horse and died from the injuries	Singer and percussionist of Bloodstone	27 years, 163 days	[42]
Wallace "Wally" Yohn	January 12, 1947	August 12, 1974	Plane crash	Organ player of Chase	27 years, 212 days	[42]
Dave Alexander	June 3, 1947	February 10, 1975	Pulmonary edema	Bassist of the Stooges	27 years, 252 days	[42]
Pete Ham	April 27, 1947	April 24, 1975	Suicide by hanging	Keyboardist and guitarist, leader of Badfinger	27 years, 362 days	[42]
Gary Thain	May 15, 1948	December 8, 1975	Drug overdose (heroin)	Former bassist of Uriah Heep and the Keef Hartley Band	27 years, 205 days	[42]
Cecilia	October 11, 1948	August 2, 1976	Traffic collision (car)	Singer	27 years, 296 days	[56][57]
Helmut Köllen	March 2, 1950	May 3, 1977	Poisoning (carbon monoxide)	Bassist of 1970s prog rock band Triumvirat	27 years, 62 days	[42]
Chris Bell	January 12, 1951	December 27, 1978	Traffic collision (car)	Singer-songwriter and guitarist of power pop band Big Star and solo	27 years, 349 days	[42]
Zenon De Fleur	September 9, 1951	March 17, 1979	Traffic collision (car) and subsequent medical complications	Guitarist of the Count Bishops	27 years, 189 days	[40][58]
D. Boon	April 1, 1958	December 22, 1985	Traffic collision (van)	Guitarist, lead singer of punk band Minutemen	27 years, 266 days	[42]
Alexander Bashlachev	May 27, 1960	February 17, 1988	Fall from a height, probable suicide	Poet, rock musician and songwriter	27 years, 266 days	[59]
Amar Singh Chamkila	July 21, 1960	March 8, 1988	Murdered	Singer, songwriter, musician, and composer	27 years, 231 days	[59]
Jean-Michel Basquiat	December 22, 1960	August 12, 1988	Drug overdose (Speedball)	Painter and graffiti artist; formed the band Gray	27 years, 234 days	[45]
Pete de Freitas	August 2, 1961	June 14, 1989	Traffic collision (motorcycle)	Drummer of Echo & the Bunnymen	27 years, 316 days	[42]
Finbarr Donnelly	April 25, 1962	June 18, 1989	Drowning accident	Singer of Five Go Down to the Sea?	27 years, 50 days	[60]
Chris Austin	February 24, 1964	March 16, 1991	Plane crash	Country singer and guitarist/fiddle player for Reba McEntire	27 years, 20 days	[61]
Dimitar Voev	May 21, 1965	September 5, 1992	Cancer	Poet, founder of the Bulgarian new wave band New Generation	27 years, 107 days	[62]
Mia Zapata	August 25, 1965	July 7, 1993	Murdered	Lead singer of the Gits	27 years, 316 days	[42]
Kurt Cobain	February 20, 1967	April 5, 1994, c.	Suicide by gunshot.[63]	Founding member, lead singer, guitarist, and songwriter of Nirvana	27 years, 44 days c.	[42][63]
Kristen Pfaff	May 26, 1967	June 16, 1994	Drug overdose (heroin)	Bass guitarist of Holeand Janitor Joe	27 years, 21 days	[42]

Name	Date of birth	Date of death	Official cause of death	Fame	Age	Sources
Richey Edwards	December 22, 1967	February 1, 1995	Disappeared near a common suicide site; later presumed dead	Lyricist and guitarist of Manic Street Preachers	27 years, 41 days	[42]
Stretch	April 8, 1968	November 30, 1995	Murdered	Rapper	27 years, 236 days	[55][64]
Fat Pat	December 4, 1970	February 3, 1998	Murdered	American rapper and member of Screwed. Up Click	27 years, 61 days	[42]
Freaky Tah	May 14, 1971	March 28, 1999	Murdered	American rapper and member of the hip hop group Lost Boyz	27 years, 318 days	[42]
Kami	February 1, 1972	June 21, 1999	Subarachnoid hemorrhage	Drummer of Malice Mizer	27 years, 140 days	[65]
Rodrigo Bueno	May 24, 1973	June 24, 2000	Traffic collision (car)	Cuarteto singer	27 years, 31 days	[56]
Sean Patrick McCabe	November 13, 1972	August 28, 2000	Asphyxiation	Lead singer of Ink & Dagger	27 years, 289 days	[42]
Maria Serrano Serrano	November 26, 1973	November 24, 2001	Plane crash (Crossair Flight 3597)	Singer of Passion Fruit	27 years, 363 days	[42]
Rico Yan	March 14, 1975	March 29, 2002	Acute Hemorrhagic Pancreatitis	Filipino actor	27 years, 15 days	[42]
Jonathan Brandis	April 13, 1976	November 12, 2003	Suicide by hanging	American actor	27 years, 213 days	[66]
Jeremy Ward	May 5, 1976	May 25, 2003	Drug overdose (heroin)	The Mars Volta and De Facto sound manipulator	27 years, 20 days	[42]
Bryan Ottoson	March 18, 1978	April 19, 2005	Drug overdose (prescription medication)	Guitarist of American Head Charge	27 years, 32 days	[42]
Valentin Elizalde	February 1, 1979	November 25, 2006	Murdered	Mexican banda singer	27 years, 297 days	[42]
Damien "Damo" Morris	May 22, 1980	December 19, 2007	Traffic collision (bus)	Member of Australian deathcore band the Red Shore	27 years, 211 days	[67]
OrishGrinstead	June 2, 1980	April 20, 2008	Kidney failure	Founding member of the R&B group 702	27 years, 323 days	[68]
Jade Goody	June 5, 1981	March 22, 2009	Cervical cancer	Reality-television personality	27 years, 290 days	[21][69]
Dash Snow	July 27, 1981	July 13, 2009	Drug overdose	Artist	27 years, 351 days	[70][71]
Amy Winehouse	September 14, 1983	July 23, 2011	Alcohol poisoning [72]	Singer-songwriter	27 years, 312 days	[50][53][73]
Richard Turner	July 30, 1984	August 11, 2011	Cardiac arrest	Trumpet player, collaborator with Friendly Fires	27 years, 12 days	[74]
Anton Yelchin	March 11, 1989	June 19, 2016	Accidental blunt traumatic asphyxia [75]	Actor, Chekov in the Star Trek reboot series	27 years, 100 days	[21]
Thomas Fekete	July 1, 1988	May 31, 2016	Cancer	Guitarist of Surfer Blood	27 years, 335 days	[76]
Kim Jong-hyun	April 8, 1990	December 18, 2017	Suicide by carbon monoxide poisoning [77]	Vocalist and lyricist of Shinee	27 years, 254 days	[78]
Fredo Santana	July 4, 1990	January 19, 2018	Cardiovascular disease and idiopathic epilepsy [79]	American rapper	27 years, 199 days	[80]
Benjamin Keough	October 21, 1992	July 12, 2020	Suicide by gunshot	Elvis Presley's grandson and son of Lisa Marie Presley and brother of Riley Keough	27 years, 265 days	[73]

from the time of the first death-Alexandre Levy in 1892 to Benjamin Keough in 2020 there's over 60 names in this 27 Club list, Brian Jones drown in a pool in 69', Jimi Hendrix overdose in 1970, Janis

Joplin one month later, then Jim Morrison of The Doors dies in 71', if they weren't dying some major bands were breaking up and going solo; bands like The Beatles, Humble Pie, The Eagles and at the later end of the seventies we had bands like Black Sabbath breaking up along with other deaths like Bon Scott of AC/DC and John Bonham drummer with Led Zeppelin then into early 80's with the death of Randy Rhoads guitarist with Ozzy, some artists went on to have very successful solo careers and others fizzled out and just faded away.

Before television came around our forefathers and families would gather around the sitting area (living room) and listen intently to the radio, whatever was being broadcasted, church service, musical production or something that involved the war and even the president speech would be aired, for many it was their favorite past time. For myself growing up in the seventies and three channels black and white TV was hardly exciting, especially whatever those stations were spoon feeding most times.

When we moved up to the north side of Edmonton in 1971, it wasn't long afterwards that we made friends at school and found similar interests in music, in little time we would go to our neighborhood friends place early enough to listen to some new music that had come out, then walk to school, this soon would become one of my favorite times, especially how you'd gather to listen to records, it was something to behold, for the most part everyone listened to what was being played, not just put it on the player and use it as background noise, the radio stations by that time was good for that.

We finally got cable around 1978 and we would connect the cable to the home stereo to get KEZE in Spokane WA., Edmonton finally got FM Stations in 1979 with K.97, much better than CHED, but those DJ's were not wise, I had more knowledge about the music they were spinning than they did, I continued buying records from my jobs and babysitting, prices were very cheap for albums, average prices were like $6 per album and $10 for double albums. By the time I was 16 in 1980, I had acquired 2500 albums!

As Pat Travers would say and sing about in The Pat Travers Band (not country) …

> *Ohhhh Hooked on music,*
> *Hooked on music.*
> *Hooked on music, I'm*
> *Hooked on Rock n' Roll-look out!*
>
> *-Pat Travers*

I most certainly was absorbed with and within the music, in the 70's you needed to do a little more digging than how it is nowadays, I would buy a book (Rock Encyclopedia) that was not bad, it was the most informative source, but still the information was dated, wasn't at your fingertips instantly, it could be six months or older, that's where social media now (2022) sure kicks ass! Sure, you have to still check your sources to be sure you have the right information, as you should.

My oh my, my addiction, albums oh love oh love just to hear them, it was the entire event though, going to the mall specifically the record store (A&A records Londonderry mall) buying 6 or 8 records, going through your favorite genre in alphabetic order would take a few hours and then going home, everything about a record was awesome, the smells and taking out the new virgin vinyl unwrapping it and putting it onto the record player and setting the needle down for the first time in anticipation of the first sound that was about to prick your ears and put a smile on your face, taking in all the art work and reading all the linear notes on the sleeves, to experience this for myself there was nothing like it, my perfect jam!

A lot of today's greatest Rock albums from the end of the sixties and through the early seventies and eighties were the debut albums for many new bands that were trying to make their way onto the scene and establish themselves eternally etched into Rock n' Roll, don't get me wrong with what I'm saying, not all albums were great, some people will argue and state their case about this that and the other album with clearly only one or two good tracks on certain records, once I started to compile a list in comparison to Rolling Stone magazines top 500 albums of all time, there's no way on this Earth or any other planet in which the so called top 271 professionals could pick and place those 500 albums. I'm certain there must have been some kind of voting system in place on how they came to those on the list! I soon realized that music is subjective, and you cannot and should not make lists, because from one person to the next, from one band or artist to the next, you cannot really say whose number 1 or 2 or even 500 for that matter, and not only that, Rolling Stone magazine mixed the genres, so like what the hell is that? How can you compare Jazz, Hip-Hop, Blues, Country, and Rock n' Roll, on an all-time list…yeah okay, I don't think so!

We all have to agree to disagree because on any given day you can come at me bro and be screaming bloody murder that all 12 of Bob Dylan's albums need to be on that list, and out of say anybody Deep Purple or AC/DC they may have had three combined! There are so many bands and or artists didn't even make that list, and many others that would leave you with your mouth dropped to the floor saying WTF…over!! Like I've stated before if it doesn't have playability, listen ability, quality, craftsmanship and originality, then how does it even fit to be an album of choice? Not many people (radio Stations) realize this,

but like the old adage says…

"There are two sides to every story."

My saying is this…

… the same goes for records …there's two sides to every album… an A side and a B side (especially radio stations, I'm certain they don't know there's a fucking 'B' side)

Okay, so for **MYSELF,** and me alone, maybe there were outside influences that really determined who you are as an individual and what you listen to, case in point; it would have to be The Beach Boys, Bob Dylan, The Beatles, Neil Young, Queen…I'm not at all bashing them or disc-crediting their abilities, I myself think they were all overrated, the media at that time played into them and that's all they played, fifty years later and most radio stations are still playing the one or two tracks by the same artist or group, I don't get it and probably never will, why FM stations have bought into this mentality of re-cycling the same music over and over and over again is beyond me. I know it's a numbers game of being number one radio station or the number one classic rock or the greatest hits stations. They all play the same songs, same rotations, how many times can you listen to Ram Jam's – 'Black Betty'? It turns a person off not only the song but also the artist.

This time when we were young, growing up in Dickensfield, must've been 1976/77,my brother Robert had grown attached to some certain records and while he was building models downstairs, he would constantly play these albums over and over again, the one's he would not stop playing were; Supertramp's – 'Crime of the Century', Rory Gallagher's- 'Blueprint', maybe Cheap Tricks debut and a couple of others, it was totally annoying having to listen to them every day, everyday…we'd have to yell at him to turn it down all the time, pretty much like every radio station that constantly plays the same shit, and that's what it becomes… SHIT!!!

It had to have been a solid year of this ongoing torture in which Robert felt compelled to bestow upon his siblings, we felt the same to do vinyl damage, John and I got a hold of these albums and used a Bic lighter to heat up certain areas in the vinyl and would push that heated area with a pen making it look like black volcanoes, ah sweet ass revenge!

Let me try to paint this picture for you…the music scene in Canada during the late 60's and in through the 70's was very slim, up until the British Invasion of music which happened into the mid to late 60's and then Woodstock, but there still wasn't an overabundance of music, let me re-phrase that, there wasn't music that fulfilled the appetite, I didn't seem like much to appeal to many others though.

I mean AM radio was constantly serving a potpourri of shit, the shit pot of all genres of music, it absolutely made you want to vomit all over the place, they had no direction of consistency, from far and wide and back again, meaning they played Country to R & B to Rock to Folk and back n forth, it's no wonder the kinfolk were hooked on Pepto Bismal, it was definitely a cause for upset stomach, a constant roller coaster of garbage in which they played. By the time FM radio stations came along, for us here, it wasn't much better, sure they had some consistency in only playing that certain genre.

In August of 2018 I was challenged on Face book to choose an album a day for 10 days, didn't need to post or say anything, just post an album a day. That was the hardest thing to struggle with, you start focusing in on all of the songs that make up an album, the playability, listen ability, character and how does it fit into my lifestyle and molded me as a person, so many factors…I can look down on this list right now and I can rearrange it again…because, now I've taken away the numbers, there's no #10 or #1 some days on any given day that ends in y it could change

The Pat Travers Band – Go for What You Know

– Hooked on Music

Max Webster – Universal Juveniles

– Battle Scar (with Rush)

Rush – Hemispheres

– La Villa Strangiato

Molly Hatchet – Gator Country

– Dreams I'll never see

Stevie Ray Vaughn – Texas Flood

– Testify

Humble Pie – Live at the Fillmore East

– I'm Ready

Pink Floyd – Dark Side of the Moon

– Time

ZZ Top – Fandango

– – Backdoor Medley

Led Zeppelin – Physical Graffiti

Kashmir

AC/DC – Back in Black

– BIB – Shoot to Thrill

So depending on any given situation per individual this list of your 10 albums could vary day to day, this list of mine is mostly from albums from the early 70's to 1982, I could really change this around with the modern era of music now in 2022, especially with the arrival of Myles Kennedy being the lead singer for the former band Creed which are now called Alter Bridge from 2004(currently in studio producing there 7th Album titled 'Pawns & Kings'), Godsmack, Chris Cornell and his projects with Soundgarden, Audioslave & Temple of the Dog (which they were planning a 25th anniversary tour of, until his untimely death 05.18. 2017) and his solo material of course there's many, many others. By now if you're close to retirement your list of ten albums will change because of life, life changes everything when you're reminded of a time/ place/ smells/anniversary's/ birthday and of course death.

Now then another challenge came forward and it was posted to pick **ONE** album that impacted you as a teenager, so from the time I was 13 in 1977 through to when I was 19 in 1983, let me just show a few albums form that timeline…

Rock albums released…

1977 - *Heart-Little Queen, David Bowie- "Heroes," Jackson Browne- Running on Empty, Eric Clapton-Slow hand, Fleetwood Mac-Rumors*

1978 - *Van Halen-Van Halen, Rolling Stones-Some girls, The Cars-The Cars, Molly Hatchet-Molly Hatchet, Joe Walsh-But seriously, Folks.*

1978 - *Pretenders-debut, Tom Petty-Damn the Torpedoes, Fleetwood Mac-Tusk, AC/DC-Highway to Hell, Blackfoot-Strikes*

1980 - *The Police-Zenyatta Mondetta, Motorhead-Ace of Spades,* **AC/DC-Back in Black**, *David Bowie-Scary Monsters, Ozzy Osbourne-Blizzard of Ozz, Loverboy-debut*

1981 - *Journey-Don't Stop Believing, Rolling Stones-Tattoo You, J. Geils BandFreeze Frame, Motorhead-No Sleep til Hammersmith, Rush-Moving Pictures, Triumph-Allied Forces, Foreigner-4*

1982 - *Bruce Springsteen-Nebraska, 38 Special-Special Forces, Asia-Asia, Roxy Music-Avalon*

1983 - *Stevie Ray Vaughn-Texas Flood, Van Halen-Jump, The Police-Every Breath, Def Leppard-Pyromania, The Police-Synchronicity, U2-War*

This is only but a few that were released during this 7-year time frame of being a teenager there are many, many more and many of these became some of the All-Time greatest albums and are still being played to this day. Christmas time 1978 I got three AC/DC albums, High Voltage, Let There Be Rock and Power age, I was all in on this group, did I mention that the rawness of these albums was and is so special I love it! There was nothing like them when they came on the scene especially with Angus Young in the schoolboy uniform playing guitar like he was getting electrocuted, this was amazing to watch and listen to, the following year (1979) they released Highway to Hell they finally make it to the big leagues then, tragedy strikes, lead singer Bon Scott found dead (Feb. 19/1980)!

I was bummed out, they were getting set to embark on a world tour for Highway to Hell, thinking that was the end of AC/DC, a short time later (2months) after Mr. Scott's death the band hired a new vocalist named Brian Johnson from another band named Geordie. In no time at all they went into recording in the Bahamas and made a 'Tribute Album' for Scott titled 'Back in Black', I had turned 16 in January of 1980 and the production date for this new album was in April / May, right on cue, I must've been the first to purchase Back in Black or pretty close, being so fricken excited to get home and put this baby on the player, I got home and with nobody at home, I put this on the big boy home stereo and cranked that volume right up, I couldn't stop listening to it…10 songs that would open up an entire international podium around the globe and would go on to becoming the second best-selling album of ALL time (50 million world-wide) even though at the time of its release many critics thought this album 'was a joke', many of those same critics would have to rescind articles and comments due to its overwhelming success!

This is my choice, my one album that impacted me as a teenager at 16 years old, is **Back in Black** it was and still is such a powerful innovative album and just sheer energy heading into a new decade and they pulled off a masterpiece with only ten songs, from the dropping of the needle on *Side A- Hells Bells, Shoot to Thrill, What Do You Do for Money Honey, Given the Dog a Bone, Let Me Put My Love into You. Side B- Back in Black, You Shook Me All Night Long, Have a Drink on Me, Shake a Leg and Rock and Roll Ain't Noise Pollution* to this last song on the B side it totally leaves you begging for more, the second best-selling album of ALL time, 50+ million copies, I guarantee you, I have bought this album 4 or 5 times and CD's probably 3 times and cassettes at least 3 times too, I have just acquired this album again, with plastic album covering so we'll see how long this next collection will grow, they're so expensive now!

Wowzers, pull my string, for the life of me I've been so certain about this event it's so mind blowing to me now, to find out that AC/DC's Back in Black concert was not my first show, like WTF? Do you remember when growing up and you have your ducks in a row and everything is laid out exactly how I left it, now finding out this date here... it's like the Mandela effect! I was checking out other shows that I attended and for some reason upon checking tour dates on Wikipedia Ted Nugent's Scream Dream Tour happened June 3, 1980with The Pat Travers Band and The Scorpions, this would be the show that brother John and I stayed out all night for tickets, ended up getting a breakfast meal bought for us at the Westin Hotel. Believe it or not the Scorpions sucked so bad and were booed off stage, I think they only played a couple of three or four songs, and if it weren't for terrible Ted's antics and swinging across stage in his alter ego loin cloth, a young Pat Travers Band almost upstaged the headliner... that's how I'd have to review the show! (This is of course Pat Travers party central-north-end-animals that have house parties with PT music)

This is also the show that Ted stepped up and gave an earful to Edmonton's faithful for throwing a Frisbee and which hit him in the leg, while the music was still playing and intense reverb, Ted is like in fast forward mode, a fuckin squirrel on cat nip, basically said, "the next motherfucker that wants to throw shit up on stage, yeah, you're going to deal with my roadies and myself coming down and wango tango all over that Edmonton Ass!! Are you with me? Edmonton? "I know it didn't seem like much but...as it was E town had a bad reputation already about being careless with stuff ending up on the stage and hitting the performers.

There's a little discrepancy on the release date of Back in Black album and the opening tour date on the North American leg, Wikipedia has the official release date of the album as of July 25, 1980 and the show in Edmonton was July 13, 1980, I disagree there must've been a pre-release date because I had the album long before the concert, unless the record store wasn't supposed to release it, I do not know… or care! I had the album and was listening to it non-stop! Anyways, on with the show…the muchly anticipation of AC/DC finally coming to Edmonton we were the opening show for North America on this leg of the tour and The Pumps opened, Northlands Coliseum there was only a little over 7k people at this show, but it sounded as loud as a sold-out arena, after the Pumps (opened up) the anticipation was just haunting when the house lights shut off and the fog machines filled the stage with heavy smoke, you could see the lowering of the bell, the cheers from the crowd so loud, ear-piercing in fact, me and my two older brothers were third row on the floor in front of the stacks of speakers, by the time the third song was being played our seats (collapsible seats / folding chairs) are being flattened to the ground, so we're hanging onto the coat tails of the row in front of us, I don't think they liked it too much, judging by the looks they were giving! I was totally wired off this show, my ears ringing for three days afterward, I was an AC/DC junkie, a concert goer addict! The energy that Angus Young brings to the table, OMG…he was absolfuckinglutely flying, running and sizzling on the ground like bacon in a frying pan, even taking oxygen through the mask as he was playing, to witness that is just totally amazing, you're in awe constantly watching as to what he'll do next! I was hooked on concerts, the build-up, hype, and the entire atmosphere, it has a lot of special people with many different smells and curiosities it's a great beast!

Next show…Ritchie Blackmore's Rainbow (IV) with each roman numeral was a different band line-up and a different year, for 1981 this line-up included Ritchie Blackmore-guitars, Joe Lynn Turner-vocals, Don Airey-keyboards, Bobbi Rodinelli-drums, Roger Glover-bass. The opening act for this show, none other than Canada's own Pat Travers Band, which by the way we ended up missing because of some miscommunication or fighting between boyfriend and girlfriend issues, you know how it goes? Certainly, the main act Rainbow didn't disappoint, the main explosive excitement was during Mr. Blackmore's guitar solo totally smashing his white Fender Strat and giving it away in the front row, who by the way ended up being none other than Cam McLeod of a local band called White Lion, long live Rock n' roll!!

The greatest thing about Rock n' Roll and music not only watching the pros and those concert bowls or stadiums, it was and all of this plus, sometimes your entire day was to prep and get ready for your outing, some days could be just one club and that was your night or sometimes you'd drive around lookin' for the hot spot! we had so many live rooms in Edmonton you could catch so many rock bands on any given night, the circuit was in no particular order, the (Beverly) Crest, MJ's roadhouse (Londonderry), Club John's, Rev rock room, Ci South, Redford Inn North, Inn on Whyte, Peoples Pub so many, many more that helped contribute to the raising of this GIANT in the night life around this E town!

in a short time within 2 years ads were coming out about an indestructible new item called a CD (compact disc), labelled as the future in music, coming to replace the thicker and bigger albums, advertisers made it sound like the CD would still play when it was scratched or damaged, I ended up selling my record collection before waiting and replacing my albums with these so-called CD's, dumbest thing I ever did!

I Turned twenty years old in 1984, and not a whole lot of direction, especially with a criminal record it was almost tempting to cross that path again, don't do the crime if you don't wanna do the time, and I really didn't like that part of the criminal life, I loved my freedom too much and found myself getting introduced to a smaller type bar downtown called the 'Club Limelight', finally a bar to call 'my home' I then made good friends with the DJ Klay that spun the records and in little time we were hanging out and partying eight days a week, entering into the fall / winter of 1984 we had our own party crowd of about 12-20 people consistently always partying until the wee hours of the mornings, Limelight opened another location in Mornville, AB., (just north of St. Albert) they included a party bus that would run back n forth to both Limelight bars, soon. Thereafter, the end of December 1984 and January 1985 the owners (Chinese mafia) owned everything in Edmonton, just about (both Limelight's, Lydo Chinese food, Chicken on the Way, Greenhouse Bar &Grill, Frank Lee's kung fu studio, the timeline 421.1111 and some others too) along with all this they've now created and opened the ultimate bar downtown on 105 street 102 ave., at an old warehouse called 'Rock City' boasting to be one of the bigger party rooms in the Capital city, it changed to a restaurant called Characters and is now a micro-brewery.

This one event that took place on a hot august night in 1985 would turn out to be one of my biggest earth-shattering events in my lifetime (didn't know it at the time), mid-afternoon Carson (a kid my mama Hope brought in) and I went to West Edmonton Mall no big deal, when we left it was so hot outside and the DJ on K-97 pipes up and says the next vehicle at the station (108 St 101Ave) will get four tickets to the Stevie Ray Vaughn show that night, I said to Carson "it's on our way home, what do we have to lose" not really speeding, okay maybe a little, burned a few red lights and made it downtown to the radio station and Walla like winning the lottery, what a great feeling having those tickets in our mitts, we go back home, to get ready for the show and to find two more peeps to join us…mmm, strange not a soul around to be found, like nobody, it was as if the Exodus happened, no cell phones, we were calling like everybody on landline phone we could think of that would want to come with us and there was no one! We finally got a hold of a couple of church girls, and they wanted to come with us.

Talk about a performer unbelievable, SRV took to the stage with his fedora and poncho on, not looking into the audience at all, head down and just starts shredding on his guitar for like fifteen minutes his shadow cast onto the audience just larger than life itself, Stevie was putting the Jubilee faithful into a trance and with great accuracy I might add! For being only 30 years old he was a master, pure, pure mastery by the time SRV played Voodoo Chile the Jubilee had erupted and begging for Stevie to keep playing!

I say earth shattering because you never know how big of an event anybody you get to see live is, it may turn out to be the one and only time you see them live, in the case of SRV it was only five short years on the exact anniversary of this show when we see him that Stevie begged for one of the last seats on the helicopter and as it went up into the fog it made contact with overhead power lines killing all that were on board, I was working at the golf course and just rolled up on a golf cart to the clubhouse when I heard the horrific news, very sad news to say the least!

Having the 'Party Bus' for Limelight / Rock City was one of the coolest ways to advertise because you had all the hooligans going to different events (mostly concerts) they just didn't have the right person for PR work, could've hooked up with other bars/pubs with industry cards and did pub crawls, football games and other sporting events, Klondike days and all the festivals! In any case it was an absolute blast when we were on it, overloading the bus for the AC/ DC -Who Made Who show was one of the biggest highlights before they shut the bus down, something to do with permits and being responsible for the party goers, I imagine the clean up afterwards wasn't any fun either, wouldn't be so bad I'm sure the Lee brothers owned a car wash too.

Much like the days and nights at Limelight, we continued partying all the time (the same little crowd grew to more like 20-30) we would stay in the club after hours and would end up making some dumb laugh tracks and other goofy soundtracks, to get everyone laughing hysterically we'd all lay on the floor and put our heads on the other persons stomach, at first doesn't seem like it was going to work, but once your head is moving and their tummy is bouncing, everyone is breaking into some pretty good laughter. For some more PRS work the night the Edmonton Oilers won the Stanley Cup vs. The Philadelphia Flyers in game 7 at home, we dressed my buddy up like the Philly goaltender Ron Hextall, I tied a rope around his waist and walked with him up to Jasper Avenue, just a few short blocks and the crowds that started to gather thought that I had really captured Hextall, during this one stoppage for the TV cameras they started beating him so bad he removed the goalie mask, and we were going to fight this mob, by the time we walked back to Rock City buddy was covered in bruises.

As we were entering into the first week of 1987 former front man with Van Halen, David Lee Roth was touring the second leg of his first solo album Eat em' and Smile with Steve Vai on lead guitar, as Klay and I were set out to embark on this show, K-97 announces next vehicle to the station will win four tickets for this concert, here we go again…(lol) I feel like I'm always chasing concert tickets, we had tickets already so I wasn't sure as to why we needed these four, I think Klay just gave them away at the door or something for promo to Rock City along with a get a free drink card.

Anyway, as we're rounding the corner to the station, we could see the DJ (with K-97) standing at the doors with the tickets, my door was already ajar and I was ready to step out and grab these tickets, it was as though I was thrown out of the car, I rolled about three or four times got up and grabbed the envelope, the DJ hauls us into the booth and puts us on air because he thought it was hilarious and was referring to it like a scene from the movie The French Connection or another mobster type movie, it wasn't planned to happen that way but it was great for more publicity for Rock City for sure.

Another great show with another climatic stoppage was with Iggy Pop opening for The Pretenders, Iggy was like on cloud nine another dimension where he's just floating around somewhere above where we walk, and his feet don't touch the ground…ever! His entire performance was two or three feet above the stage, talk about flying high. We almost were making it through this show without an event, then out of nowhere Chrissie Hynde stops the show, has the house lights turned on and has these two hecklers on the floor removed from the show, seemed like we almost made it through a show without an interruption, oh so close.

(2022) whereas now you can get music from anywhere and everywhere downloads, Spotify, YouTube, google all social media platforms it doesn't take much to find it. Although it was still available back in the day you just had to wait a little longer it was like waiting for regular snail mail compared to like drive through. I was still getting access and filled up for sure, my older siblings bought records and went to all the shows at the Kinsmen Field House, plus going to my friend's house listening to music and smoking some cigs before school (gr. 3) the only radio station then was 630 CHED (AM) and that was garbage, they were playing everything on that station.

Blackie's E-fuckin-ssential Vinyl

Not in any fucking order because music can't be put into lists or compared between genres, music is subjective and is personal but shared universally, people can share similar interests and dig the same artists, but I found that throughout my life, like a good pop-up friend or acquaintance some bands and artists didn't stay but for some strange reason when you listen back to some of them, it brings you back to that moment in time of your life, like visiting a good old friend and it speaks to you maybe the same way as when you first heard it but maybe now has a different meaning for your situation. The most influential music can vary from the genres you inject for your listening pleasures and depending on what is going on in your life, some days maybe could be filled with just a certain artist within different groups like a Chris Cornell, Soundgarden, Audioslave kind of day or maybe it's a Sammy Hagar, Montrose, Van Halen day. It could vary especially if you're on a road trip or sitting by a fire pit reminiscing on your memories, whichever the case if you're an album junkie and want to have some great vinyl added to your collection then this is what you should incorporate into your library on your island…

- Jimi Hendrix – Are you experienced / Axis bold as love.
- Alter Bridge – Blackbird / One day remains / Fortress.
- Pink Floyd – The Wall / Dark side of the Moon
- Led Zeppelin – Physical Graffiti / LZ II / IV / Celebration Day
- Ozzy Osbourne – Blizzard of Ozz
- The Rolling Stones – Exile on Main St. / goat heads soup

- Rush – Moving Pictures / 2112 / Hemispheres / All the world's a stage.
- Black Sabbath – debut / Heaven & Hell / Paranoid
- Deep Purple – In rock / Perfect Strangers / Machine Head
- Metallica – Black / kill 'em all/ master of puppets
- Free- Fire & Water
- The Pat Travers Band – Heat in the Street / Crash & Burn / blues tracks / makin magic
- Uriah Heep – Demons & Wizards
- Budgie – Never turn your back on a friend.
- Montrose – Montrose
- Nirvana – Nevermind
- The Doors – the doors
- Gun's n' Roses – Appetite for Destruction / Use your Illusion I & II
- Rory Gallagher – Irish tour '74 / Blueprint
- Bad Co – Bad Company
- Aerosmith – toys in the attic / pump
- Rainbow – on stage / rising / Long live rock n roll.
- Boston – boston
- Bob Marley – legend / exodus
- Creed – human clay
- Soundgarden – king animal / Badmotorfinger
- Van Halen – debut / for unlawful carnal knowledge
- AC/DC – If you want blood/ Back in Black / Flick of the switch.
- Thin Lizzy – Live and Dangerous / black rose/ china town / jailbreak

- Judas Priest – Point of entry / British steel.
- Motorhead – Ace of spades
- Iron Maiden – Iron Maiden / Killers / number of the beast
- Saxon – Wheels of steel
- Scorpions – blackout
- Dio – Holy diver
- ZZ top – Fandango and earlier material / first album
- Def Leppard – Pyromania / Hysteria
- Whitesnake – 1987
- Queensryche – operation mind crime
- Jane's Addiction – nothings shocking.
- Faith no More – the real thing • The Cult – sonic temple
- Pearl Jam – Ten / vs.
- Temple of the Dog – temple of the dog
- Red Hot Chili Peppers – Blood sugar sex magic
- Alice in Chains – dirt
- The Black Crowes – The southern harmony and musical companion
- Linkin Park – hybrid theory
- Queens of the Stone age – Songs for the deaf
- Vol beat – guitar, gangsters Cadillac's / beyond hell above heaven
- Shinedown – leave a whisper / amaryllis.
- Molly Hatchet – Flirting with disaster.
- T*Rex – Electric warrior
- Joe Satriani – what happens next / the extremist.
- Slash – world on fire

- Triumph – never surrender.
- Webb Wilder – doo dad
- Jeff Beck – Wired / blow by blow
- Johnny Winter – second winter
- Humble Pie – rock on / performance rocking the filmore.
- Chris Cornell – higher truth
- God smack – when legends rise.
- Frank Marino – tales of the unexpected
- Max Webster – mutiny up my sleeve / universal juveniles.
- Age of Electric – Age of electric / make a pest a pet.
- Stevie Ray Vaughn – Texas flood / live alive/ couldn't stand the weather.

There are many, many more albums that were left on the shelf, and that in itself could be an entirely different book , mostly for a lot of these artists their earlier material is more pleasing to me, like early U2 or AC/DC the raw energy harnessed on vinyl is just candy for the ears, plus the B sides to many records would get over looked and never played, mostly FM radio stations killed the play of so-called no name artists because there needle was stuck skipping on one song, and that pretty much killed it for me with the classic rock that's been over played for fifty years, it was quite a buzz when these records came out and we listened to them first hand, not knowing they'd still be played into our retirement years…I mean wholly shit if I were the artist or band still making royalties off some album they made a half a century ago, that's bank $$$

List of deaths in rock and roll (1980s)

From Wikipedia, the free encyclopedia

Jump to navigation Jump to search.

This is a dynamic list and may never be able to satisfy particular standards for completeness. You can help by adding missing items with reliable sources.

The following is a list of notable performers of rock and roll music or rock music, and others directly associated with the music as producers, songwriters or in other closely related roles, who have died in the 1980s. The list gives their date, cause and location of death, and their age.

Rock music developed from the rock and roll music that emerged during the 1950s and includes a diverse range of subgenres. The terms "rock and roll" and "rock" each have a variety of definitions, some narrow and some wider. In determining criteria for inclusion, this list uses as its basis reliable sources listing "rock deaths" or "deaths in rock and roll," as well as such sources as the Rock and Roll Hall of Fame.

Just within the pages on this list below from January 1980 through December 1989 there's around 450 names with some of the most influential people to create Rock n' Roll!

Georgeanna Tillman The Marvelettes	35	January 6, 1980	Inkster, Michigan, U.S.	Complications from sickle cell anemia and lupus
Larry Williams	44	January 7, 1980	Los Angeles, California, U.S.	Suicide by gunshot
Carl White The Rivingtons	47	January 7, 1980	Los Angeles, California, U.S.	Acute tonsillitis
Professor Longhair	61	January 23, 1980	New Orleans, Louisiana, U.S.	Heart attack
Jimmy Durante	86	January 29, 1980	Santa Monica, California, U.S.	Pneumonia
Edward Lewis Record producer for Decca Records	79	January 29, 1980	Chelsea, London, England	Cancer
Warren Smith	47	January 30, 1980		Heart attack
Bon Scott AC/DC	33	February 19, 1980	Dulwich, London, England	Alcohol poisoning [1]
Janet Vogel The Skyliners	38	February 21, 1980		Suicide by carbon monoxide [2]
Jacob Miller Inner Circle	27	March 23, 1980	Kingston, Jamaica	Traffic accident
John Poulos The Buckinghams	32	March 26, 1980	Chicago, Illinois, U.S.	Heart failure
Ricky Lancelotti	35	April 7, 1980		Unknown
Anna Jantar	29	April 14, 1980	Warsaw, Poland	"MikolajKopernik" plane crash [3]
Tommy Caldwell The Marshall Tucker Band	30	April 28, 1980	Spartanburg, South Carolina, U.S.	Traffic collision
Ian Curtis Joy Division	23	May 18, 1980	Macclesfield, England	Suicide by hanging [4]
Carl Radle Derek and the Dominos, Eric Clapton	37	May 30, 1980	Claremore, Oklahoma, U.S.	Kidney infection
Charles Miller War	42	June 14, 1980	Los Angeles, California, U.S.	Stabbing [5]
Malcolm Owen The Ruts	26	July 14, 1980	London, England	Heroin overdose
Keith Godchaux The Grateful Dead	32	July 23, 1980	Marin County, California, U.S.	Traffic accident
George Scott III	26	August 5, 1980	New York City, New York, U.S.	Heroin overdose
Jimmy Forrest	60	August 26, 1980	Grand Rapids, Michigan, U.S.	Heart failure
John Bonham Led Zeppelin	32	September 25, 1980	Windsor, England	Asphyxiation on vomit [6]
Pat Hare	49	September 26, 1980	Saint Paul, Minnesota, U.S.	Lung cancer
Lincoln Chase	54	October 6, 1980	Metro Atlanta, U.S.	Unknown
Bobby Lester The Moonglows	49	October 6, 1980		Lung cancer
Steve Peregrin Took T. Rex, Shagrat, Steve Took's Horns	31	October 27, 1980	Ladbroke Grove, London, England	Asphyxiation [7]
O. V. Wright	41	November 16, 1980	Mobile, Alabama, U.S.	Heart attack
Darby Crash Germs	22	December 7, 1980	Los Angeles, California, U.S.	Suicide by heroin overdose
John Lennon The Beatles, Plastic Ono Band	40	December 8, 1980	New York City, New York, U.S.	Murder [8]
Tim Hardin	39	December 29, 1980	Los Angeles, California, U.S.	Heroin overdose
Robert Pete Williams	66	December 31, 1980	Rosedale, Louisiana, U.S.	Unknown
David Lynch The Platters	52	January 2, 1981		Cancer
Felton Jarvis	46	January 3, 1981	Nashville, Tennessee, U.S.	Stroke
Alice Mae Buschmann Spielvogel The Chordettes	55	January 6, 1981	North Little Rock, Pulaski County, Arkansas, U.S.	
Blind James Campbell	74	January 22, 1981	Nashville, Tennessee, U.S.	Unknown
Carl Feaster The Chords	50	January 23, 1981		Cancer
Bill Haley Bill Haley & His Comets	55	February 9, 1981	Harlingen, Texas, U.S.	Brain tumor or heart attack
Mike Bloomfield The Paul Butterfield Blues Band	37	February 15, 1981	San Francisco, California, U.S.	Accidental drug overdose

Name	Age	Date	Location	Cause
Little Hat Jones	81	March 7, 1981	Naples, Texas, U.S.	Unknown
Tampa Red	77	March 19, 1981	Chicago, Illinois, U.S.	Unknown
Bob Hite Canned Heat	38	April 5, 1981	Los Angeles, California, U.S.	Heart attack caused by heroin overdose [9]
Kit Lambert	45	April 7, 1981	Middlesex, England	Cerebral hemorrhage after falls downstairs [10]
Austin Pitre	63	April 8, 1981	Elton, Louisiana, U.S.	Unknown
Steve Currie T. Rex	33	April 28, 1981	Vale de Parra, Algarve, Portugal	Traffic accident
Bob Marley The Wailers	36	May 11, 1981	Miami, Florida, U.S.	Acral lentiginous melanoma
Ernie Freeman	58	May 16, 1981	Los Angeles, California, U.S.	Heart attack
Roy Brown	55-60	May 25, 1981	San Fernando, California, U.S.	Heart attack
Mary Lou Williams	71	May 28, 1981	Atlanta, Georgia, U.S.	Bladder cancer
Joseph Santollo The Duprees	38	June 4, 1981		Heart attack
Polka Dot Slim	54	June 22, 1981	Oakland, California, U.S.	Unknown
Chuck Wagon The Dickies	24	June 28, 1981	San Fernando Valley, Los Angeles, California, U.S.	Suicide by gunshot
Rushton Moreve Steppenwolf	32	July 1, 1981	Los Angeles, California, U.S.	Traffic accident
Hubert Johnson The Contours	40	July 11, 1981	Detroit, Michigan, U.S.	Suicide by poison and gunshot
Harry Chapin	38	July 16, 1981	Jericho, New York, U.S.	Heart attack/Traffic accident [11]
Guy Stevens Record producer and band manager from Hapshash and the Coloured Coat, Mott the Hoople, ProcolHarum and The Clash	38	August 28, 1981	South London, England	Prescription drug overdose
Sandra Tilley The Velvelettes, Martha and the Vandellas	35 or 36	September 9, 1981	Las Vegas, Nevada, U.S.	Complications from brain surgery
Furry Lewis	88	September 14, 1981	Memphis, Tennessee, U.S.	Heart failure
Hazel Scott	61	October 2, 1981	Mount Sinai Hospital, Manhattan, New York, U.S.	Pancreatic cancer
George de Fretes	59	November 19, 1981	Los Angeles County, California, U.S.	
Big Walter Horton	60	December 8, 1981	Chicago, Illinois, U.S.	Heart failure
Pigmeat Markham	77	December 13, 1981	The Bronx, New York, U.S.	Stroke
Tommy Tucker	48	January 22, 1982	Newark, New Jersey, U.S.	Food poisoning [12]
Lightnin' Hopkins	69	January 30, 1982	Houston, Texas, U.S.	Esophageal cancer
Alex Harvey Sensational Alex Harvey Band	46	February 4, 1982	Zeebrugge, Belgium	Heart attack [13]
John Belushi The Blues Brothers	33	March 5, 1982	Los Angeles, California, U.S.	Speedball overdose [14]
Randy Rhoads Quiet Riot	25	March 19, 1982	Leesburg, Florida, U.S.	Plane accident
Floyd Smith	65	March 29, 1982	Indianapolis, Indiana, U.S.	Unknown
Lester Bangs music journalist	33	April 30, 1982	New York City, New York, U.S.	Opioid, diazepam, and NyQuil overdose
Neil Bogart Record producer for Kiss and music executive from Casablanca Records	39	May 8, 1982	Los Angeles, California, U.S.	Cancer
Rusty Day The Amboy Dukes	36	June 3, 1982	Longwood, Florida, U.S.	Murder
Addie Harris The Shirelles	42	June 10, 1982	Atlanta, Georgia, U.S.	Heart attack
Art Pepper	56	June 15, 1982	Los Angeles, California, U.S.	Stroke
James Honeyman-Scott The Pretenders	25	June 16, 1982	London, England	Cocaine overdose [15]
Warren Ryanes The Monotones	45	June 16, 1982		Unknown

Name	Age	Date	Location	Cause
Jane Vasey Downchild Blues Band	32-33	July 6, 1982		Leukemia
Bill Justis	55	July 15, 1982	Nashville, Tennessee, U.S.	Cancer
Sonny Stitt	58	July 22, 1982	Washington, D.C., U.S.	Heart attack
Nick Lucas	84	July 28, 1982	Colorado Springs, Colorado, U.S.	Double pneumonia
Joe Tex	47	August 13, 1982	Navasota, Texas, U.S.	Heart attack
Doyle Wilburn The Wilburn Brothers	52	September 27, 1982		Lung cancer
Hoyt Hawkins The Jordanaires	54	October 23, 1982		Heart attack
Dave Torbert Kingfish, New Riders of the Purple Sage	34	December 7, 1982		Heart attack
Marty Robbins	57	December 8, 1982	Nashville, Tennessee, U.S.	Heart attack
Lazy Bill Lucas	64	December 11, 1982	Minneapolis, Minnesota, U.S.	Natural causes
Rebop Kwaku Baah Traffic, Can	38	January 12, 1983	Stockholm, Sweden	Cerebral hemorrhage
Lamar Williams The Allman Brothers Band	34	January 21, 1983	Los Angeles, California, U.S.	Lung cancer
Billy Fury	42	January 28, 1983	London, England	Heart attack [16]
Lorraine Ellison	51	January 31, 1983		Ovarian cancer
Sam Chatmon	86	February 2, 1983	Hollandale, Mississippi, U.S.	Unknown
Karen Carpenter The Carpenters	32	February 4, 1983	Downey, California, U.S.	Heart attack due to anorexia [17]
Dig Richards	42	February 17, 1983	Sydney, Australia	Pancreatic cancer [18]
Cliff Trenier The Treniers	63	March 2, 1983		Cancer
William Walton	80	March 8, 1983	La Mortella, Ischia, Italy	Natural causes
Danny Rapp Danny & The Juniors	41	April 5, 1983	Parker, Arizona, U.S.	Suicide by gunshot
Pete Farndon The Pretenders	30	April 14, 1983	London, England	Drowning after heroin overdose
Felix Pappalardi Mountain	43	April 17, 1983	New York City, New York, U.S.	Murdered by his wife Gail Collins Pappalardi
Earl Hines	79	April 22, 1983	Oakland, California, U.S.	Heart attack
Muddy Waters	70	April 30, 1983	Westmont, Illinois, U.S.	Heart attack
Clarence Quick The Del-Vikings	46	May 5, 1983		Heart attack
Stan Rogers	33	June 2, 1983	Hebron, Kentucky, U.S.	Asphyxiation of smoke on airplane
J. B. Hutto	57	June 12, 1983	Harvey, Illinois, U.S.	Cancer
Douglas "Buzz" Shearman Moxy	32	June 16, 1983	Toronto, Canada	Motorcycle accident
Walter Jackson	45	June 20, 1983	Chicago, Illinois, U.S.	Cerebral hemorrhage
Larry Darnell	54	July 3, 1983	Columbus, Ohio, U.S.	Lung cancer
Chris Wood Traffic	39	July 12, 1983	Birmingham, England	Pneumonia
Frank Fenter Record producer and music industry executive of Atlantic Records and Capricorn Records	47	July 21, 1983	Macon, Georgia, U.S.	Heart attack
Jimmy Liggins	64	July 21, 1983	Durham, North Carolina, U.S.	Unknown
Wild Bill Moore	65	August 1, 1983	Los Angeles, California, U.S.	Unknown
James Jamerson The Funk Brothers	47	August 2, 1983	Los Angeles, California, U.S.	Complications of cirrhosis, heart failure and pneumonia
Klaus Nomi	39	August 6, 1983	New York City, New York, U.S.	Complications due to AIDS
Ira Gershwin	86	August 17, 1983	Beverly Hills, California, U.S.	Cardiovascular disease
Willie Bobo	49	September 15, 1983		Cancer
George "Harmonica" Smith	59	October 2, 1983	Los Angeles, California, U.S.	Unknown
Hugh Mundell	21	October 14, 1983	Kingston, Jamaica	Murder by gunshot
Merle Travis	65	October 20, 1983	Tahlequah, Oklahoma, U.S.	Heart attack
James Booker	43	November 8, 1983	New Orleans, Louisiana, U.S.	Renal failure related to chronic abuse of heroin and alcohol

Name	Age	Date	Location	Cause
John Grimaldi Argent, Flux, Cheap Flights	28	November 15, 1983		Multiple sclerosis
Tom Evans Badfinger	36	November 19, 1983	London, England	Suicide by hanging [19]
Gene Bricker The Marcels	45	December 10, 1983		Unknown
Jimmy Nolen	49	December 18, 1983	Atlanta, Georgia, U.S.	Heart attack
Dennis Wilson The Beach Boys	39	December 28, 1983	Marina del Rey, California, U.S.	Accidental drowning
Alexis Korner	55	January 1, 1984	Westminster, London	Lung cancer
Jackie Wilson Billy Ward and his Dominoes	49	January 21, 1984	Mount Holly, New Jersey, U.S.	Pneumonia
Paul Gardiner Tubeway Army, Gary Newman	25	February 4, 1984	Northolt, Middlesex, England	Heroin overdose
Ethel Merman	76	February 15, 1984	Manhattan, New York City, New York, U.S.	Brain cancer
Joey Vann The Duprees	59	February 28, 1984		Heart attack
Tom Jans	36	March 25, 1984	Los Angeles. California, U.S.	Drug overdose
Marvin Gaye	44	April 1, 1984	Los Angeles, California, U.S.	Murdered by his father
Ral Donner	41	April 6, 1984	Chicago, Illinois, U.S.	Lung cancer
Red Garland	60	April 23, 1984	Dallas, Texas, U.S.	Heart attack
Count Basie	79	April 26, 1984	Hollywood, Florida, U.S.	Pancreatic cancer
Z. Z. Hill	48	April 27, 1984	Dallas, Texas, U.S.	Heart attack
Moses' "Whispering" Smith	52	April 28, 1984	Baton Rouge, Louisiana, U.S.	Unknown
Nate Nelson The Flamingos	52	June 1, 1984	Boston, Massachusetts, U.S.	Heart attack
Meredith Willson	82	June 15, 1984	Santa Monica, California, U.S.	Heart failure
Harmonica Slim	49	June 16, 1984	Texarkana, Texas, U.S.	Unknown
Guy McDonough	28	June 26, 1984	Melbourne, Australia	Pneumonia
Jimmie Spheeris	34	July 4, 1984	Santa Monica, California	Motorcycle accident
Philippé Wynne The Spinners	43	July 14, 1984	Oakland, California, U.S.	Heart attack
Big Mama Thornton	57	July 25, 1984	Los Angeles, California, U.S.	Heart attack
Esther Phillips	48	August 7, 1984	Carson, California, U.S.	Liver and kidney failure due to long-term drug abuse
Percy Mayfield	63	August 11, 1984	Los Angeles, California, U.S.	Heart attack
Lenny Breau	43	August 12, 1984	Los Angeles, California, U.S.	Murder by strangulation
Hammie Nixon	76	August 17, 1984	Jackson, Tennessee, U.S.	Unknown
Trummy Young >	72	September 10, 1984	San Jose, California, U.S.	Cerebral hemorrhage
Titus Turner	51	September 13, 1984	Atlanta, Georgia, U.S.	Unknown
Shelly Manne	64	September 26, 1984	Los Angeles, California, U.S.	Heart attack
Geater Davis	42	September 29, 1984	Dallas, Texas, U.S.	Heart attack
Teddy Reig Record producer, record company executive and co-founded of Roost. Records	58	September 29, 1984	Teaneck, New Jersey, U.S.	Unknown
Steve Goodman	36	September 30, 1984	Seattle, Washington, U.S.	Leukemia
Wells Kelly Orleans	34	October 29, 1984	London, England	Morphine and cocaine overdose
Keith Hudson	38	November 14, 1984	New York, U.S.	Lung cancer
Razzle Hanoi Rocks	24	December 8, 1984	Redondo Beach, California, U.S.	Traffic accident
Mal Spooner Demon	39	December 10, 1984	Leek, Staffordshire, England	Pneumonia
Ron Tabak Prism	31	December 25, 1984	Vancouver, British Columbia, Canada	Brain blood clot

Name	Age	Date	Location	Cause
Eddie "Bongo" Brown The Funk Brothers	52	December 28, 1984	Los Angeles, California, U.S.	Heart ailment
Paul Hewson Dragon	32	January 9–10, 1985		Accidental drug overdose
Georgie Stoll Musical director from Metro-Goldwyn Mayer	79	January 18, 1985	Monterey, California, U.S.	Pneumonia
Kenny Clarke	71	January 26, 1985	Montreuil, France	Heart attack
Matt Monro	54	February 7, 1985	Cromwell Hospital, London, England	Liver cancer
David Byron Uriah Heep	38	February 28, 1985	Reading, Berkshire, England	Alcohol-related liver failure
Robert Blackwell Record producer and arranger	66	March 9, 1985	Hacienda Heights, Whittier, California, U.S.	Pneumonia
Bob Shad Record producer for Big Brother and the Holding Company	65	March 13, 1985	Beverly Hills, California, U.S.	Heart attack
Willie Mabon	59	April 19, 1985	Paris, France	Cancer
Johnny Fuller	56	May 20, 1985	Oakland, California, U.S.	Lung cancer
Lloyd Green	75	May 23, 1985	Los Angeles, California, U.S.	Myocardial infarction
Pee Wee Crayton	70	June 25, 1985	Los Angeles, California, U.S.	Heart attack
Wynn Stewart	51	July 17, 1985	Hendersonville, Tennessee, U.S.	Heart attack
Kay Kyser	80	July 31, 1985	Chapel Hill, North Carolina, U.S.	Heart attack
Kyu Sakamoto	43	August 12, 1985	Mount Osutaka, Ueno, Gunma Prefecture, Japan	Plane accident
Jimmy Stokely Exile	41	August 13, 1985	Richmond, Kentucky, U.S.	Complications from hepatitis/Chronic liver disorder
Philly Joe Jones	62	August 30, 1985	Philadelphia, Pennsylvania, U.S.	Heart attack
Jo Jones	73	September 3, 1985	New York City, New York, U.S.	Pneumonia
Little Brother Montgomery	79	September 6, 1985	Chicago, Illinois, U.S.	Unknown
Brian Keenan The Chamber Brothers	42	October 5, 1985		Heart attack
Blind John Davis	71	October 12, 1985	Chicago, Illinois, U.S.	Unknown
Ricky Wilson The B-52's	32	October 12, 1985	New York City, New York, U.S.	Complications due to AIDS
Big Joe Turner	74	November 24, 1985	Inglewood, California, U.S.	Heart attack
Ian Stewart The Rolling Stones	47	December 12, 1985	London, England	Heart attack
Curley Moore	42	December 14, 1985	Algiers, Louisiana, U.S.	Murdered
D. Boon The Minutemen	27	December 22, 1985	Tucson, Arizona, U.S.	Traffic accident
Gus Jenkins	54	December 22, 1985	Los Angeles, California, U.S.	Unknown
Tommy Blake	54	December 24, 1985	Haughton, Louisiana, U.S.	Murdered by his wife
Andy Chapin The Association, Ricky Nelson	34	December 31, 1985	De Kalb, Texas, U.S.	Plane accident
Ricky Nelson Ricky Nelson	45	December 31, 1985	De Kalb, Texas, U.S.	Plane accident
Bobby Neal Ricky Nelson	38	December 31, 1985	De Kalb, Texas, U.S.	Plane accident
Pat Woodward Ricky Nelson	35	December 31, 1985	De Kalb, Texas, U.S.	Plane accident
Ricky Intveld Ricky Nelson	22	December 31, 1985	De Kalb, Texas, U.S.	Plane accident
Clark Russel Sound man for Ricky Nelson	35	December 31, 1985	De Kalb, Texas, U.S.	Plane accident
Phil Lynott Thin Lizzy	36	January 4, 1986	Salisbury, Wiltshire, England	Heart failure and pneumonia caused by alcohol and drug use [20]
Joe Farrell Return to Forever	48	January 10, 1986	Los Angeles, California, U.S.	Myelodysplastic syndrome

Gordon MacRae	64	January 24, 1986	Lincoln, Nebraska, U.S.	Pneumonia
Albert Grossman	59	January 25, 1986		Heart attack
John R. American disc jockey and record producer	75	February 15, 1986	Nashville, Tennessee, U.S.	Lung cancer
Robbie Basho	45	February 28, 1986	Berkeley, California, U.S.	Stroke
Richard Manuel The Band	42	March 4, 1986	Winter Park, Florida, U.S.	Suicide by hanging
Sonny Terry	74	March 11, 1986	Mineola, New York, U.S.	Natural causes
Mark Dinning	52	March 22, 1986	Jefferson City, Missouri, U.S.	Heart attack
O'Kelly Isley, Jr. The Isley Brothers	48	March 31, 1986	Alpine, New Jersey, U.S.	Heart attack
Dorothy Ashby	53	April 13, 1986	Santa Monica, California, U.S.	Cancer
Hank Mobley	55	May 30, 1986	Philadelphia, Pennsylvania, U.S.	Pneumonia
Benny Goodman	77	June 13, 1986	New York, New York, U.S.	Heart attack
Dean Reed	47	June 13, 1986	East Berlin, GDR	Suicide by drowning
Clarence Garlow	75	July 24, 1986	Beaumont, Texas, U.S.	Unknown
William B. Williams American disc jockey	62	August 3, 1986	New York City, New York, U.S.	Acute anemia and respiratory failure
Thad Jones	63	August 20, 1986	Copenhagen, Denmark	Cancer/Bone cancer
Cliff Burton Metallica	24	September 27, 1986	Ljungby Municipality, Sweden	Traffic accident
Moses Asch	80	October 19, 1986	New York City, New York, U.S.	Unknown
Esquerita	50	October 23, 1986	Harlem, New York, U.S.	Complications due to AIDS
Eddie "Lockjaw" Davis	64	November 3, 1986	Culver City, California, U.S.	Hodgkin's lymphoma [21]
Bobby Nunn The Coasters	63	November 5, 1986	Los Angeles, California, U.S.	Heart failure
Tracy Pew	28	November 7, 1986	Melbourne, Victoria, Australia	Brain hemorrhage
Bea Booze	74	November 11, 1986	Scottsville, New York, U.S.	Unknown
Scatman Crothers	76	November 22, 1986	Van Nuys, California, U.S.	Pneumonia and lung cancer
Lee Dorsey	61	December 1, 1986	New Orleans, Louisiana, U.S.	Emphysema
Billy Rancher The Malchicks, Billy Rancher and the Unreal Gods, and Flesh and Blood	29	December 2, 1986	Portland, Oregon, U.S.	Kidney and liver cancer
Desi Arnaz	69	December 2, 1986	Solana Beach, California, U.S.	Lung cancer
Hollywood Fats Canned Heat, The Blasters	32	December 8, 1986	Los Angeles, California, U.S.	Drug overdose
Kate Wolf	44	December 10, 1986	San Francisco, California, U.S.	Leukemia
Tommy Keifer Krokus	29	December 24, 1986		Suicide by hanging
Peter Lucia, Jr. Tommy James and the Shondells	39	January 6, 1987		Heart attack
Handsome Ned	29	January 10, 1987	Toronto, Ontario, Canada	Accidental heroin overdose
RauliSomerjoki	39	January 14, 1987	Helsinki, Finland	Alcohol-related ailments
Ray Bolger The Scarecrow from The Wizard of Oz	83	January 15, 1987	Los Angeles, California, U.S.	Bladder cancer [22]
Alfred Lion Record executive and co-founder of Blue Note Records	78	February 2, 1987	San Diego, California, U.S.	Heart failure
Liberace	67	February 4, 1987	Palm Springs, California, U.S.	AIDS
Tony Destra Cinderella, Britny Fox	32	February 8, 1987	Pennsylvania, U.S.	Car Accident
Seymor Spiegelman The Hilltoppers	56	February 13, 1987	New York City, New York, U.S.	Heart defect
Jimmy Holiday	52	February 15, 1987	Iowa City, Iowa, U.S.	Congestive heart failure
Jim Connors Radio personality and disc jockey	46	February 24, 1987	I-95, Virginia, U.S.	Car crash
Danny Kaye	76	March 3, 1987	Los Angeles, California, U.S.	Heart failure from Hepatitis
Norman Harris MFSB	39	March 14, 1987	Philadelphia, Pennsylvania, U.S.	Cardiovascular disease

Don Gant	44	March 15, 1987	Nashville, Tennessee, U.S.	Complications following a boating accident
Tony Stratton-Smith Record producer and manager from The Nice, Van der Graaf Generator, Bonzo Dog Doo-Dah Band, and co-founder of Charisma Records	53	March 19, 1987	London, England	Stomach cancer
Dino Martin Dino, Desi & Billy	35	March 21, 1987	San Gorgonio Mountain, California, U.S.	Military aircraft crash
Buddy Rich	69	April 2, 1987	Los Angeles, California, U.S.	Respiratory and cardiac failure
Maxine Sullivan	75	April 7, 1987	New York City, New York, U.S.	Seizure
Carlton Barrett The Wailers	36	April 17, 1987	Kingston, Jamaica	Murder by gunshot
Irving Ashby	66	April 22, 1987	Perris, California, U.S.	Unknown
Billy Johnson The Moonglows	59	April 28, 1987	Los Angeles, California, U.S.	Unknown
Paul Butterfield The Paul Butterfield Blues Band	44	May 4, 1987	North Hollywood, California, U.S.	Accidental heroin overdose
Allen Jones Record producer for The Bar-Kays	46	May 5, 1987		Heart attack
Victor Feldman	53	May 12, 1987	Woodland Hills, California, U.S.	Heart attack
Gary Driscoll Rainbow, Elf	41	June 8, 1987	Ithaca, New York, U.S.	Murdered
Kid Thomas Valentine	91	June 18, 1987	New Orleans, Louisiana, U.S.	Unknown
Fred Astaire	88	June 22, 1987	Los Angeles, California, U.S.	Pneumonia
Elizabeth Cotten	94	June 29, 1987	Syracuse, New York, U.S.	Pnuemonia
Snakefinger The Residents	38	July 1, 1987	Linz, Austria	Heart attack
John Hammond Record producer for Columbia Records	76	July 10, 1987		Stroke
Lee Gaines The Delta Rhythm Boys	90	July 15, 1987	Helsinki, Finland	Cancer
Pete King After the Fire, BAP, The Flys	28	July 15, 1987		Testicular cancer
Howard McGhee	69	July 17, 1987	New York City, New York, U.S.	Unknown
Todd Crew Bassist for Jetboy	21	July 18, 1987		Heroin and alcohol overdose
Alex Sadkin Record producer for Arcadia, Simply Red, Thompson Twins, Boom Crash Opera and Duran Duran	38	July 25, 1987	Nassau, Bahamas	Traffic accident
Joe Liggins	71	July 31, 1987	Lynwood, California, U.S.	Stroke
David A. Martin Sam the Sham & the Pharaohs	50	August 2, 1987		Heart attack
Scott La Rock Boogie Down Productions	25	August 27, 1987	New York City, New York, U.S.	Gunshot
Peter Tosh The Wailers	42	September 11, 1987	Kingston, Jamaica	Murder by gunshot
Lorne Greene	72	September 11, 1987	Santa Monica, California, U.S.	Pneumonia
Jaco Pastorius Weather Report	35	September 21, 1987	Fort Lauderdale, Florida, U.S.	Brain hemorrhage following beating [23]
Ted Taylor The Cadets	53	October 2, 1987	Lake Charles, Louisiana, U.S.	Traffic accident
Woody Herman	74	October 29, 1987	West Hollywood, California, U.S.	Pneumonia following ulcer surgery
Luke "Long Gone" Miles	62	November 22, 1987	Los Angeles, California, U.S.	Unknown
Little Willy Foster	65	November 25, 1987	Chicago, Illinois, U.S.	Cancer
Richard "Ricky" Taylor The Manhattans	47	December 9, 1987		Cancer
Slam Stewart Slim & Slam	73	December 10, 1987	Binghamton, New York, U.S.	Congestive heart failure

Name	Age	Date	Location	Cause
Conny Plank Record producer and also known as Moebius & Plank	47	December 18, 1987	Cologne, North Rhine-Westphalia, Germany	Cancer
John Spence No Doubt	18	December 21, 1987	Anaheim, California, U.S.	Suicide
Gene "Bowlegs" Miller	54	December 25, 1987	Memphis, Tennessee, U.S.	Unknown
Nat Tarnopol Record producer for Brunswick Records	56	December 25, 1987		Congestive heart failure
John Dopyera	94	January 3, 1988	Grants Pass, Oregon, U.S.	Unknown
Joe Albany	63	January 12, 1988	New York City, New York, U.S.	Respiratory failure
René Hall	75	February 11, 1988	Los Angeles, California, U.S.	Heart disease
John Curulewski Styx	37	February 13, 1988	Chicago, Illinois, U.S.	Brain aneurysm
Alexander Bashlachev	27	February 17, 1988	Leningrad, Russian SFSR, Soviet Union	Fall from the window (most likely suicide)
Memphis Slim	72	February 24, 1988	Paris, France	Kidney failure
Pearl Butler Carl Butler and Pearl	60	March 1, 1988		Unknown [24]
Divine	42	March 7, 1988	Los Angeles, California, U.S.	Heart enlargement after years of obesity
Gordon Huntley Matthews Southern Comfort	62	March 7, 1988		Cancer
Amar Singh Chamkila	27	March 8, 1988	Mehsampur, Punjab, India	Murder by gunshot
Andy Gibb Younger brother of the Bee Gees	30	March 10, 1988	Oxford, England	Myocarditis worsened by drug addiction
Moody Jones	79	March 23, 1988	Chicago, Illinois, U.S.	Unknown
Dave Prater Sam & Dave	50	April 9, 1988	Sycamore, Georgia, U.S.	Traffic accident
Brook Benton	56	April 9, 1988	Queens, New York City, New York, U.S.	Pneumonia from spinal meningitis
Pony Poindexter	62	April 14, 1988	Oakland, California, U.S.	Unknown
John Banks The Merseybeats	45	April 20, 1988		Throat cancer
Barbara Robison The Peanut Butter Conspiracy	42	April 22, 1988	Billings, Montana, U.S.	Toxic shock poisoning
Carolyn Franklin	43	April 25, 1988	Bloomfield, Michigan, U.S.	Breast cancer
B. W. Stevenson	38	April 28, 1988		Heart valve surgery complications
Claude Demetrius	71	May 1, 1988	New York City, New York, U.S.	Unknown
Howie Johnson The Ventures	49-50	May 5, 1988		Cancer
Paul Wilson The Flamingos	53	May 6, 1988		Unknown
Chet Baker	58	May 13, 1988	Amsterdam, Netherlands	Fall from hotel window after heroin and cocaine abuse
Gil Evans	75	May 20, 1988	Cuernavaca, Mexico	Peritonitis
Ted Dunbar	51	May 29, 1988	New Brunswick, New Jersey, U.S.	Stroke
Dick Jacobs Record producer from Decca Records, Brunswick Records	70	May 30, 1988	New York City, New York, U.S.	Unknown
John Jordan The Four Vagabonds	74	June 16, 1988		Unknown
Finbarr Donnelly Five Go Down to the Sea?	27	June 18, 1989	The Serpentine, Hyde Park, London	Drowning accident
Jesse Ed Davis	43	June 22, 1988	Venice, Los Angeles, California, U.S.	Drug overdose
Hillel Slovak Red Hot Chili Peppers	26	June 25, 1988	Los Angeles, California, U.S.	Heroin overdose
Jimmy Soul	45	June 25, 1988	Spring Valley, New York, U.S.	Heart attack
Nico	49	July 18, 1988	Ibiza, Spain	Cerebral haemorrhage after fall from bicycle [25]
Priscilla Bowman	60	July 24, 1988	Kansas City, Missouri, U.S.	Lung cancer
Jean-Michel Basquiat Gray	27	August 12, 1988	Manhattan, New York, U.S.	Speedball overdose
Fred Below The Aces	61	August 13–14, 1988	Chicago, Illinois, U.S.	Liver cancer

FAST LANE IN A 97 STREET... POOL HALL

Name	Age	Date	Location	Cause
Robert Calvert Hawkwind	43	August 14, 1988	Ramsgate, England	Heart attack
Roy Buchanan	48	August 14, 1988	Fairfax County, Virginia, U.S.	Suicide by hanging
Tim Davis The Steve Miller Band	44	September 20, 1988		Complications related to diabetes
J. C. Heard	71	September 27, 1988	Royal Oak, Michigan, U.S.	Heart attack
Cliff Gallup Gene Vincent and His Blue Caps	58	October 9, 1988	Norfolk, Virginia, U.S.	Heart attack
Son House	86	October 19, 1988	Detroit, Michigan, U.S.	Laryngeal cancer
Johnnie Louise Richardson Johnnie & Joe	53	October 25, 1988	New York City, New York, U.S.	Stroke
Black Randy Black Randy and the Metrosquad	36	November 11, 1988	Los Angeles, California, U.S.	Complications due to AIDS [26]
Janet Ertel The Chordettes	75	November 22, 1988	Sheboygan, Sheboygan County, Wisconsin, U.S.	
Roy Orbison Traveling Wilburys	52	December 6, 1988	Hendersonville, Tennessee, U.S.	Heart attack
Bill Harris The Clovers	63	December 6, 1988	Washington, D.C., U.S.	Pancreatic cancer
Herbert Rhoad The Persuasions	44	December 8, 1988	Sacramento, California, U.S.	Aneurysm
Sylvester	41	December 16, 1988	San Francisco, California, U.S.	AIDS
Paul Jeffreys Steve Harley and Cockney Rebel	36	December 21, 1988	Lockerbie, Scotland	Pan Am Flight 103 bombing
Bobby Baylor The Solitaires, The Mello-Moods	54	January 4, 1989		Pneumonia
Patti McCabe The Poni-Tails	49	January 17, 1989		Cancer
Whistling' Alex Moore	89	January 20, 1989	Dallas, Texas, U.S.	Heart attack
Steve Wahrer The Trashmen	47	January 21, 1989		Throat cancer
Donnie Elbert	52	January 26, 1989	Philadelphia, Pennsylvania, U.S.	Stroke
Blaze Foley	39	February 1, 1989	Austin, Texas, U.S.	Gunshot
Paul Robi The Platters	57	February 1, 1989		Pancreatic cancer
Kenneth C. "Jethro" Burns Homer and Jethro	68	February 4, 1989	Evanston, Illinois, U.S.	Prostate cancer
Joe Raposo Television writer and lyrics from Sesame Street	51	February 5, 1989	Bronxville, New York, U.S.	Lymphoma
King Tubby	48	February 6, 1989	Kingston, Jamaica	Gunshot
Hip Linkchain	52	February 13, 1989	Chicago, Illinois, U.S.	Cancer
Vincent Crane The Crazy World of Arthur Brown, Dexys Midnight Runners, Atomic Rooster	45	February 14, 1989	Westminster, London, England	Suicide by barbiturate overdose
Roy Eldridge	78	February 26, 1989	Valley Stream, New York, U.S.	Heart failure
Odie Payne	62	March 1, 1989	Chicago, Illinois, U.S.	Unknown
Marek Blizinski	41	March 17, 1989	Warsaw, Poland	Cancer
Ray Agee	68	April 15, 1989	Los Angeles, California, U.S.	Unknown
Dmitry Selivanov	25	April 22, 1989	Novosibirsk, Russia	Suicide
Lucille Ball	77	April 26, 1989	Los Angeles, California, U.S.	Aortic rupture
Ron Wilson The Surfaris	44	May 7, 1989	Placer County, California, U.S.	Brain aneurysm
Keith Whitley	34	May 9, 1989	Goodlettsville, Tennessee, U.S.	Alcohol poisoning
Good Rockin' Charles	56	May 17, 1989	Chicago, Illinois, U.S.	Unknown (ill health)
John Cipollina Quicksilver Messenger Service	45	May 29, 1989	San Francisco, California, U.S.	Emphysema
Vivian Carter Record producer, company executive and co-founded of Vee Jay Records	68	June 12, 1989		Hypertension, diabetes, and stroke
Pete de Freitas Echo & the Bunnymen	27	June 14, 1989	London, England	Traffic accident

Name	Age	Date	Location	Cause
Vic Maile	45	July 11, 1989		Cancer
Nesuhi Ertegun Record producer, record executive of Atlantic Records and Warner Music Group	71	July 15, 1989	New York City, New York, U.S.	Complications of cancer surgery
Paul C East Coast hip hop pioneer, producer, engineer, and mixer	24	July 17, 1989	New York City, New York, U.S.	Murdered [27]
Bull Moose Jackson	70	July 31, 1989	Cleveland, Ohio, U.S.	Lung cancer
Larry Parnes	59	August 4, 1989	London, England	Meningitis
Sonny Thompson	65	August 11, 1989	Chicago, Illinois, U.S.	Unknown
Mickey Hawks	49	August 31, 1989	North Carolina, U.S.	Unknown
Keef Cowboy Grandmaster Flash and the Furious Five	28	September 8, 1989		Heart attack after crack-cocaine overdose
Tim Hovey New Riders of the Purple Sage	43	September 8, 1989	Watsonville, California, U.S.	Suicide by drug overdose
Pérez Prado	72	September 14, 1989	Mexico City, Mexico	Stroke
Gene Nobles American disc jockey	76	September 21, 1989	Nashville, Tennessee, U.S.	Unknown
Irving Berlin	101	September 22, 1989	Manhattan, New York City, U.S.	Natural causes and Heart attack
Cousin Joe	81	October 2, 1989	New Orleans, Louisiana, U.S.	Natural causes
Alan Murphy Go West, Level 42	35	October 19, 1989	London, England	Pneumonia resulting from AIDS
Ewan MacColl	74	October 22, 1989	Brompton, London, England	Complications following heart surgery
Dickie Goodman Record producer	55	November 8, 1989	North Carolina, U.S.	Suicide by gunshot
Freddie Waits	49	November 18, 1989	New York City, New York, U.S.	Kidney failure
Billy Lyall Bay City Rollers, Pilot	36	December 1, 1989		AIDS
Patti Santos It's a Beautiful Day	39	December 14, 1989	Near Geyserville, California, U.S.	Car crash
Floyd Jones	72	December 19, 1989	Chicago, Illinois, U.S.	Unknown [28]
Lance Railton "Earl Preston & the TT's"	40's	December 24, 1989		Unknown

The reason for going to any show because it might be the only chance you ever get to see a performer…maybe, case in point earlier I mentioned about Stevie Ray Vaughn, five short years after I had seen SRV, he died in a helicopter crash, what about those last tour dates of such performers like; Bon Scott singer with AC/DC, John Bonham drummer with Led Zeppelin or how about Randy Rhoads guitarist for Ozzy Osbourne, any of them, look at the list above that was only up until 1989, and there's like 400 names here and the list has continued to grow, on some articles the average age of musicians in the industry is late 50's to early 60's, with that being said many young ones between 27-32 also have died.

Another great short story was my two oldest sons (Calum and Isaiah) and myself back on July 23, 2016, went and parked purposely at the Jubilee Auditorium, there was an afternoon football game at Commonwealth Stadium and a sold-out Chris Cornell at the Jube, so we proceeded to the game by way of the LRT and came back to the Jube to check at the box office it there were any tickets or chance to get in to see Mr. Cornell, we go up to the box office window and I ask "any tickets left for the show?" and before he turns the computer monitor my way to view the screen he replies; "yeah, we saved the last three best seats in the house for you guys" as I'm about to say: "you don't need to be a smart ass jerk about it!."

He turns the monitor towards us and there they are highlighted in red, eleven rows back from the stage, middle seats together on the floor, $100 per seat and we got to witness one of the best singer/musicians play for nearly three hours! Sad to say Chris Cornell passed away (05.18.17) not even a year later after a show with Soundgarden in Detroit in his hotel room, the coroners called it death by suicide, my opinion it was murder with some foul play covered up to look like suicide.

Why? Mr. Cornell and good friend Chester Bennington (Linken Park) were going to expose the pedophile ring scandal, which included child porn and trafficking, in Hollywood and beyond and bring down many, many high-profileprofessionals. Two months later what would have been Cornell's birthday, Mr. Bennington was found dead in the same way as his good friend. Truthfully after these two have died and the pedophile scandal has come to the surface, I find it really hard to believe that both Cornell and Bennington took their own lives by way of suicide, call me a conspiracy theorist or whatever you want, I will call them who believes otherwise the same for believing in false and mis-leading news.

This is my poem dedicated to Chris Cornell, simply not titled…

Untitled

Shredded talent pounds the endless
Pavement…another
Overcast Seattle sky,
Busking on a street corner
I play for my next meal,
Waiting…on a record deal,
The same drop of rain beads
Down my nose, again
This is how my story goes,
A rendered poem I spoke, another lyric that I wrote…
Out from the shadows a freak
Knells down beside me, out from his cloak
Slips a dastardly deed, read this…
As he chokes out a…sign here…
Shook the world for an open stage.
Soaring wings, left the 'Rusty Cage.'
Reverberated winds from the crossroads
Where the mallet strikes many deal
On the souls that they would
Steal…away
Your hopes and trust and
The spotlights no longer
Shinedown,
Your planted seed
Will always grow in this…
'SOUNDGARDEN'

There's many that won't go to a concert, they feel it's a total waste of time, money, and energy, they feel it's just like putting a record on anyway, no change up. I'm the opposite, it's like a super event, everything about it is on a grand scale, seeing the fans and just to be part of the show is such a great feeling of emotion, the atmosphere before the band comes on stage, the 'high' of anticipation and excitement that fills the arena, everyone is filtering into the bowl, the lights are dimmed kind of like a blue grey color and all the different aromas soon are rising like smoldering ashes, the buzz is like a beehive as the time is drawing ever so close, the fanbase is getting antsy as the chatter is getting louder and louder, with the house music playing there's some side parties and cheers being tossed around like the beach balls and Frisbees start to circulate and everyone tries to anticipate hitting or throwing one.

As the roadies do a little check with the instruments on stage there's peeks and cheers with the anticipation now gets very loud…the foggers start to smog the stage and the big tease now is the house lights go off, the quick premature eruption of applause and cheers go up and stays on a steady roar, lighters are being lit around the stadium and the anticipation for the band to arrive, like a volcano bursting, among the darkness the outline of a bell being lowered center stage, smoke all around the ship.

The pirates are losing their voices already, the lights haven't even been turned on as the mallet strikes the bell, people losing their minds, as the bell gets stroked again, again and again after the eighth gong of the bell, the stage lights and guitar are turned up, the crowd is all on their feet erupting with every chord and starts then the words "I'm rolling thunder, pouring rain I'm coming on like a hurricane, My lightning's flashing across the sky, you're only young but you're gonna die", man…what a show to be part of…(AC/DC-Back in Black tour- July 1980, first leg of the North American Tour) 16 years old, witnessing one of my favorite bands with two of my bros, three rows back on the floor, you can't experience that by just listening to records…sorry. Every show has different sights, sounds, and smells but to experience it, it's a buffet to all of your senses, take it all in and overdose on everything, seriously.…do it!!

Another show that was a total rush for me to be part of was a smaller venue downtown Edmonton at the convention Center, Max Webster / Kim Mitchell, this show was about my fifth time seeing Mr. Mitchell on a previous occasion at the prime-time nightclub I was able to have a chat with him and another member of the band Peter Fredette (vocalist, bass player), a little time before the forementioned show at the convention Center, Mr. Mitchell and his wife had their first child, so for this show I made a huge congrats poster card for Kim Mitchell on becoming a Canadian Daddy Rocker, I was wearing my signature orange coveralls as per Universal Juveniles and pre-concert start up I was getting everybody in attendance to sign the poster card and gave it to Mr. Mitchell up on stage.

Certainly not every touring act will have a 'Bang On,' 'Light em up' smokin' show and give a spectacular performance every single night, they're expected to, the fan base anticipates it, with high demands too! I went to Calgary once to see Bon Jovi a highly anticipated show, and they absolutely sucked eggs, their best and only good song was 'Wanted Dead or Alive', other times bands don't have a strong frontman and the showmanship is flat and ends up being you could've just spent the night and time at home and spun their records and had a much better time.

Then there are times you wished and hoped the night wouldn't end, the entire event from pre-show, drinks, dinner and the friends that you're with, everything is just better than what you even anticipated it to be…there's also other times when you just so happened to be at a nightclub / pub or bar where a band whether they're on tour or local, everything about the night is perfect, and it was a total surprize.

Dirty Deeds Done Dirt Cheap...

As the doors would soon be closed on the little (BIG) bar of the Limelight(106 St. just North of Jasper Ave) nearing the end of 1985, it would be relocating under a new name (Rock City-105 St. 102 Ave) much bigger room (an old warehouse) and an oversized atmosphere, ushering in the new era of monster size nightclubs, along with some asshole bouncers (steroid junkies, all pumped up) that had egos bigger than the club itself, I witnessed some of the pain they'd inflict on some of the party goers and it wasn't very pretty and was totally unnecessary, using that excessive force was totally uncalled for, Klay and I were actually totally turned off by that and never condoned that behavior for a place that we were a part of, and yet the owners and managers would hire these apes all the time.

The transition to move over to Rock City wasn't easy, much of the faithful were holding on for dear life, the comfortable confines of Limelight which brought us so close and so many great times, was now on the chopping block, the building was going to be demolished for added parking! Once we made the move over to Rock City it wasn't long thereafter to make new memories and establish this as a new staple in night clubbing, branded and made it your own was to be established, where does everyone fit in? now that the room is different, limelight was long and narrow and Rock City is roomier and squarer.

The strange part was having familiar faces that encompassed or had ownership of a particular spot or seat, like on the scene of TV series Cheers, for so long you knew where everything was, even in chaotic clutter you knew who is where, and everything is how it should be, then in a blink of an eye, welcome to a whole new place, do we accept and embrace the change? Or what? It still possessed the same patrons we just needed to re-establish a new order and recreate a bigger party atmosphere totally out of this world! Something that the nightlife scene has never been a part of, and now many new faces are flocking on our turf, how dare they?

As we came to terms and accepted the fact, we moved from Limelight to Rock City we enjoyed the holiday atmosphere of Christmas 1985 and busted in the New Year of 1986, with many new joys and meeting new people, tragedy was looming around the corner, fucking again!

Dedication to Cindy Blackburn (nee McClure), a bubbly spirted beautiful girl, hairdresser at Angie's Hair salon (WEM), Cindy absolutely loved life and liked to party (with the 97 St. gang) wasn't that many of our downfalls? Cindy reached her limit at a party and passed out on the couch, some others took liberty to inject her with some more cocaine, much like the lyrics in Lynyrd Skynyrd's song 'That Smell.'

"That Smell"

Whiskey bottles, and brand-new cars
Oak tree you're in my way.
There's too much coke and too much smoke.
Look what's going on inside you.
Ooooh that smell
Can't you smell that smell?
Ooooh that smell
The smell of death surrounds you.

Angel of darkness is upon you.
Stuck a needle in your arm.
So, take another toke, have a blow for your nose.
One more drink fool, will drown you.
Ooooh that smell
Can't you smell that smell?
Ooooh that smell
The smell of death surrounds you.

Now they call you Prince Charming
Can't speak a word when you're full of 'ludes.
Say you'll be all right come tomorrow.
But tomorrow might not be here for you.
Ooooh that smell
Can't you smell that smell?
Ooooh that smell
The smell of death surrounds you.

Hey, you're a fool you.
Stick them needles in your arm I know I been there before.

One little problem that confronts you Got a monkey on your back.
Just one more fix, Lord might do the trick.
One hell of a price for you to get your kicks.

> Ooooh that smell
> Can't you smell that smell?
> Oooh that smell
> The smell of death surrounds you.
> Ooooh that smell
> Can't you smell that smell?
> Ooooh that smell
> The smell of death surrounds you.

Maybe they were thinking it was going to bring her to life, spring back up and start partying again! No, it did the complete opposite, it sent her into a coma for a little more than a week with life support, once they unplugged the machine there was no brain activity, she died right around her 21st birthday January 11/86. One of the guys received a 2-year manslaughter sentence for injecting Cindy with a chemical substance. Mama Hope woke me up that morning to tell me that Cindy had passed away, I said "I know, I dreamt about it."

Like most of us Cindy led a (Jekyll and Hyde) life style, she was a born again Christian and had (open) struggles or demons with drugs and the party life which ultimately consumed her, my brother Grant was chasing her for courtship and dating, which led him right into church, in the process also would lead the rest of the Blackburn family down that pathway into Killarney Christian Fellowship (92 St 132 Ave.,) church, this started when I was doing my weekends under lockup, after finishing my time, it was refreshing to start a new slate and be clean and sober for a little while, or at least until 1984.

Soon enough I was keen on these two sisters(Patti & Sam) that also frequented the Limelight and also moved over to Rock City, in true form Patti would interrogate me as if I were on trial, she questioned me over and over, testing my loyalty, friendship and wanted to be sure I was legit, we would talk for hours about everything under the sun, previous relationships, who I was in love with? Who did I still have feelings for? Non-stop questioning and once you thought you were safe; she'd come at you again from another angle.

I should've learned from a previous relationship when I was the maintenance and Mr. Do Everything guy at The Greenhouse, I became involved with a bartender who also was four years older than me, is it something about the process? The rejection? the flirting? We (or I) some of us, get entangled in the lust web and in doing so, waste so much time and good energy on the wrong relationships, think of it…think of how much time you spend and waste on trying to be with somebody (usually the wrong somebody), who may have had similar thoughts and desires during the early meet and greet, the excitement, the joy and overwhelming sensations you spend on the early moments of being with that person.

The intriguing mystery that lay within and keeps drawing you back to them, the lengthy times of staying up all night, then going home and continue to spend more hours on the phone with themas you both fall asleep(with phone pressed to your ear) together, then wake each other up, because you can't get enough, you want to overdose on them, know everything about each other, really you become a gluten, constantly pigging out and taking in all the shit and processing it to satisfy the lust machine, pretty much a human garburator fulfilling the vacancy in your soul and trying to find a resident to fill the open spot.

I was all in, gave in to her prenuptial verbal contract demands, I was liquified and I caved just like that, threw in the towel on the party life and signed into a new life, because why? isn't that what everybody wants? That's what society says, friends and family make you believe, find true love they say, get married they say, have children they say, that's the cycle, true?

The hardest and difficult thing about relationships is when there's children, and yes Patti had a young daughter named Jade, we hit it off quite well, I wasn't trying to be her father figure just mostly a friend to her, Jade seemed to acquire these stickers for her sticker book, some collectable book where it required you to peel the backing off and find the location to place it into the book, always seemed like Jade would have so many of these and would want me to do it upon staying up all night, I was always so tired, having that to do plus stay awake for episodes of inspector gadget cartoons.

Some of the best moments with Jade was always Christmas mornings, being up all night, again we would buy a real spruce tree and set it up and decorate it, then the morning of I'd walk through the house with my boots on and leave snow on the floors, leave cookie crumbs on the plate along with the milk glass half emptied, Jade would wake up early and run through the house screaming, just losing it "He Was HERE," "HE WAS HERE!!", then pull my hair to wake me up and come and see.

The Oilers won their third Stanley cup in 1987 against Philadelphia, my DJ partner Klay (dressed like the flyers goalie Ron Hextall) and as we took to the streets of Jasper Ave between 105st and 108st, to do some promo stuff for Rock City hand out free drink cards, the media would try to get some film footage on us with the crowd, the crowd would just start beating on Klay like he was the real Philly goalie, one time in front of Audrey's Bookstore it got so intense, Klay ripped off the goalie mask and wanted to take on this fucking mob.

Within the next few weeks Klay was offered a position in Grand Prairie and it was such a lucrative offer you'd be silly not to go, our first-time going up was at the end of July 1987, when Edmonton was declared a state of emergency and twenty-seven people were dead from the worst natural disaster in Canadas history (known as Black Friday), eleven tornadoes ripped through the east side of Edmonton's corridor, and left a massive trail of destruction in its path.

Hours before we were about to leave to go party in GP, I was standing on a balcony in Clearview watching this massive twister to the right of me and to the left was the open field where Clearview Rec Center is situated, the field was like snow had fallen from the hail, the trees in front of me were blowing so hard the tops of them were touching the ground, and it was raining down two by fours and shingles from houses that were being gutted apart from mother fucking nature, it was so surreal.

At around six pm the Sun came out and it was so calm and peaceful, like nothing had happened, we then left for Grande Prairie, which was by far the worst trip I've ever taken, in an old truck that five of us travelled in, this friend of a friend new a short cut and oh my fuckin gawd, GP is only four and half hour drive, the way in which he took 'his short cut' was nine and half to ten hours, his uncle had to come meet us with gas, probably by far the worst feeling in the world, being part of this trip, the deep degrading, humiliating lowlife feeling when you discover in an instant that you don't wish to be with anybody at that moment, let alone losers that don't know there fucking way around Alberta! I phoned mama Hope in Swan Hills and they had just declared Edmonton a state of emergency, I remember feeling like such a schmuck and a loser for leaving, I just wanted to go back home at that point.

One of the best road trips was to go see U2 in concert in BC Place the Joshua Tree Tour (11.12.1987)this actually should've been on the film Rattle and Hum which was U2's film basically footage of the Joshua Tree tour, we were on the second level and watching the antics on the floor was absolutely comical, the patrons on the floor were like breathing all night, when I say "All Night" I mean from the break between Los Lobos and U2 people were rushing onto the floor, back and forth the security in front of the stage were spraying the crowd with water hoses and pulling some of the partygoers out because they were passing out with heat exhaustion, the problem with the floor being over populated was due to the fact that a group of rockers would gather on the second level then jump to the floor level the first person would try and hurdle the protective fence the top of their foot would catch and they'd fall over with the gate making way for the others to run through and filter there way among the others on the floor, security would only catch a few but the others would get through creating this overabundance of rockers on the floor!

We weren't sexually active just lots of foreplay that was very close to having sex, without verbally saying she wanted me to in BC, that was the time in which Patti had fully and completely surrendered and desired to have me, and because she hadn't given me the go ahead, I regretfully did not take advantage, remember nice guys do finish last.

The trip home was as bizarre as it gets, it was Carson, Patti and me and we were driving back the same way, so we thought, the first thing was the fog was pretty intense and as we were driving along the highway all of sudden without warning signs, detour signage or any indication that the fucking road is closed all of a sudden there's jersey barriers going across the lanes! which had we hit we all would've perished, once we got going again, counting our blessings, just then with no warning lights or railroad cross arms (an uncontrolled crossing) Carson slams the breaks on, there's a train crossing inches away from hitting it! like what in the hell is going on? Talk about a stressful start to the road trip back home.

The eighties were drawing to a close and my career choices were slim to none, after the bottom fell out from Alberta and a few of my educational choices like; make-up artistry and broadcasting media at Columbia Academy on the west side of Edmonton, one of the counselors there had the scoop on a DJing gig at the Coliseum Inn (DJ, shooter bartender and a bouncer) it was a great gig until a high school buddy and his stripper gf Sheri, was stripping one night during reading week, while the young students around pervert row got a little carried away and when the strippers would take off their clothing, these students would take the clothes and were not keen to give them back, my buddy took exception to this and the fight was on, not in the bar, they were all waiting for him outside, only thing was he wasn't leaving, not until he called up some BIG boys, so he bought nachos and beers and told them "your foolish to stick around," he forewarned them and gave them ample time to leave, maybe they just thought since he was a short haired, smiley kind of dude, who would he know?

I'll tell you who he knew…they were possibly the biggest, ugliest Viking sized mudderfuckers this side of both oceans, I've known some pretty big ugly boys before, these boys were from Popeyes - Alice the goon types!! What was I to do, or going to do? I watched as they threw some tables and chairs around, and cleared out the bar, took all the punks outside and dealt with them out there. As for me, I wiped up and closed around 11 pm, a little earlier than normal not too bad, the next day I was called in the office and relieved of my duties for not performing my job description! I laughed and said "later," that was unfortunate because I liked strippers, they would give me some good tip money for getting the crowd going plus, I made tips at the shooter bar and my wage.

Not getting a break with landing a secure job, I went on driving taxi in the late winter of 1988/89 the company had lots of favoritism going on, they would send you on a phantom or ghost calls and as you fished for it, the next car up was usually the dispatchers buddy that would always get those good fares, along with car rental and expenses I had enough of that shit show!

The stress level on this relationship was through the roof, I've never experienced so much negativity and bad luck, we were two dogs constantly chasing our own tails, enabling each other's addictions, trailer park trash without the trailer, we were not good for one another at all, being gamblers (bingo) mostly 3 or 4 times a day every day, criminal like-minded mixed with fraudulent activities was a very toxic and dangerous lifestyle.

Constantly our shit would end up in hawk, to get some cash to go play bingo and try to win the jackpots, and endless cycle, you'd get the shit back from the pawn shop, only to go back a few days later and repeat the process, it's the most dumbest thing, it makes you feel like such a low-life!

I finally landed a great gig in Ontario at a gold mine, making around $1k per week, not bad at all, hardest thing was being away from home, working hard sending all my money home to satisfy my gf's addictions, I was gone for five weeks, then I would come home for seven days off, upon going back to the mine on the third week, this cook and me went to his room to have some drinks, soon some others would join us, then this cook stood up and started breaking shit in his room, I stood up to just tell him to settle down, we're going to get the boot, then the fucker takes a swing at me, I dodged that one then popped him on the chin, soon the room got very small and the other workers were just trying to contain me, so I'd move out of the way and punch them, I escaped the clutches of anyone that tried to grab me, bad thing was I hit everyone in the room including my foreman, not feeling too good in the morning I got my walking papers and had to leave site. Very shitty timing, I couldn't re-adjust my plane fare, and the train was full, so that left the Greyhound Bus, a 3-day bus ride, talk about feeling like a low life scum bucket, losing my job then having to spend three days on a bus. OMG!!!

As I was licking my wounds and trying to figure out what I was going to do next, I guess the City of Edmonton had called just before I had left and went back out east, so I figured what have I to lose, I called the City back, she said leave it with her and she would call me back, by that Friday she called me and said that I was to start in Millwood 'son Monday morning, I was there one week then got transferred to Golf courses where I was employed in golf for 20 years .

I finally put myself through enough of the torture of basically being demoted to a roommate or a provider and getting sweet fuck all in return, no nothing, communication, friendship, or love. The lies and cheating took its toll on me, I wasn't sleeping or eating, walking around the city in a zombielike state. The first time she cheated on me, I knew it all along, my feelings were gone haywire, mostly my Spidey senses were in a blender on high speed, the one thing that we promised each other, if you fall out of love and into the arms of another person, we will tell each other and not hurt the person.

I actually wrote a poem titled 'A Stranger Trespassed' basically it was about a gardener who had this beautiful garden and how he looked after it, had a nice little fence around it and he would weed it, water and look after it, then when the stranger trespassed, he disrupted the garden broke the fence, pulled out flowers and violated the nice garden. I gave her the poem six months after the fact waiting for her to tell me, she read it and asked "were you following me? Spying on me?" I replied "no," I just looked at her… and said, "are you for real?"

Even after forgiving her the first time the continuation of the deceit and the ongoing cheating took its toll on this once a young stud, I walked into the doorway of the bedroom as her and her sister lay laughing and joking, I announced I'm moving back to mama Hopes on the morrow, it ended, it's over, I came to terms with it and had enough, I first moved out owed twelve-hundred dollars on a student loan, when I left, I owed $25k, not saying it was just her, it was my fault too for staying in that toxic relationship.

Mike Burke came to my rescue on the night for New Year's Eve 1990/91hall party at the Evansdale community hall, which was a really good thing for me, not only to get out and get my mind refocused, it helped to dust that (Pigpen feeling off(Charlie Brown) the endless cloud of dirt that surrounded me (negativity and bad vibes), when Mike left, he said and pointed out this girl, Stevie that was going to take me home, which really helped put the final nail in the coffin and solidify the end of the of my time with Patti.

There are some things that I took away from that relationship though, being encouraged to continue being and doing artistic talents, drawing, and entering art contests, writing my first poems and actually being creative with thoughts, some of my early writings about her...

My Treasure

Not too long ago there was a place to go.
It wasn't for fancy dress, but a place none the less,
Across the room of confusion was a being of opposite mink,
The movement for them to meet was neat,
That through a lustful link, made him think; it was behind the wink.
After, when realizing not by choice, he heard a voice,
That his motive in doing wrong, saw something special, and meant to do no harm.
Sleepless and endless nights together, made their friendship grow stronger
and would help them weather anything...forever!
To realize the beauty God created, you could sense a warm human crying inside.
Although making mistakes, it was her, whom you could not hate
She can't be read like a book; she cares and loves you a lot
and will gently hold you within the pages of her look.
You hold on because there's something more worth finding,
Through patience and understanding
Never say goodbye, pick her up high, where eagles fly,
With love as endless as the sky.
In her is something that will last forever,
In her is a treasure.

I Met Her

I met her on a chilly night, but it was warm inside, and
        We had warmth running through our bodies.
We smiled, talked, and laughed; we have memories.
        We travelled and walked; we have memories.
I met her, we enjoyed each other, shared confidences,
Thoughts, and special moments, we have memories.
I met her, with ice, fruit and honey, laughter, sadness, and
        Tears, sharing all we have, we have memories.
I met her, a while ago; it's been a lifetime with her.
        Time: it stands still for us. We have memories.
        I met her, I never want to let go of her,
She's a perfect woman, we have memories.
I met her, and for her I want nothing but the best!
I met her; we still have all these moments and more.
For a lifetime, I met her, she's _____ _____
        I met her; I don't want her to change.
        We have loving memories, forever & ever.

My Inspiration

        A strong, strong wind blows in all directions, it's coming!
        It stirs up the creatures in the night, shhh, it's coming!
Everyone rushing getting things done, here and there, shhh, silence! It's coming!
        She is raging and the earth explodes in your eyes! Who suffers?
Who's left in the cold? She runs to grab hold, take cover! It's here, shhh!
Something about this storm, something about this storm, it should rage in everyone.

Louder, louder! We cry, we wonder, louder, louder! Damn it!

       Open up the windows!

Louder, louder! We cry, we wonder…why can't we all have this storm?

       Shhh, silence! You can't, you can't, can't what? Shhh, silence!

       You can't touch it! she is raging, she arrives.

In the calmness of the night, gently she comes to me,

Picks me up within the clouds and polishes off the rough edges.

       Louder, cry louder! Shhh, silence! It's a woman…

       Shhh, silence! It's you…

This Moment

       This moment with you, I would like to share.

       Because I know you care.

       I pause…for this moment with you,

To take a glimpse of your face, and lock that look in its place.

       That place where you and I will be lost in a desired place.

       I pause…for this moment with you.

What makes me wander into that garden of your love?

It's a garden where not many can relate, but a place where I can escape.

To frolic and dream, dream of a fantasy, where you and I will become a reality.

       I pause…for this moment with you.

       You're like a sparkle and it's remarkable that.

You're like a precious diamond, cut and polished within its brilliance and excellence.

       A diamond made for you; would be you.

You're like a dove; the purity and innocence, the meaning of what's white and free.

       You are the dove and the one I want to love.

       I pause…for this moment, and more with you.

Wildflower

She sprung up, amongst the most beautiful of
Daisies, tulips, and daffodils.
She is strong, upright and to the fullest.
She sprung up, amongst them all, porcelain skin, rosy, red lips,
Blushing cheeks and Spanish brown eyes, and the tallest of all.
She sprung up, while the rest took their time, she sprung up!
To waste no time, among the laid-out garden and all the colors of the rainbow.
You sprung up, outstanding in the flower patch, you sprung up.
And you stayed up and you stayed beautiful because you are…beautiful!
You stayed up, because while the rest are taking their time and
Dying at the stem side, you keep growing.
Staying young and gorgeous
You, you are the most precious…
Water me, water me…I'll water you forever!
Because, among all the flowers, you are my Wildflower.

Beauty in Motion

Beauty, beauty who is she now? She is my 'Wildflower,'
'My Inspiration' when 'I Met Her' she is 'My Treasure' and the
One whom I'll be with forever! But, for 'This Moment" is something.
I don't want to hide; it's her beauty I want to describe. Motion, motion
Ooouuu her gentle stride, how she struts.
Her frame with such enormous pride…
Ooouuu look at people, stop and stare at this brunette with wild hair.
Ooouuu check out her features, a masterpiece.

Slender silky skin and a perfectly balanced face right down to her chin.

Mysterious dark brown eyes with whites as pure as snow.

A high-class stuck-up nose, full set of lips that will make your
Mouth swell up with moisture, when extended will highlight her laughter,

And make you want to go after.

Ooouuu the curves of her feminine body, covered in the harmony of markings.

She should be placed high on a pedestal and crowned.

Queen, goddess.

Now about this one I love.

I don't want to cause a commotion.

But this is…'Beauty in Motion.'

That was a very young Paul, just totally blinded by lust and life of being infatuated by someone who wasn't in it for the same reason(s), truth be told, don't believe everything someone says, people change, they commit and say shit and make vows that they cannot keep! Look at these next poems and see how broken I was… **The Break…**

Life

Why is it so cold? Please, shut the door…

It's not open! Why is it so cold? It's you,

It's you I want to hold.

Don't walk, don't run.

Come back, don't hide.

Don't give me that selfish pride!

You were in it once before, why now?

You took my heart and headed out the back door.

It wasn't just a fling, or is that just your thing?

Why is it so cold? Please, shut the door…

It's not open!

It's…

…it's

LIFE

Breakdown

Many things were said, a lot of tears were shed.

I guess the relationship is dead!

But we will remain friends…after all, this is not the first kick in the head.

Locked in a chamber of my own confusion, surrounded by clouds of steel blue grey.

When will it stop? I have a case of pain stay…

When will it go? Go away.

My imagination has run wild, just like a bronco buck.

Nothing to surprise me though,

like everything in this world is…

…Fucked!

Lost-Hope

Everything lost, nothing gained.

What happened?

I woke up...

From a perfect dream, now I'm back in reality.

In a state of confusion,

Lost in a world of depression.

Unlock this dark room.

Let me escape back to my dream.

With my fantasy

Woman.

Drained

Your beauty is like the ocean.

Ohh so smooth, with each wave

That pounds the pure golden white sand.

It gives me a new breath of fresh life.

...but now, it feels like somebody.

...pulled

...the

...plug!

Stone Cold Love

In our youthful days we danced on clouds
   We surrendered all,
Even dreamed about making vows.
    The secrets and memories that
      We once shared.
I couldn't erase your scent from my bed,
    Shedding this callused layer of skin
That's caused humming and vibrating in my head.
    I've released this displeasure.
      Set from within
Another seventy-two hours wasted away…
      Crimes of passion
What else could I say? A bouquet of dead flowers
A blank card with empty or blurred words
    All I wished was for you to stay.
Now alone, I've paced this town.
    With this molded look starring down
My fever is running cold.
    With this stone-cold love
      No longer
        Left to hold.

As you can read, I was all in, ready, willing, and able to continue even after the lies and cheating, I don't understand why? why would I put myself through that? Like geez man…what was going through my head? That's the difference though, when she was laying down the dos and don'ts she wasn't buying into her own program, and I was making it work because she had a young daughter.

Many of us in one form or another has gone through the stages of either 'puppy love' 'attraction(s)' or 'infatuations' with people in and around our lives or even having crushes on somebody in the entertainment industry (music or Hollywood). How many times did you mail away a letter to get a signed picture? Or stood in a line-up to get up close and personal with maybe a meet and greet or a photo with your crush celebrity? Some of you are in denial and trying to be 'manly' and snort "I've never done that!" "wouldn't catch me doing such a thing!"

You'd gladly sit back and mock those of us who did, the one's that let our guard down and showed some weakness. Some of the Hollywood babes back in the 70's Linda Carter (Wonder Woman), Catherine Bach (Daisy Duke), Farrah Fawcett (Charlie's Angels) the list goes on and on, for some of these woman or sex objects you could see them live at usually some car shows that would tour, I actually sent a letter to Linda Carter and didn't receive anything in return.

There's been a few times of mistaken identity, one of the best one's was the time we were at Uncle Albert's restaurant after clubbing at Rock City, it just so happened that the band Heart had played at Northlands Coliseum in Edmonton, while we were ordering from the waitress she informed us about this other co-worker that couldn't stop talking about us, she was so nervous to come to our table because she thought we were the band Heart, our waitress asked if we wouldn't mind play along and asked if we'd sign our autographs on one of the placemats, we played along and signed it, that poor girl.

Multiple times after the break up with Patti, upon walking into restaurants or public gatherings, many times the conversations would stop and everyone would stare at me, maybe they were thinking I was somebody famous or something, in recent years I've been told I look like the lead singer for the heavy metal band Testament, Chuck Billy another dude, WWE wrestler Chuck Palumbo and also Meatloaf singer Michael Lee Aday.

The one that really surprised me and caught me off guard was, while shopping at a clothing store in Hawaii and one of the workers was following me throughout the store, thinking they had nothing better to do and watch me to see if I was shoplifting, she was very noticeable and I thought of entertaining the notion by being obvious and stuffing a tee shirt or something down my shorts, after a good half hour of this, the store clerk finally approaches me and asks "are you Ted Nugent?", maybe it was how I was dressed that day with a black dressy button up shirt with black shorts and nice tan Reebok sandals with my black shades atop my head, but my hair in those tropical places always turns out like crazy hot, poof, Monica off the TV show Friends (not that bad) With a sheepish grin I had to just say no, not today, "no I am not!"

The few times I've been to Las Vegas card dealers and pit bosses alike have starred and given me the nod, like they know me personally, here's hoping that I'm not on the wrong end of those nods like owing a huge amount of money for gambling debts, good thing it has never been that kind of a nod, it's been more like a happy to see you again, great happy to see you too!

Identity noun in Merriam Webster dictionary means,

Plural identities:

1 a: the distinguishing character or personality of an individual: INDIVIDUALITY

Paul vs. Blackie (Dr. Jekyll/ Mr. Hyde)

Paul – with much thought about these two characters in my life and being very much a part of me, I actually was Paul and Paul alone for the most part growing up, no nick names, no aka id's just little Ol me Paul, I actually always had a strong sense of humor which was a very good trait, throughout my school years it was one thing my teachers always made comments about, my quick wittiness the ability to make people laugh without really trying, most of the time, people set themselves up to walk right into a punch line, which makes it really easy to be the butt end of a joke or a one-liner, and for the most part it happens on a whim, unplanned and as it unfolds it's there for the taking.

When I realized this very early especially with teachers, they always seemed to leave themselves wide open for a nasty one liner and most times, I couldn't resist, it became a really big part of my character, I would not only munch on the openness I would absolutely devour it, and for the most part it came with a price, usually the teacher in their embarrassment would exercise their authority and then kick me out of the class, much to the chagrin of my audience. All is fair in love and words I guess, in my high school years it became a daily routine almost, and some of my classmates would come to class just to see how long I could last, they informed me many times that it was there only reason to come to class that day, was to see how long before I got the boot! There was probably a Vegas fuckin wager on it that I wasn't aware of.

The beginning of grade 11, Mrs. Tate's English class, the chatter is low but there's ongoing conversations around the room, the unsettling and wrestling about finding your seat and shit, Mrs. Tate starts the roll call, gets to my name, I say "present", she replies in her stern English accent "No you're not, get out!" there's an automatic HUSHHHH in the classroom "I don't want you in my class" I'm like "what the FUCK!" why? She's like "I know what you're like and I'm not having any of it!" "Get out!"

As I'm packing up my belongings the class is in a state of shock also, because I haven't even done anything to warrant this, I start mimicking her and making out right fun of her, why not take advantage of this situation, the audience was on my side so anything I said or did they were lapping it up, she brought it on herself, what could I do but make a grandiose exit. Another class, industrial ed., Mr. Hrycun'sa very big grumpy Ol German man, very dry sense of humor, a few times throughout the year I would make him chuckle or smile, I would also end up getting das boot from his class too.

One time I'm wearing a tee shirt that has a little old lady in a rocking chair and it says, 'Express Thyself' and she's giving the middle finger, it's on underneath my jean jacket, you can barely see it, and I'm now working on the lathe, my back is facing the class, Mr. Hrycun comes to me has me shut the machine down and proceeds to tell me to turn my shirt around, I was confused because I had my jacket on so you couldn't even see the shirt, in his broken English I figured okay you dumb fuck, it's on!

I took my jacket off and placed it on the chair, then turned my shirt around to face him and the class, I started working on the lathe again and was smiling bigtime, within a few minutes he's yelling at me, but I have him on ignore, the machine is loud and I have head muffs for hearing protection on, and I can hear him, he comes to me again and is just flipping his lid, I said "I did what you told me to do" and he tries to back track and say "you know what I meant" I played it cool and was being facetious, I started yelling back at him and basically said "say what you mean then!" and told him to take an English class to learn how to speak, none the less, I was kicked out of that class too!

One of the greatest though was the Sociology class, there was only a dozen of us in this class and I brought out the best of myself here, on more than one occasion she'd ask if I wanted to teach the class so I would, other times if she left the room, she wasn't coming back in, she'd be locked out and not let back in, other times we'd drive her crazy with putting her purse on the speaker or other items that she needed out of reach, she would end up taking stress leave and not return to school that year!

Paul vs Blackie

Who is Paul? Who is Blackie? I was touched when the author (Paul Blackburn) asked me to take a stab at answering this enigmatic and intriguing question. Perhaps I can do so, at least partially, by two short stories.

A fond memory I have from the early 1990's is Paul, and I were departing on a road trip to Vancouver/Victoria (my current home) at 11:30pm, rocking out to The Wizard by Black Sabbath driving through the rugged Canadian Rockies in the pitch black with lightning crackling in the sky. What could be more metal than that?

Another memoir is from when Paul and I worked at Edmonton's Victoria Golf Course and Driving Range. Because he and I both had long, brown hair, black sunglasses, and bandanas. Customers at the Driving Range thought we were the same guy who just worked all day, every day. One customer even asked me "don't you ever get a day off?"

Poet, musician, DJ, nightclub vampire, amateur plumber, man of faith, father, brother, son…friend. Is that Blackie? Is that Paul? The simple answer is…yes. Blackie is Paul and Paul is Blackie. I say this because both are authentic, both are sincere, both are passionate.

Some call him Blackie, some call him Paul. I call him…my friend.

Eric Sehn

Upon meeting Klay(the DJ) in 1984, I only went by my first name, Klay started calling me Blackie at first, I wasn't crazy about it, mainly because it was my sperm donors nick name, but I figured you know I'll go with it and make it my own! Like I've stated before, or I mean Mr. Sehn said, "I know how people know you, on the Northside they know you as Paul, and on the Southside, they know you as Blackie".

Blackie, to me was/is my alter ego, and I was able to hide behind that name, mainly because it was a stage name that really was popularized when Klay and I became the K & B roadshow at Uncle Charlie's, the events that followed upon returning from Mexico and the Bachelor Auction and being involved in promos was on another level, cocaine was finding its way up my nose at will…along with doing mushrooms, they were being given to us freely, like when you ask your guests "would you like something to drink?" oh here, stick this up your nose! Dah, okay… Blackie, was invincible, immortal, God-like or so I / he thought.

It was another level of being cocky or overconfident, being up on the stage or the spotlight people (your patrons or followers) treat you like you're from another planet, a superhero and whether it's just being a DJ or part thereof, the common people want a piece of that or have a sense of ownership, belonging and to hang out maybe even to have somewhat of a relationship with you.

Most nights (weekends) I'm going to say at the very least (minimum) just myself, I'm not speaking for Klay here…me, myself and Blackie could have had ways with five different girls per night, above and beyond numbers with Klay, we were, after all somewhat respectful, then other times we were like Bruce the shark off Finding Nemo, "I'M HAVING FISH TONIGHTTTTT!!!" I met some nice girls along the way and others I probably messed them up, being messed up myself, at times I tried to apologize, and many times it repelled off their skin like rain drops on a waxed car.

For the most part, being on an open stage, you're better off being single, because being in that spotlight with a girlfriend watching you on those nights, she's going to question every fucking entire motive, flirtation or kiss you make with another girl, it absolutely stones your creativeness and freewill to do anything, because you're being judged, no matter what they say like "it's alright" no "I don't mind you doing your business" until you do it, then they have daggers in their eyes and want to take that other girl to the washroom and have a cat fight!

It was bad vibes sleeping with or having relations with a lot of those girls looking back, and again they knew me as Blackie there, nobody knew my other life (only a select few), so it was easy to hide behind Blackie's cape.

Most of the times after our antics and DJing(Fridays & Saturdays) you'd want to try and unwind and relax, 'don't want to come back down from this cloud' lyrics by BUSH, a lot of times we would be invited or expected to make appearances at other clubs or afterhours parties, this one time we went to this popular after hours place just north of Whyte Ave., 104 St. upstairs around back, we went in grabbed a beer and made a tour of the place to see who was around, then just as we thought of leaving there but there was a perfect spot on the west floor, just to veg and sip our beers and be a spectator for a change, plus the vibe was very cool.

As we sat and looked on, watch and chill, in walks a couple that are not local, they were imports from L.A or New York, they were a smashing good looking couple straightway from a vogue magazine cut-out (looked like Marilyn Monroe and James Dean) both dressed in import fashion too, now as we sat there on the floor in the darker shadows (out of the spotlight) this couple walked in and around the room not sure if they were looking for somebody or just checking it out, it's also after 4 am, so not like there's other places to go, it looked as though they were leaving, when all of a sudden she walks over to us and bends down to my level and says "you're such a handsome man, what are you doing in a place such as this?" then smiled, winked and blew me a kiss and left.

For the most part even though I am both Paul & Blackie, Blackie was the more outgoing and had no reservations, maybe it was the spotlight, maybe it was my ongoing chemical warfare and the overwhelming courage, energy or power you feel when doing mind altering drugs. There was an unbelievable sensation when crowds of people know who you are and when we had the capability of exercising our abilities to bring someone in a line-up to the doors of any bar, pub or nightclub in the city and get them inside on a nod.

You live and die by the sword…

The saying "live by the sword, die by the sword" is an idiom that basically means "what goes around comes around." More to the point, "if you use violent, forceful, or underhanded methods against other people, you can expect those same methods to be used against you."

Idiom or karma, whichever the case Paul and Blackie, I am still that person, and something had to change, was I too big for my britches?

too big for (one's) britches.

Overconfident in one's importance, skill, or authority; behaving as if one is more important or influential than one is.

As you'll read in the upcoming pages the **'turning point'** in my life March 28, 1993, my snow globe world will be shaken to the core!

Happy New Year's 1991 , moved back home at 27 years old, it had its perks but....my 3 year reign on partying is about to start, firstly, the same guy that made off with the profits from our scooter, was a manager at Redford Inn on Whyte ave., he called me up to come DJ / host at the bar called Peoples Pub, I was on it like fly's to shit, great gig to get my mind off the shitty relationship that ended and started giving me confidence again, not that I was lacking confidence, I guess I just became a little reserved in not partying so much.

Back in Black(i.e.) is about to be re-birthed my alter ego or as a good friend and coworkers told me "I know how people know you,

NorthsideEdmontonians know me as Paul and once I cross the river (North Saskatchewan), they know me as Blackie"?

My good friend Klay, had called me up to do some guest appearances and party in the DJ booth at this south side bar called 'Uncle Charlie's' this was the start of something big for this little pub with a downtown club atmosphere, before and during renovations one of the weekends before closing for a few weeks, we had this room on fire, it was some of the greatest atmospheres of a bar with just DJ's, close to 2 am before last call we were just crazy electric, we spread out this poly on the dance floor and dumped a 5 gallon pail of Mazola oil over top the plastic, customers were stripping to their underwear and diving into the oil covered plastic dance floor, never seen anything like this, this bar was crazy and was about to get more crazier after the Reno's.

The start of 1992 wasn't looking good out of the gate, by March we had new direction and were re-focused, we had posters made, a new contract and now being the highest paid entertaining goof balls in the City, that new room was insane, there was a games area a sit down area like a kitchen, then bar stools around the counter top outlining the dance floor and an upper seating area with big booths, never a dull moment then you had us two in a giant sized booth that looked like it was from outer space, a stage right next to it, to perform any silly antics we had going on, there was wigs n' make-up & air guitars.

We had a beach party in the wintertime with two hot tubs and when you walked in the bar you had to step up the entire floor was covered with sand, the Halloween contest was for 2 days (Friday, Saturday) then stayed up all night on the Saturday because we left for Mexico the next day, ohhh and what a start of a trip this was, talk about being ill prepared, who knew you needed ID or your wallet to leave the country? We get to the airport at like 03:00 am I don't have my wallet, what? We had to call a lawyer, wake him up and come to the airport and pay him like $75 to swear me in as a Canadian citizen then pay another $75 for a name change on the ticket because I wasn't on the ticket initially, so we're already $150 and haven't got on the plane, ohh the plane….we had to run through the entire airport exactly like on any movie set, just making it…they actually were holding the plane for us, taking our seats on the plane and laughing so hard, what a shit show!

This is just the start of our 7 day tour of Puerto Vallarta, omg, we messed up, not sure how we didn't get more seriously injured , when we arrived the first day it was a wash staying up all night then not sleeping on the plane, we crashed hard, woke up to get alcohol and go shopping, we spent 3 hours at a store called Gigantico (the Superstore) trying to shop wisely and use our kitchenette, because down in Mexico we're going to cook our own food, ha-ha, everything on the shelf had a layer of dust you needed to wipe off first to even see what the hell it was, the meat section was so gross, the chicken is corn feed so there skin is all yellow, you couldn't tell corn meal from salmonella, we ended up buying hamburger with peanut butter and chocolate bars quite the experience, the liquor store was much better, let me say…we bought this old A&W root beer style bottle had to be a gallon of this disgusting red wine, we named it the Elcid of wines, your lips would quiver when putting the jug to your lips to have a swig after the bars were closed and you couldn't get any more drinks on the resorts. The next day we went on a booze cruise, it's a 3 hour cruise on a boat unlimited booze for $20 US per person great deal, my partner was so loaded I had to pour his liquid ass back at the resort and I went bar hoping with these two chicks, one was from Texas and another from Chicago, we went to every bar around and it was not happening I got back to the room at 3:30am and we had set up a Bora Bora for 9 am departure omg, I thought my head was caving in, we get on the boat and I'm drinking coffee by the pot and once we started going I thought I would be too, going over the side rails to puke, sea sickness and hung over wasn't a good feeling , so I did what any great white Canadian would do… start drinking alcohol again, that's the saying 'avoid a hangover. Stay drunk' came from!

The boat docked by 1500 hrs. we had a nap before venturing out to Senor Frogs the local hot spot to party, we turned that bar every which way but loose, it was electric, people dancing on the tables, I was playing air guitar like Angus Young of AC/DC on this small uneven table as I was getting into it, I biffed it off the table , not skipping a beat I made it to my feet and still playing , the place erupted like I was actually playing I made it atop that little table again only to biff it another time , my knee swelled up like three times the size but I kept going, beautiful tanned ladies exposing their breasts and the bar was happening, they had these sirens and lights go off then they would be playing the theme from ghostbusters and these other workers would come around with an old style fire extinguisher full of margarita one guy would put a sheet over you like a bib and the other would have a coal miners hat with a light on it shining it in your eyes while they pump some shots of margarita in your mouth or with good intentions to! A spectacular night!!

After a night like that we thought we'd just stick around the resort and try to recover maybe ice the knee while enjoying some sunshine and coco locos (a coconut with the top lopped off and the bartender tips about 8 bottles of whatever he grabs and pours it directly into the coconut) one of these will give you a nice glow on, my DJ buddy Klay all of a sudden sits up and wants to go para sailing, alright you go me and my swollen knee will watch, as he's coming back in to land, the communication is lost or just not happening between ground guy and boat guy and my Klay is heading straight for the wall on the Holiday Inn resort, he pulls away from the balcony with like zero time remaining talk about a close shave, that would've hurt for sure , looked like a scene from the Flintstones whew!! Let's go sit poolside and enjoy the scenery, you know try to survive the rest of this trip, yeah let's!

Gimme drugs…gimme drugs part II

Upon returning from the Mexico trip, I was starting up another trip, my chemical romance, I was getting cocaine given to me everywhere I turned, almost like I had a tee shirt that said; I'll do your blow, donations gladly accepted!

We were rocking Uncle Cs like mad men when we returned from vacation, we did a fundraiser with the fireman with their calendar plus a bachelor auction ahh yes! and they wanted me in it, of course management wants me in it! all suited up with tuxes and more free coke we were all set, let the bidding begin…the deal was whomever bid the highest for the bachelor they were bidding on got to go on a dinner / movie date with them.

I ended up going for $650 which was the highest amount paid only because they wanted a date with Blackie, turns out it was a married woman who just wanted to get some excitement back into her life, funny thing during our dinner date she was so nervous I could hardly get her to talk, the entire time I was doing all the talking, gets boring pretty fast, good thing we met up with the other couples for the movie!

After Christmas of 1992 and heading into the New Year of 1993, the party life style continued 8 days a week we were checking out other establishments to see what was hot and what was not, we were still the hottest act in the city on the weekends, we had lineups around the outside of the building to come see these two lunatics, we were giving out our autographs on our posters to patrons whom took them down and we signed them, it was soo crazy, we were only DJ's, that got red carpet treatment all over the place, cocaine was flowing like beer on tap, after hours parties always wanted us to make an appearance, no cover charges most times drinks were complementary.

This one night off I went bar hopping with a good hairdresser friend and my brother, just keeping it low key have some drinks and go dancing, we parked ourselves at the Gas Pump downtown Edmonton, the place is full and it's a more mature crowd and we're having a wonderful time, then this gorgeous blonde waitress from another downtown bar Teddy's (during the daytime) she knew who I was from the golf course in the river valley, we'd come and have drinks there after work. She approached me and first asks me why I never ask her out? I said, "you have a boyfriend, why would I ask you out?" she wants to dance so I oblige her and while we're dancing, she says we should go to this after-hours place and I'm like where's your bf? She said "they broke up", without hesitation I'm off with her in a back of a taxi, I couldn't get her off of me, it was almost like date rape, we show up to this after hours place in a back alley second story in the sketchy part of Edmonton off 95st, I was really feeling uneasy about going there because it was an Asian after hours place and her bf happened to be Asian , we go in and my only reprieve was I knew the doorman (bouncer) he was like Paul what are you doing with her? And I told him she wanted to party here, he said "be careful and don't be making out with her in here", I said "for sure I won't be", the little stand up bars in between the pool tables had little piles of coke like bird seed for the road runner, help yourself these Asian pool players would say, aside from that I had many guys coming up asking if they could dance with my gf, I said go ahead she's not my gf, staying there until the wee hours of the morning we caught a cab out of there, she was all over me still, she wanted to have sex in the cab, it wasn't cool with the driver he kept saying stop, stop as we were driving down Jasper Ave, she passed out, I dropped her off behind Teddys where she lived and then I made my way back in front of Teddy's and there they were, omg was my hairdresser friend pissed! I had the keys to her car with me, it was going on 5 am, she almost didn't want to drive me home. A few days later the doorman who happens to be my neighbor commended me on not getting involved with that waitress, she was still seeing her Asian bf.

As the party life was getting more and more reckless, the management at Uncle C's started to blame us for lack of people coming to the bar during the weekdays, we made a plan that Uncle Charlie's would only remain open from lady's night Thursdays, Friday and Saturdays, they were still unhappy and blaming us for lack of people coming out, not the location of course not, had they opened that bar on Whyte Ave it would've been a completely different situation. They tore us apart and had me host lady's night and my partner in crime finish up the weekends, there was other financial problems that existed behind the scenes and within the year they were closing the doors of Uncle C's.

Little did I know everything was happening for a reason and I was being set up for a Grand Finale, the last piece of the partying puzzle, March 28, 1993, what a day, game changer….

Pretty much like any other day, except it was Guns N' Roses day, it was there 'Skin n' Bones tour', a dozen of us wound up at the Northlands horse race track up in the clubhouse for brunch, betting and beers what an awesome afternoon, winning most of the races we were feeling on top of the world, you know the feeling when you don't want moment in time to end? That was that afternoon, even though we were there for five hours, I wish it had been another five! Only a couple of us were going to the G n' R show so we made our way to the Coliseum Inn for more pre-concert drinking, just before heading across the street for the show, my good friend and I took these mushrooms I had been saving for this occasion, after watching the opening act Brian May (Queen) the mushrooms still didn't take effect we strolled around the concourse for seemed like a lengthy time, G n R were notoriously late to start their show, we continued to walk around for an hour before going back to our seats, the house lights went off and the anticipation and cheering seemed like another half an hour, my buddy lit a joint and I partook of it, G n R still taking their sweet ass time, another joint was lit and again I smoked some more, prior to this I hadn't smoked any drugs since around 1983, all of a sudden and almost simultaneously as G n R hit the stage and the coliseums patronage erupted, it felt like a hand giving me a push and holding me down in my seat.

With periodic peeks at the stage, I couldn't look for long Axl Rose was wearing a tee shirt with 'Charles Manson's face on the front and the saying ; Charlie don't surf on the back, it was (in my state) very disturbing to look at, I would then turn my head to watch the faithful cheering their band on, as I peered out I could see waves after waves of their souls being sucked towards the stage, all I could do was pray to God for those losing their souls, I could hear my friend saying "get up! This is so excellent!!" I tried I couldn't move from my seat, as much as I wanted to, I was being shown something and it wasn't a great feeling, a twisted version of Alice in Wonderland , the hurt and pain I had caused to many females using them for sexual satisfaction and hating them for the way I was treated by some of my earlier relationships, all the while well this show was going on, I'm talking with God like he's sitting next me, and as each name came to me, I'd pray for them and ask God to forgive them and me, this wasn't just one or two females, this was the entire Paul & Blackies black book from when I was a young lad throughout my entire 29 years of age, you have to remember I was raised by my mom I never really had issues with females, I loved them, the thing was I loved All of them!

During all of this praying my mouth was so dry I needed to get a drink up in the concessionaire, first I had to negotiate with myself how I was going to go about doing this feat, trying to slay these dragons that kept oppressing me, at one point I felt if I left my seat I wouldn't find my way back, it would be like a roulette wheel being spun and the coliseum was like a child's spinning top toy, I was in the middle of a row surrounded by concert zombies, feeling stuck with no way out…*Too frightening to listen to a stranger, Too beautiful to put your pride in danger, You're waiting for someone to understand you, But you've got demons in your closet, And you're screaming out to stop it, saying life's begun to cheat you, Friends are out to beat you (lyrics to hide in your shell by Supertramp).*

I finally felt the release to get past the protectors of the staircase they were the size of Vikings, I had to breakthrough and I did like a freedom fighter, Rocky Boaboa atop the steps in Philadelphia, I took those concert cheers as victory and made it up to the concourse hill only to see the concessions were all closed…WTF!!! My inside voice was screaming noooooooo!!!!!! I was dying of thirst!!!

I figured I'd go to washroom it wasn't far, I got this…as I had my sights set on that, two uniformed policemen were walking towards me and I was trying to be calm, I'm stoned, the mushrooms kicked into gear when I smoked those two hash joints, I'm hallucinating BIG time, the cops were giving me the stare down (as they should've, I was thinking of grabbing their gun and shooting them, what the hell? Just get to the washroom and drink some tap water and wash my face, as I'm down in the sink lapping water out of my hands like a guy that's been in the dessert for days, I start washing my face too, as I go to look up into the mirror I'm covered in blood, I start thinking had I killed those two cops, wholly fuck! I start washing my face some more to be sure…whew, now to try and find my seat again, after getting turned around I ended up walking the concourse for a few laps until a hostess helped me find my seat.

Now believe it or not…I was the designated drunk (stoned) driver, not proud of this, I shouldn't have been playing that video game, we made plans to meet friends at Boston Pizza just off 97 street 118 Ave traffic circle, along the way I was still very thirsty I had to stop at a Mr. Submarine as I go in alone the guy in there has this look of terror like, I'm going to rob the store, I was going to say "gimme all your money" but I wasn't sure if he had a gun so I didn't, just give me a chocolate milk and I'll be on my way.

We get to the Boston Pizza and we have a pretty big table with our friends, then my buddy knows some other friends from his hometown of Lac La Biche and invites them to join us, they don't sit with us but they spoke for a long, long time, I usually have a keen sense of character and my Spidey senses were buzzing off the charts, I tried very hard not to make eye contact, I was still being very stoned and minding my own business, it was definitely a vibe killer and the air had tension no doubt, after he left my friend tells me he's a big time drug dealer and he packs a pistol too. It's no wonder I felt so uneasy!

We finished up at the restaurant and said our goodbyes, I thought I was feeling not bad still a little high but didn't seem bad until I was travelling solo back to mama Hopes place, going northbound on 97st just after the Yellowhead trail, I had thoughts of driving right Into the concrete overpass support, all of a sudden my arms are locked in stiff heading right towards it, at the last second I was able to pull away, suddenly my high went down a dark path, a very, very demonic state, I was being chased by demons and it was very intense, I still was driving and I had to separate my hallucinations from reality, not sure of the speeds I was driving at but I made it to the parking lot parked the car and ran to the door, they were all around me, I just wanted to get into my bed and pass out, I ran to the door fumbled with my keys and dropped them I'm like so freaked out I couldn't get rid of them , I made it in, and they couldn't enter probably because it's a Christian home covered by the blood, whatever the case I'm in the house drinking water before I go to bed, I just want to pass out or go and puke and I cannot I'm being haunted and taunted with all my thoughts on a merry go round over and over, beating and kicking the shit out of all the confidence that was in me, I had gone over every thought and scenario, beating my pillow into submission it was actually my pillow beating me I went over 15 rounds, I was pretty worn out by six am.

Needless to say, my snow globe world was shaken to the core, I knew that if I escaped the clutches of Hell that night I would be returning to church, I still had to sort out some other issues like; being involved with many women even some that I cannot say to this day because it will ruin some of the bonds that have been formed.

Looking back on the decade that was or wasn't it was the darkest ten years of my life filled with unlimited sex, drugs and Rock n Roll, if you do the math, there's 3,650 days in that span and I was out and about on 3,600 of them , I was labelled as ; Mr. Night Life, King of the Night Life and the Godfather of Nights, if there was a line-up to get into any bar in this city and you were anywhere in that line I could bring you to the doors and get you in.

Nobody really wants to retire at the top of their game, and it was the same for me, I wasn't prepared to call it quits, but after the G n R concert I had to process the situation, there's no possible way for me to carry on that lifestyle without ending up in the grave. ATTENTION! ATTENTION!! We interrupt this program…OMG, along with all that was going on with my snow globe being tossed here, there and everywhere…I had a beautiful interruption, well, not me directly, she served us at the Coliseum Inn the night of the G n' R concert, with no direct flirting or anything of the sort, I did not know she was remotely interested in me let alone going behind my back to a buddy to find out everything about me, I didn't believe him at first, he was like, so there's someone who is very interested in you (me) like wants to know all the details, I'm like your full of shit! He's like No for real, had a phone number if I was interested and wanted me to call her. I was like floored to say the least, she was like Edmonton's version of a young super model Tawny Kitaen, talk about messing with my Zen, like I'm on the mend here, and I'm trying to get my shit together.

I had to call her, to be certain it was for real and like why now? OH, it's for real and this is happening, she was very serious and as a matter of fact this is what's going on, I'm like great a fine-looking young lady that knows what she wants and isn't afraid of going after it, was I prepared for everything she wanted and was after? I was still pinching myself to see and feel if this was happening, yes, it is! Whatcha going to do about it? Exactly, I had sorting out to do and some scrambling, I wanted this so bad and didn't, I was covering all the angles or at least I thought I was. What a mess, the good angel on my right shoulder the devil on the left scenario, gut instinct was a non-factor, I couldn't rely on anything I was feeling, fried scrambled brains…lol

You know that everyone always thinks it's about them, there's something wrong or this, that and the other, noooooo, STOP IT… it's not, really, I'm just fucked up, how does one keep explaining that I'm really trying to sort out some shit, and if you just don't pressure me into dating or asking questions, it'll be fine really, I like you… but let's just remain friends hangout for coffees and go to movies or shopping, with all that being said why not? Men and women are not so different, sometimes men can be on Mars and sometimes we can be on Venus, at times…yes, it's just a matter of the planets being in alignment, because there's times when everything is grooving like a well-oiled machine, then what? A timing chain or belt breaks, maybe a gear slips, does all Hell break loose over it? I've had friends not married date and be dating for ever, time frame. Maybe twelve or fifteen years, no issue no problems, put a ring on the finger get married, divorced within two years! Why? I'm no dating fucking guru or even Hitch! In fact, if you want a healthy relationship, fight, and dis-agree, have fun, and pee your pants together in laughter, you want to laugh? Start quoting lines from movies as your lying-in bed together late at night, dance, dance outdoors in the weirdest spots, go for walks, enjoy each other's habits and quirky shit, do stuff together, garden, karaoke, knit, bowling, shoot pool, take a class dancing or something, go to movies, spin music together, spin pottery, create something that you don't normally do, cooking or baking classes, ride bikes, go for weekly dates.

I'm not totally sure what the breaking point was or why we parted ways...? I don't know (weird yeah, I know) I usually have a good memory like an elephant, pretty sure the excitement wasn't all there, because the lack of my ability to keep entertaining people, really, yeah, I could be sometimes and possibly be Mr. entertainment for a little while but to stay in that mindset all the time was very exhausting, you know? When everyone expects you to be a fucking marvel or always turned 'ON,' it's draining both physically and mentally. Plus, at that stage of the game (life) maybe I came across a little heavy, like leaning towards a steady and meaningful relationship, like marriage and not playing games, I was around thirty and she was twenty-six anyway not that age matters, does it? When you're both consenting adults.

I wrote this poem for her in (1994) and ended up not giving it to her, so she hasn't read it...

Polishing Petals

In times of lost generations, human nature has taught or not,
We as the 'men' of today, seems so easy, to waste away.
That part of another person, in which we betray!
Understanding you as, who you are! Listening to you as when you communicate.
Respecting you as; not to hate, to desire you as; to romanticize not just...
Separating your thighs! The anticipation deeply set within our thoughts the
Craving to re-capture, our innocence is what's to be shared,
I would like to treat you fair; I have an offer for you to be,
So please...accept my arm and accompany,
With me enter and explore, walk through the hazy mist and
Bleed your colors onto my...canvass...
Scenery of pastel floral so we can roll around in heart.
Shaped leaves and hold each other into fits o' laughter.
Gazing upon my reflector over years, I've had times.
For tears when I turned to start over,
I saw another shadow re-appear I was.
Trying to catch my breath...I peered back and saw.
You in the mirror. That is all...that matters!

There did exist a time frame where I had dates with some women outside the church, they had been previously pursued and then by happenstance I would run into them and in the flirtation ask if they'd like to go for lunch or a drink sometime, most times meant within the next days off, which wasn't a bad thing, except my days off at the golf course were Tuesdays or Wednesdays, not ideal for a dinner, drink and dance type date, but maybe a lunch at the buffet at Hotel Mac or the restaurant over the River Valley on the deck, there's always romantic places or things to do, you just need to be up on your game and know the Hot Spots!

Sometimes being a player gets you in a situation(s) where it can look or appear to be really bad, usually not taking other woman to the same place as a previous date is key, making or creating new memories (you never know) when you're going to be with 'The One' that sweeps you off your feet and ends your time as a player in the dating pool game…plus, it gives you the opportunity to really find awesome spots throughout the city, one of the best places of course (no longer there) was Nellie's Tea Shoppe (Tom & Nellie) two of the greatest that ever ran a restaurant along 118 Ave and 126 St, such a romantic spot with the greatest food.

Another place and date which was across from Earls Tin Palace was Maxwell Taylor's no better place during Happy Hour, there was a time on a date there in the evening where the sunset was beaming upon her beautiful blonde locks and wearing a black turtleneck, sharing the brie, apples and fresh bread and being very straightforward about what she wanted. What did she want you ask? While we were having wine and our brie she described in great detail (I must add) I was in a state of being in a trance, looking deep into her kaleidoscope of hazel-colored eyes twirling in that sun that was shining in and throughout her aura, her full sparkling desired lips, she had my full attention, I was a sponge, just thoroughly absorbed at that moment.

Oh yes, what she wanted…was to have my baby (I don't have one), no, no…I want to take you home and I want you to impregnate me, so that I can have your child, no strings attached, no nothing, I don't want alimony or you in the child's life, she would raise the baby on her own, that was the conversation, after the wooing and the dinner we wound up back at her place and we did what she stated and had it all planned out, to this day, I have never seen her again, and don't know if she got pregnant or had my child at all.

There were some crazy times during the early 90's after moving back home, I started to pay attention to myself (appearance, clothing, hair) the finer detailing of ones being, focus, focus wow I didn't really notice how handsome I had become, for real? Yes really, I wasn't so self-absorbed with myself, until I peeled back some layers (of onion) that was abused by previous relationships, cleaning myself up by getting my hair done at the Pink Lime Hair Group (PLHG)I also shopped at Henry Singers, I was on the market and looking very hot and sexy. The PLHG wanted me to become a model and be a hair model for them and they were going to look after me in that regard, I had a photo shoot for my one and only modelling time, didn't think it was for me.

The parties that the PLHG threw were out of this world spectacular, we're talking red carpet extravaganza style, top notch all out, lifestyles of the rich and famous, had I paid more attention, the first one was held at this club at the entrance of these lofts on 110St., and 99Ave just before the high-level bridge, they had limo service, Hors d'oeuvres that I have never been a witness to and entirely looked after by the owners of PLHG, they had become also good friends and I would hang out with Bassam until he moved away to Calgary, the other brothers would relocate to Vancouver.

They had another brother that owned a pizza / pub eatery in Ottewell neighborhood too that Bass and I would go to when went tearing up the city.

The second PLHG party was beyond WOWZERS, held at the Citadel Theatre downtown Edmonton, was Bigger than BIG, they spared no costs, and the clients were all the high-end personalities, sport athletes and anyone that was a Who's Who in Edmonton, okay there may have been some imports from Hollywood and possibly New York, you kinda want to be solo at these events, because the single ladies in attendance are ouuu la la, everybody is dressed to the nines,(that's an under in Vegas, it should be on a scale of 1-10, I'd say most were 12's)it's by far the BIGGEST and BEST event or any outing that you can be part of in this city!! Out of this high-end flirtatious party were some gorgeous (North side) single girls that I knew but didn't expect to see them here, didn't know they were clients, so I was able to introduce Eric to Janice and Tammy, we didn't connect with them this night but eventually we would re-connect on separate occasions, on Whyte Ave., pubbing.

It turned out that I re-connected with Tammy after seeing her again at People's Pub and got her phone number, anyway after the smoke cleared and I finally called her to set up a date, and like I've said before, my days off would not coincide with normal people, if I went on dates that is, so it turned out we connected on my days off, and from that I wrote this poem titled…

A Notable Tuesday

I can't remember how it was that I was able to hook up with you.

I know, maybe it was in the stare that we generated at People's Pub

As our eyes were communicating something different than the language we were speaking.

Somehow in our conversation we got connected.

And the phone lines crossed paths.

We set up a rendezvous to have a liquified date.

Oh, those martinis were delish!

Our motives got mixed together with lingo and laughter.

We blended well, so we strolled.

We spilled onto the floor of a sushi restaurant and

in our freedom, we enjoyed feeding each other.

Wisps of your hair still appeared wet like a Nagel graphic,

I desired watching you,

The confidence of licking that lone piece of rice on your upper lip

Aroused my sensual awareness like set off explosions on a minefield.

Our entertaining drew to a close, we meandered back to your apartment for a night cap.

The night was so intoxicating.

I had to stay, Adam and Eve in the Garden of Eden...

Oh, what a night, definitely

A notable Tuesday.

The next series of problems that were following me was that I didn't want to date single Christian Church girls, I still had other woman that I was trying to release from my bar days, one of the last ones was one I didn't want to break up with but eventually I had to because she did not believe in God and had no interest in coming to church with me, it was easier to let her go but I still had feelings for her, plus I would've been going to church having a gf, being on the open market poses some problems, issues and rumors with lots of drama, I was still trying to clear my name back at church when some of their so called faithful would spread shit about me when I wasn't even going there, one guy made up this story how he partied with me this entire weekend filled with sex and drugs, he didn't even apologize when I came back, totally believed his own pack of shit lies! He didn't even confess that he made up those stories to clear my name, so the rumors lived on, and everyone believed them and didn't want to hear what I had to say, I could care less, believe what you will!!

Be it as it may, I was trying really hard to keep a low profile, many would say otherwise or even disagree, there was a certain excitement in the air now that I was back in church, I held a certain aura about me, I'm not saying that to be cocky or conceited, I've been known to have an entire restaurant or room fall silent when I walked in, I think maybe people thought I was a celebrity or somebody famous they just couldn't pin-point which it was. With that everyone wants a piece of that no matter what whether it's the criminal look the bad boy look or just love to be in the spotlight, it was great attention while it lasted!

With going back to church there was new activities, which was awesome, Tuesdays we had a gymnasium to use at Londonderry junior high, getting there early to play badminton then when we had enough people we would usually play volleyball, because on Thursday nights we would overtake the outdoor volleyball at Rundle Park in the northeast side of Edmonton to play beach volleyball, then we would have a fire couple of people would bring guitars and we would just end the night off singing, great times, sometimes on Thursdays when it was raining and cool during the daytime and by the time the afternoon rolled around it was sunny and warm, never missed a Thursday.

Going into the Fall / Winter this die-hard activity group, we created what we called "Ugly Night" it was a night to do as many crazy activities as possible throughout the entire night into the morning hours. Without falling asleep or quitting, the first official winter event was New Year's Eve / day 1994/95, starting out at a sleigh ride north of Edmonton, tobogganing at Gallagher's hill, bowling on Whyte Ave, breakfast at a Humpy's restaurant and with most people dying out or tapping out the remainders would have to play games usually an intense battle of Rook! Going into summertime "Ugly Nights" they seemed would be easier or more activities to do but including 18 holes of golf was the tough way to end the night / morning, the last three of us dragging our sorry asses down the 18th fairway at Riverside Golf Club, gimme sleep, gimme sleep!

It was during those volleyball days at the gym that I would invite Crystal to come we enjoyed each other's conversations and liked hanging around going to rundle park for those Thursday beach volleyball nights, it was very therapeutic for the both of us at this time, with her not sure what was going on with her relationship other than the mental abusiveness and me I was just trying to stay away or clear of having any girlfriend in church, I was just coming out of the world nightlife and I was abusive in every way shape and form, not giving a shit about anyone and my own selfish desires, and just was still sorting out my life from the mushroom trip at the G n'R concert and having a very attractive worldly girlfriend that could not understand what I was putting her through, plus the few gf's in church that wanted to be in my life and just could not understand that I only wanted friendship, just hang around play pool or darts, go eat some food have coffee and talk. With the breakup of my last gf of the nightlife it was like nobody cared what I was going through or feeling, my snow globe world was turned upside down, my confidence my inner being was shaken to the core and there was really nobody to turn to and talk to, mostly everyone one was reading me wrong or just not at all, usually when I wanted to go for coffee or do something was to get my mind off what I was thinking and feeling.

With that many guys would've loved being in my position, that's all that we had been doing for years coming in and out of people's lives just to fuck around with them and throw them back in the water. At one time maybe I did, just not give a shit, but that's not who I am or was about, I realize when you start getting served the nasty shitty stick, you want to infuse that same poison onto somebody else, it's not their fault that happened to you so why I turn do you want to administer that behavioral garbage onto someone else, Is it because? You let your guard down and, in your weakness, you got walked on or cheated on? And you can't get back at the person that did you wrong because you got in a huff and moved on, but you feel wronged so your thoughts have built up anger and resentment towards females and now I have to get these bitches back and must make them all feel that they're in the same boat together, even after doing more wrong and hate fucking them or developing negative thoughts and treating (all) of them the same way, it doesn't make me feel better, dumping my trash over a lot of innocent girls that were totally off the wall in love with Blackie, I'd have my way with them for a little bit, say what needed to be said, did what I needed to do, maybe woo their hearts with flowers, cards and chocolates or just a nice elegant dinner. Then just end it, dump their ass, no phone calls or be an asshole and say it's over, it's been swell, but the swelling is gone down. A true genuine player could make them be head over heels in love with you, dump them in complete asshole form, then win them back and do it again! Time and time again I would do it, it's such a hurtful, demeaning, and painful thing to do to so many innocent girls, it was such a cold hearted and horrible thing to do. All I could usually say was sorry, just because most times it wasn't me that wanted to break off with any of them, as DJ's and entertainers of this city's night life, we felt it was necessary to remain available and single not tied down to anyone. Just blame Blackie he was more that kind of character anyway!

Going into the summer of 1996, Crystal and I kept our friendship rolling along and into Klondike Days we ended up going there almost every night, riding the Ferris Wheel to see if we could time it right by being in the line-up and getting on the ride for the 11pm fireworks, they would stop the rides for the fireworks and in our infinite timing we actually timed it three or four times during that week and we were close to the top each time when they stopped the ride.

Halfway through these Klondike days we decided to start dating as in seeing each other, as in boyfriend / girlfriend, excuse me…hold the phone…wow, did this raise many eyebrows and concerns!

Eh' Love Tune

The night was electrifying as we stared into the TV screen,
    Desperately racing to catch our breath.
Our eyes were trying to focus on the endless sea of
    Whatever it was we were watching.
    As we soldered our hands together,
  they became entwined, and our hearts were
    Beating like a marching band drummer.
Together in unison the electrodes pulsated.
  God inscribed on our lives
  'Two hearts beat as one.'
  The Heavenly host rejoiced.
We tried to remain, but it was too much for us mortal frames.
If you fix your eyes on Him and gaze into the universe,
You can try to capture our song still beating along…

And I thought the rumor weed mill was outta this fuckin world when I wasn't even going to Church, this was just fuckin wackedmade-up shit, that didn't make any sense, we were actually trying to remain pure and not have a relationship based on physical contact or touch, and we were, as hard as it was already if that wasn't enough, then the rumor weeds had to rear their ugly heads and appear around every corner, OH my fucking gosh people, seriously?? No matter what we did, just being seen at a movie theatre turned into us having a full on make out session, please…I had my own apartment for fuck sakes!

Another afternoon to get my haircut, I would usually have lunch or a coffee with my hairdresser friend after she cut my hair, and lo and behold one of the elders of the church runs into us, the wheels were in motion…I could see the and read the headlines now, "Church goer Paul out with pretty Worldly Girl" it was so predictable, I gave Crystal the heads up, and that Sunday, dimes to doughnuts the ol gal was probably stewing in her borsht for the entire week and went directly to Crystal with the news of seeing me with another woman. I could've got Crystal to totally play into this and we could turn it into just more drama, but there lay the problem, we were so sick of the weekly drama we just wanted nothing to do with it! Escape room escape room where the fuck were, they are then?

It's no wonder the reason Christian do gooders go wondering off figuring out shit the way they do, because fellow Christian so-called brothers and sisters shut you out of their lives because they all end up believing the rumor weed lies and keep you out of the circle, it's the way it is, does anyone really want to give you the benefit of the doubt? Or believe in the Hollywood fuckin' lie because its hot n' nasty shit, its make believes and sounds so real! I was done with it all, it was like water beading on the nicely waxed vehicle, done, finished, wax on wax off! It's funny with these mental dumb fuckers that make up these rumors never want to actually do drama and help write a play or anything like that, they just want to try and mess you up and you know, he who is without sin cast the first stone or second and third, fifth & tenth, there's an old adage of someone who points a finger, there's three pointing back at them, be careful how you shoot that pointed trigger!

The time hadn't come, and I chose to move out of mama Hope's place (don't ask me why? I had it so good at home, I was the only one at home finally) what was I thinking? I'm still at a loss as to why? I think it was because the Arlington apartment downtown Edmonton had vacancies, once the most sought-after places to live (in the mid-eighties you had to put your name on a list) Everything in the Arlington was designed for luxurious living. The front doors opened into a marble atrium, the floors were of maple, and the trim of oak. Each of the 49 apartments featured built-in oak furniture, including a reversible Murphy bed and oak buffet, China cabinets, writing desks, and bookshelves. The building also had electrical lighting, steam heat, and gas-powered stoves. There was even a tearoom in a partial sixth storey on the roof where residents could entertain their guests (like on the show How I Met Your Mother).

Built in 1909 it was a beautiful designed 5- storey red brick building the suites had hardwood floors and wood trim with built in book shelves, Murphy beds, pull chain toilets and claw foot tubs, was a very trendy place it also had mmm, spirits or ghosts apparently, it had people were murdered in that building over the years, couples that fought like crazy and killed each other, I lived there for three months and never slept there, every time I tried I would get comfortable in bed then just about asleep then the chains would drag across the floor and stop at the end of my bed and watch me, a very uneasy uncomfortable situation, I had to move out of there!

It turned out I moved out on Crystal's 19th birthday, I ended up taking her out to the Hotel Macdonald for a very elegant dinner and wine and also helped knowing the Hotel Matradee and he sent over a bottle of fine wine, the night was so divine, it left your lips soaking the flavors of the awesome meal along with your tongue keeping on indulging on the aftertastes, again those nights that you wish would never end…

Those sexual desires to return to my apartment, and still with the rumors and bullshit going on I was still manly, and I didn't touch Crystal on her birthday night, I dropped her off at home before midnight, we kept it pure, it wasn't until a few months later that we finally caved, and I'm not blaming anyone, we're all adults and can make our own decisions, what's the saying, 95% of Christian couples fool around or bring it to a point where it's pretty much crossing the line of so called 'Sin' the remaining 5% are just lying, and I don't really care I'm not the Judge, Jury or executioner, nor should anyone else be or try to be! ***Sinners judging sinners for sinning differently.***
— Sui Ishida

Everything was cruising right along, I mean as well as it could be, I was still working my City job at Victoria Golf Course in Edmonton and Crystal was working as many as three or four jobs depending on the week, I set up my apartment in Bay Wood like a little cow palace, just a few cow pattern (white & Black) splashes like the folding futon the two sided cover was cow pattern on one side and pure black on the other side, the kitchen had painted white cupboards so I had red handles and red highlights and Knick knacks in the kitchen, the bedroom was made into the computer room with one of the most expensive computers / scanner (3 pass) and printer at the time state of the art technology $10k, was still trying to pimp myself out with the graphics but now that computers hit the stage, everyone was jumping into the same pool. It was crazy times trying my best to keep up and learn Corel draw and doing my Horticulture courses through Old's College, adult learning correspondence courses.

Picking up odd jobs and working in the city arenas during the fall / winter time I was able to keep my apartment for a few more months lol, nah wasn't so bad rent was still cheap and so was everything else, besides there was always mama Hopes place, or church friends and pool or dart nights could always dine out, just had to have good timing, timing was always everything within the church body, I wasn't in to many good books anyways so I kept to myself and hung out with my golf pro buddy since we were also neighbors too, plus, still had a few worldly friends that still enjoyed hanging with me for a soda or two, which at times we may have lost count, ha-ha, DT would start calling them going for pails, this one time we found a local pub that served Corona's in tin pails for very cheap, not as cheap as Ezzie's on Tuesday night draft night at 0.50 per draft, I'll tell this story about a cheap night at Ezzie's, so another one of my good friends from Uncle Charlies him and myself go out to draft night and kindly indulge or consume a good amount, how many would that be? What's a decent amount? 10 or 20 Beers each...? Try over forty beers each, then we left for an after-hours party with buddy driving, the traffic circle that is on 118th Ave and 101styes the same one I went to high on mushrooms after the Guns n' Roses concert, all I'm going to say is we were entering the circle at 160Km/hr. and as a passenger I really believed we were going into the Uncle Alberts pancake house for breakfast and not by choice, his car pulled away from the sidewalk at the last second, I still think the tires kissed the sidewalk curbature on my side just ever so nice, like you were kissing somebody you didn't want to kiss, like the Auntie with the plastic orange Avon lipstick that was bleeding past her smokers lines on her cracked up lips...yikes!! Yeah, you know those lips!!

Only a few seconds later we were pulling into a parking stall by you guessed it... the same Asian after-hours bar I so happened to take that blonde waitress from Teddy's to, we park, kill the lights, buddy's like Oh Shit! As I'm turning to look at him to say "what?" I could see the flashing lights reflecting off the windows from the Police car, we just sat there for what was only seconds but felt like eternity, quite like two mice stealing food at Gasteau's Restaurant in Ratatouille, then like Bugs Bunny always said, "You zip out of the scene", like fucking gone, like what just happened? The cop took off down the back alley, chasing some real bad motherfuckers! Leave us drunks alone! Yeah, I'm sure they seen a donut shop open up.

Another great story when I was out very late with DT at the casino at Klondike Days we were at little loaded okay maybe more than a little, when we came outside of the casino at the Agricom complex which is at the very north end of the Northlands parking lot and his car was out the south east corner of Borden park, a very long walk when you're sober, so low and behold somebody parked and left us a golf cart right outside when we came out, and golf cart keys are a universal item, they all fit, and we just so happen to have our key with us (both of us worked at a golf course) so we escorted ourselves off the premises with the cart and parked it safely on the guys lawn where DT's car was parked, we would've left a note but we didn't have a pen, and apparently everyone was asleep in the house. I'm sure everything was alright; there were no damages, and we didn't hear anything on the radio or read any news stories in the newspapers.

This is my segment of How I Met Your Mother...

When I did finish serving my time on weekends (January 18,1982) I was 18 that morning and it was like FREEDOM...it really was and wasn't all at the same time, but it didn't really matter, the bottom fell out of Alberta there were no jobs, unless you knew someone or you belonged to a union, and the biggest thing on job applications was if you had a criminal record, there were odd jobs going on through the congregation at church, so I started attending regularly and within a short time, I was doing landscape and clean up out at the Pastors cabin at Sylvan Lake and then was available for the reno at church, getting to know some of the same age group or little younger because they all thought I was cool being in jail and shit makes you acceptable into their culture, I friended most everyone, cuz I'mMr. friendly. Still the biggest issue was and still is, the long hair, oh if I had a quarter each time, I heard about getting a haircut, I think I would've stopped working long ago! Talk about hearing a broken record.

I became friends and was hanging out with the girls that babysat Crystal and happened to be over one night when they were dropped off for sitting, I was around twenty years old, and a young seven year old Crystal came and sat on my lap and said "I'm going to marry you one day" I was like you have to go to bed little girl, there's no possible way, as it turned out with their family having to move to California and me backsliding right into the nightlife and finding ah er some kinda nichein my rock n roll diary of a partier, our lives grew worlds apart and I went down to the lower depths of Hell, so for almost that entire decade I was nowhere close to entering the doors of church again.

I was also in a relationship from around 1987-1990, which at the time we (thought) were all in, thinking we were going to get married, with the abortion and then her cheating on me not once but twice, I had enough and moved out near the end of 1990/91, back to the partying lifestyle, OMG, just more and more of it, being part of the entertainment group at the Inn on Whyte (People's Pub) was another great and awesome time, although short lived, the hotel was sold and they were going to be tearing it down to make a new one, of course.

So, then my time with Uncle Charlie's came into play, and my bad mushroom trip in March of 1993 and going into my 30's after 1994, the only thing that was secure and always there was my City of Edmonton job at the Golf Courses and Arenas.

Crystal returned from her Chasity tour across Canada in 1995 and then after Klondike Days of 1996 we started to date, I turned 33 in 1997, with the rumor mill hot n' heavy over creating bullshit stories of us, it turned us to turn to one another and in our weakness we ended up sleeping together, our courtship was tarnished by the same people that made up the stupid (stupidity & tabloid) stories, nobody had anything to talk about or discuss, cell phones and the World Wide Web wasn't quite a thing yet, so, we were the next hottest ticket, wow, really?

There were some other activities that went on during our courtship the main one was people being on edge or just not giving us a chance, thinking I was just out to have sex with her and that was it, that wasn't the case, but I guess I didn't have a good enough lawyer to represent me.

I was approached at my own residence asking if I had slept with Crystal, now kids and everyone reading this, I could've lied through my teeth and what would that have gotten me? Probably the same result! Nobody even knew that I planned on asking Crystal to marry me, so there were a lot of disgruntled people (close family) and tensions were being raised within the leaders and elders of the church body, nobody knew how to deal with this so-called Christian that's been back in their midst amongst the faithful, get a rope and hang this prick or put the scarlet letter on them and make them walk through the city and throw stones, you know…the Christian way right? It's alright to be part of our congregation and socialize into every group and be invited to every party or gathering, but whoa right there buck a roo, you crossed the wrong line of who's available for courting, you see, you can only date these ones over here boy!

They (the church body) and whomever else were treating me as though I was a divorced man.

Let me tell you, it doesn't matter how cleaned up a person is or becomes, Christians (some) the righteous ones that have never sinned or done any wrong, there's nobody like that? The judgmental hypocrites, yeah them. I wrote this poem specifically for the church when we were newlyweds, this was burning on my heart for such a long time as we went there, I couldn't stand the hypocrisy and the phoniness, how they can preach that it wasn't alright to do this that and the other, but don't mind me I'll be over here in my closet, doing whatever the fuck I want to!

After the smoke had cleared (somewhat), I got engaged to Crystal, it wasn't a very romantic take out for candle light dinner with wine or champagne, not sure what I was thinking, I was just a little kid all giddy and shit, went to the old neighborhood restaurant where I spent many of days having coffee, it had changed hands and ownership a few times since I started to go there when I was just seven, the original Capital was full at lunchtime, so we went up the road to the new Capital II (Dickensfield Mall), and yes my mama Hope was with us, it wasn't like I intended on asking her there either, I had the ring in my pocket and wanted to just give her a peek of it underneath the table, however it goes down as a bad way to propose to somebody.

Maybe It's...

Sitting in a pew pondering life, remote on pause...
Am I still alive? For it seems to be an eternity,
What will be? Maybe it's, the way...Jesus says.
"Go after the one and leave the ninety-nine."
How many more will head out into the cold?
The unity of the rainbow once had a pot of gold.
Now it bleeds with what's been sold...30 pieces of silver?
These men should we honor? Who stands? Who fights?
For the business is a flourishing, but the souls are for sure diminishing!
This land once flowed with milk & honey,
Now is barren by Armani grasshoppers.
Ephesians says, "we are no longer foreigners or aliens but fellow.
Citizens with God's people and members of His house."
Maybe it's...I no longer belong,
God's laws in Leviticus nineteen are not to be defiled!
Yet you make way with your fabricated smile, as you give praise
To the Lord, it gives me quivers...I am abhorred!

Pleased to meet you…

"It's Gonna Be a Golden Day!"

I've met many, many strange and wonderful people, isn't it funny that when you're young growing up you make these pacts with your besties like; if you move away and lose touch everyone says, "let's meet back at this place in 20,30 or 40 years from now," we'd make up crazy things by being blood brothers, slicing your thumb open and pressing against your buddies open wound thumb and laughing and giving each other a friendship hug. When we moved away from the slums of Dickensfield, those friendships grew apart and dissipated, like sands through an hourglass the tenure with most of them quickly became someone in your distant past, now an acquaintance, that sure changed all of a sudden, what was that time for?

Becoming so inseparable, like a daily dosage of coffee and smokes, never skipping a beat you're joined at the hip, for the most part the neighborhood had these little gangs that hung out and did shit, either just to hang out and listen to the newest records and smoke cigs, walk to the strip mall and drink coffee and smoke at the restaurant or the little candy store around the corner in the same mall.

Highschool was very similar, separated into little groups of people, there were the North enders mostly the cool kids and stoners either by the doors or the open courtyard, then the smoke pit was very smelly small room, teachers hated it when I was there, I mostly hung out like a door keeper most times just had it open to air out the pit, through the next double doors we had mostly all jocks and the trades wing;

industrial ed and shop mixed with all these jocks and jokette's, the front of the school was for the international students and the west side was mostly Italians and Lebanese, upstairs in the cafeteria was the clubbies (nerds) and a dumb shag carpet room where some would study or sleep.

For the most part and being a social lite, I got along with everyone just a great part of my character, going back at the start of grade eleven at fifteen years old and being a seasoned veteran, I had my sights on meeting this girl, lust at first sight, standing in front of me in the smoke pit with her back to me, long hair halfway down her back on a skinny little frame, oh oh wait a minute…this just in…it wasn't a girl, it was Bruce, haha, something to add to our storyline.

Once we actually had met, we became inseparable, our daily routine and diet of getting high and drinking beers, I couldn't get into the bars just yet, not until the new year when I turned sixteen, didn't matter, Bruce was two years older than me and would get the alcohol, the antics and good times we had, this was late seventies early eighties by the way, riding the newly built LRT (light rail transit) with a few joints to light up along the way with some laughs at the people on board, this is where Bruce would actually meet and marry his first wife in 1982.

We were always taking out his motorbike in the springtime even before all the snow and ice was gone, also the sandy gravel from the winter months, this resulted in us wiping out a few times, laying their laughing because it was so dumb and silly, most times you knew it was coming which made it more hilarious.

Another ride we were coming out of the Strathcona Science Park, and the railroad tracks come across the roadway at the entrance to the park, we could see the front tire was going to get stuck in the track, sure enough in went the tire and down we went onto the roadway, that one hurt a little, we needed to hurry and pick up the bike, there was a car coming up towards us. There was this time going out to Sandy Beach to the west of Edmonton, Bruce's brother Lenard came along with us, we ended up staying the night in the cook house, laid on the concrete floor wearing our bike helmets, it was pretty comfortable, we had no camping gear, this is where the saying "it's going to be a Golden Day" was birthed, I woke up at the crack of light and said that, and for forty years has been brought forward with some great laughter as well, it has been mentioned for a business name such as a landscaping company or merchandizing on tee shirts and coffee mugs, lol.

One time four of us buddies (Jeff, Rob, Bruce and myself) rolled a one-ounce joint of red Lebanese hashish, it took something like twenty rolling papers, nearly a dozen cigarettes and a cardboard filter to assemble and about forty-five minutes to smoke out on Bruce's balcony while we were smoking the heater on the end was so big Bruce flicked it towards Rob and it went down his pants Rob was doing his version of a jig on the balcony like fuck, fuck, fuck, talk about being nicely baked, we were charcoaled. This one-time Bruce and I painted our faces with acrylic paint (fast drying) artistic paint, for shits n giggles we got high and wanted to see who could last the longest without your face cracking, in no time at all we would be in gut wrenching laughter with tears streaming down our faces looking like a broken and cracked porcelain vase.

When we did work together it was strictly business and we would get our work done first and foremost, but be on guard when it was slow, we worked at this industrial cleaning supply company at an old warehouse downtown (I believe it's the 107st lofts now), boxes were stacked pretty high and we arranged them so that we could have our lunch without being harassed by the front office to pick orders, some days we'd have time for horseplay and that crazy fucker chased me around that warehouse with this long dirty mop head on an extension pole, I started throwing urinal pucks at him, when these pucks hit the floor they exploded, leaving a nice mess to cleanup afterwards, bonus points when I hit Bruce though because they fucking hurt!

Being part of Bruce's first wedding was an awesome honor, when we drove up town to do the final measurements on the suit rental, Rob was driving this little shitbox of a truck, think it was first model Ranger that barely fit the driver, and Bruce and I were small, whoever sat in the middle had to change the gears ha ha, anyway, we just picked up breakfast at McD's and was spread over the entire dash, now the drive back to Bruce's place, as we turn the corner at Jasper Ave and 97st going North, a yellow cab is in our lane and heading for us, there's a car to the right of us, so really one option, and without hesitation or skipping a beat Rob took it, he swerved left into what should be the cabs lane and back to our lane covering us all with this shitty McD's breakfasts, very good, no I'm not hungry right now, thanks!

Earlier I mentioned about a horse tranquilizer that we were selling at the Snooker Shack, it was a total fuck you up pill, Bruce and I were going to split the pill and take half each, as we were driving around Bruce forgot his wallet and needed to go back home as he ran up to the apartment, he indulged in taking the entire pill, all I could think was, this is not going to turn out well, just like I expected, we returned back to his place, with his wife there and not too crazy about us still doing drugs together, we sit in the living room and we start to play some records and talk about music, an hour or so expires and Bruce wants to go out on the balcony for a smoke, while outside he starts telling me about his high that he's going through, he had thought we were rambling on for hours inside about music and thought he wasn't making an sense.

Now Bruce is getting higher and higher, he's telling me about his high, and how he wants to jump off his fourth storey balcony to avoid walking in his place by his wife, I said we'll wait for her to go to the bathroom and then go downstairs, he couldn't wait any longer, he said to me, "fuck Paul, we have to go in or I'm going to jump down" I convinced him to let's just go in, we'll say we're just going for a walk, that worked all right, now we went and lay on this hill close by with him telling me about this high for hours, it was very interesting considering I was pretty sober, I was just overseeing my friend so he didn't bring harm to himself or others, remember now, back at the Snooker Shack, others that took this capsule resembled a concrete pillar, unable to move around, let alone communicate at the same time about their hallucinated trip! It wasn't my ideal night, when a friend is in need though you should step up to the plate.

There is however a time when we were at a lake party or BBQ, and Bruce, my brother Robert and I were out in a boat not far from shore, although a little ways out, swimmable if you're sober, anyway…Bruce said "I'm going to jump in to take a piss," both Robert and me thought he said he was going to swim back to shore, initially when he came up to the shore looking like a drown rat, he was so pissed off, it was a lot further to swim than what it appeared, "good thing I'm an excellent" swimmer he scoffed, I offered my apologies with a beer and soon enough all was forgiven and we continued to party.

Throughout our lives we both had different events going on, having different warehouse jobs and Bruce had his first child, we still met up on occasion to party on weekends, Bruce would end up divorcing his first wife and then invited the Blackburn clan to his second wedding and reception, it was one of those nights you wish could go on forever or at least stop the clock and rewind the time, it was like a high school reunion as well, even one of Hopes besties was there, it was a gala event with non-stop conversation, laughter and probably one of my all-time favorite memories of a wedding reception.

As the sand continued to pass through life's yearly glass and life grew on in separate directions with life choices and relationships, Bruce would marry wives three and four, while I was working on my first marriage and having babies almost yearly, life gets in the way with work especially after my years with the City of Edmonton which mostly was shift work too, once I took the leap to change my career to an Equipment Operator in the industrial sites and my shift was mostly 14/7 away from home, the one week off at home was not even enough time to spend with the family let alone trying to hook up with friends.

Bruce finally found his treasure with his fifth wife Jill, and is doing really well with her, it's probably the longest he's enjoyed being with someone too, I met Jill at Bruce's fifty fifth birthday gathering, and we hit it off really good, this November will be six years (2022) since we've met, and she is the best woman in his life for sure! I still enjoy my visits with both when I get the opportunity, if not when I phone them, we always talk with the speaker on for a party line.

I've enjoyed all my times with Bruce in the forty plus years of knowing him and his family, it wasn't all pie in the sky happy times, we've lost many close friends over the years and recently both of our mother's mama Hope in 2016 and a few weeks after I attended Bruce's mom's birthday, she passed away around 2021, both very hard losses.

As I was two years younger than Bruce, I also had another friend in the same high school in which I was two years older than him, Mike Burke, I met Mike when I was entering my first of three years of grade twelve, he was in grade ten, Mike was born in Burma and had a natural darker complexion with long hair, he resembled a California beach bum, also, had the beautiful tall blonde girlfriend, he was on the high school football team and during lunch breaks or just hanging in the north end where all the soccer and fields were, we would throw the football with each other in a fashion that nobody else would want to join us, only about twenty or thirty feet would separate us and we'd throw the ball as hard as possible to one another, causing aching and very red palms, this ritual carried on throughout the years.

Mike and I would also would carry the partying lifestyle to the extreme, often led to poor decision making (sometimes lol), in the early part of 1984, Mike was keen on this stripper she wanted him to come to Vegreville AB (home of the giant Ukrainian egg) to come and cheer her on to get her title, it's like being crowned in a beauty pageant, so they get this banner to wear also like in a pageant, he convinced me to come with him, keep in mind this is a local red-necked hick bar, where everyone knows each other a farming community, we're both long haired city slickers, needless to say we're under the watchful eye of this local crowd.

We are both pretty much fun-loving guys (not with each other) easy to get along with, not violent by any means, were here for the beers and to have a good time, this is not just a couple of hours type event, it took a while, it was coming up on midnight and we cheered for her really hard, she ended up getting her title, then all of a sudden doesn't want anything to do with Mike or us, now Mike is feeling really ripped off and pissed off, he wants to take on the locals in this bar and engage in a bar room brawl, not a chance Mikey, they had their pitch forks and sheep shears out ready to feast on our carcasses!

Without hesitation I was grabbing Mike, and we are going to get the hell out of dodge, like NOW!!! Mike was a little to inebriated to drive, yours truly took the wheel, he had this Diplomat car possibly late 70's early 80's model, not washed mostly lived out of at times, you could hardly see out of the windows, let alone tell that I was driving my way out of town with the high beams on, as we were exiting the town limits back to Edmonton, an RCMP was coming toward Vegreville as we passed each other, they spun a U-turn on the highway turned their lights on and pursued us, I pulled over gave her all the proper documentation, the female cop asks "do you know why I pulled you over?" as I said "no" she says "you always drive through towns with your high beams on?" the lights were so dim I couldn't even tell, "follow me back to the station" while we are in the station, the RC's were going through Mikes car without us present, they found an open bottle of whiskey under the drivers' seat and give me the ticket for that and they would confiscate the vehicle.

So this is a great turn of events, in the middle of butt fuck Vegreville over a 120Km's from Edmonton with no wheels, then for shits and giggles the pigs won't let us stay in the station and its cold out, they gave me one chance to make one call, I had to call my DJ in crime partner Klay to come and get us, within a little time Klay pulled up in the Iroc Z-28, it was a good thing, hypothermia was about to set in especially with Mike spooning me and stealing all my body warmth, haha crazy story, we were laying in a sleeping bag outside across the cop shoppe.

Another road trip…lol, we're taking off, yeah not by plane or train, we're driving, flying high again…on mushrooms this time, to Banff AB during spring break (probably should've checked on this first) one would've thought, right? Not so, for this trip, we're going blinders on and whatever happens, happens. That was it, we get to Banff and it's like bare, the carnival packed up and left like yesterday type thing, there's absolutely not anybody here, we were lucky the shops on main street were open, talk about scratching your head and saying like "WTF, over!" I think the mice even packed up and left, as we are trying to figure out what to do, I was reading a See Magazine paper it was a local rag paper about what's happening around different towns and cities, lo and behold their it is in black n white.

Our buddies from high school (Hells Bells)were scheduled to playin a bar in Calgary, without hesitation off we went to Calgary, racing a Mazda sports car along the way, we'd trade off the lead vehicle, back and forth each car would take control until we got to Cowtown in about twenty minutes, not exactly sure the speeds we were travelling at, looking at it now at the distance is almost 130km we were maintaining speeds between 170-200km/hr., I knew it was fast.

We chimed in at the bar on Electric Ave to see the boys in Hells Bells, everybody happy to see one another and as we continued this mushroom trip, we were anticipating to find a party but it wasn't looking very good at the start of the night, Mike was working on this little slutty girl who looked like a secretary and at first glances appeared to be heading into the right direction to score, it turns out she was our connection in finding a house party, what a party this turned out to be, we arrive at this house and has no furniture, it has a bed in the bedroom, I was having a good buzz on, I decide to pull up the floor and make comfy spot in front of the living room window and play it cool.

No sooner I'm adjusting to my seat, these two chicks are naked in front of me making out and going down on each other, muff diving, Mike walks by me and says "you gotta love Calgary Paul!" in a little bit all twelve of us are all on this one not so lonely bed, all horned up, making out with whomever and getting close and personal, what a trippy time! We hope you enjoyed your time in Calgary, we can make the most out of any situation, we are the Wild Party!!

This would hold true for the eighties and early nineties, Mike pulled up residence above this business on Ft Road, some loft style type apartment that became party central all the time, quite a cool location and not far from any of the bars we were frequenting.

Isn't it how amazing how an area of a city or even friends in your life can have such an impact on your development of who you are to become, bear with me here…I wasn't or didn't even have any knowledge about this area until after grade seven, I was urged to attend a different school for grade eight, this changed I believe in who I would become, my school Cardinal Legere was within a little walk across a field, they no longer wanted me there and I was to transfer to St. Francis of Assisi, the area in which would impact my life and most likely changed my course in life. During lunch time I would go to the Ft. road pool hall, I was intrigued with foosball and wanted to get better at it, I would put my money up to play the best players that played I would get destroyed all the time 9-0, the other kids would call me stupid for wasting my money, I didn't think I was wasting my money at all, I was learning, in little time I started to score on them, one or two then, three or four within that school year I started to have game, I was still losing but the games now were 6-3, 5-4 periodically I would sneak in a win, then by grade nine the tides were changing and most games were very close but now I was winning them.

This would become beneficial in the upcoming years not just playing and learning foosball, but everything housed in a billiard room, you soon become knowledgeable about all the table games.

At the end of the street was the Transit Hotel and around the corner was Bruce's first apartment, then our buddies from high school (band members of Sweet Leaf), rest in peace Robert Roggeveen and Jeff Porter, they had an extreme party house a few blocks to the west, then all of the local watering holes along Ft. Road the Londonderry Hotel with MJ's roadhouse, a little north of that was Club John's, The Beverly Crest and across the North Saskatchewan was The Rivera (rock room).Mike and I would frequent many of these rooms depending on who was playing (live bands) and tour around, then end up at his flat for a party or at another house party.

Much like with Bruce, Mike and I would have separate career paths, I started with the City of Edmonton and soon after Mike would become an Insulator with the union (heat and frost) many times Mike would try and urge me to join the union he was with, but in the early years I had my sights set on becoming a Superintendent in Golf Courses, which ultimately I would have to change my career path as well, to raise a family, I joined a different union and became an equipment operator with local 955, it was a no brainer with making three times as much with the income.

Victoria Golf Course was as part of me as any of my limbs, I was married to this course, I finally found my niche, from the first day I worked there I bought into it, I had the keys to the kingdom, there's nothing like working at a golf course and for twenty years it was my bloodline. From all the staff that came and went, with all the patrons over those years along with everybody in the clubhouse and proshopand driving range, it was the greatest experience of my lifetime.

The first day starting at the driving range was the same day as Juliette (Julie) and I hit it off right from the start and developed a really great bond, she was very much my older sister that I never had, we both were in toxic relationships and we consoled each other the best we knew how, we joked around quite a bit too, working with some older ladies in which we made some good humor out of, had us in stitches most days. Some of the best practical jokes came at Julies expense, she had the biggest fear of bees and wasps, one night shift near closing, and I knew Julie was to open in the morning, I caught this huge wasp and strung him up from the ceiling right at her level when she'd walk in, we left the fan on so that it would sway back n forth, not seeing it when she first walked in, but when she turned around, it was right in her face…she screamed so loud, apparently the morning guy came running, she said "I'm Going to Killlll You Paullll"

The city got rid of the cashiers at golf courses and thus Julies job ended, we still remained friends and have a great relationship to this day, the evolution of cahiers would now be run through the pro-shop and they now were younger with less pay, I still developed a great working relationship with most of the new cashiers, but got a little too close for comfort with Lexus, and a few times would get too steamy in the back building, very, very steamy…out of our fling I wrote this poem titled…

'The Kiss'

The heat of hot summer's passion as we anticipate
    Another minute together, T-I-C-K,
Ever so slowly frozen to our wrists as I stare,
    Your tongue gently moistens your lips.
Beads of your glow evaporate, again, ever so slow.
The excitement to zoom in couldn't happen a moment.
Too soon as I'm glued into the de' ja' vu feeling with you,
    waiting…patiently to share your occupied room.
My shadow embracing your sweet-smelling perfume.
    Pressing against you all seems but true,
Zoned into your presence chamber, again…waiting for you.
    Holding your expressions like; silken lace, deep sighs,
        Loud cries, silent whispers of licking your eyes.
    Sharing magical touches that melt drops of desired smiles.
        Heartbeats waltzing to the music box dancer.
    Awakening from our journey, clearing out the star spots
    Glazed into our look, still waiting…patiently so I can.
        Lean towards you, and give you…
            'The Kiss'

Developing some great relationships lead to some of the most extravagant stories on and off the golf course, one of the best was put on by the head pro Kevin Hogan along with his assistant pro would do a year end tournament (by invite only) it was called the 'Steak n Beans' tourney, it was divided into two teams from the pros, usually about forty people aside and you would start on a designated hole (8 players / two foursomes) and play Texas style, everyone would tee off and then select the best tee shot and play from there until you holed out, sometimes it didn't matter how well you played, you can win your points from your match and still end up losing overall with all the other matches going on, as it turned out a long-time member of Victoria Golf course Fred Dawson and me would always be paired up because of our ahh…hum winning ways haha, NOT! I wrote a tribute poem for this event and dedicated it to Mr. Dawson.

It Was a Pleasure Dining with You Fred Dawson

   Another year back at the old Victoria golf course
Everyone eagerly hitting balls, putting on the big practice green and chipping.
   Getting there 'A' game together
  Golfers, hackers, whackers and sclaffers
Just as fast as the majestic course gets greened up, and your game comes together.
   So does another season.
  You can see the discoloring of leaves starting to turn in the river Valley.
  Then the whispers and rant fill the air about the season finale,
   The Fall classic 'Steak & Beans' tournament.
  The head pro and assistant pro choose and divide the teams.

Close to forty men aside, the first annual S & B in 93' was terrible weather conditions Windy, blowing snow and light rain, it was hovering around zero but felt like minus ten All of us in toques, parkas and big snow mittens, could hardly grip your golf club Anyway, the winners ate steak, and the losing side ate beans, Tallied up the points and it was determined, Fred and myself would eat beans.

Not only on this occasion, but for eight years in a row.

Fred and I were amused with the entire event, it gave everyone lots to talk about.

Now Fred you are gone, but truly not forgotten, wherever you are, I salute you!

It was a pleasure dining with you Fred Dawson.

Another great event that I was a part of was the 'Longest Day of Golf' with then assistant pro Robb James, for four years Robb would try to establish a record and raise money for cancer too, he would use the front nine golf holes and play it over and over for the entire twenty four hour period, Robb would utilize as one of the drivers of the golf cart for each year, and on the final year when he established the record, he didn't want me to stop driving, so he carried on with me and I drove him into the Guinness book of world records 2004, playing 851 holes.

It was never a dull moment with some of the matches with playing golf with the pros and assistant pros, it was an honor to play as many rounds as I was invited to play with them, it certainly helped me to improve my game.

One of my best friends in golf, was golf pro Don Toth, D really took me under his wing and we played everywhere, if he didn't have a pro event happening we were sure to be golfing somewhere, we were mostly on the same shift my work at the Driving Range was 1400 hrs. – 2200 hrs. so we would golf before shift in the mornings, Donnie would teach lessons at the range, plus we had become neighbors in the same complex at Baywood Apts on Groat Road in Edmonton, we had become really good friends, having coffees at Westmount mall at the Grabajabba where we had become friends with the owner and had many good conversations about everything under the Sun.

We did make it camping early in the Springtime of 2005 Jasper AB., to tent, fish and golf we made a plan to go fishing in the early hours and we actually did get up early because we couldn't sleep it was so cold during the night, we were laughing about it and jokingly said we had hypothermia, fishing was good for Don he very rarely had any issues, I kept him in hysterics because I was having the worst fishing luck possible, we checked with a local restaurant if they would cook our fish, they agreed and the bill was just the same as if we ordered from the menu, we talked about the big scam the cooks probably just served us whatever they had going on in the kitchen. The following day we ended up getting on at the Jasper Park Lodge (JPL) golf course, I didn't bring any golf clothes with me, so Donnie persuaded the pro shop to lend me some rain pants from whatever they had in the back, and that worked so off we went playing.

Turned out to be a good getaway with plenty of outdoor festivities, filled with lots of great stories and laughter maybe a few pails.

Speaking of pails, haha, we got into drinking Coronas during the summertime while it was hot outside an all of the local watering holes were charging import prices on these watered-down beers, we stumbled across a pub close to our place that served them in pails, you could get them four in a small bucket or six in a large pail at really cheap prices, we would drink our forty-eight and then walk home. We joked about going out for one or two drinks and that would be all, it always turned into pails.

Another great time was when D registered to play in the Canadian Open held at Wolf Creek golf and country club down in Ponoka AB., he wanted me to caddy for him and I happily said, "for sure, little buddy", we arrive down there in Tin Cup fashion, late and hungover, D pulls out this oversized tour bag and I'm like "what the hell is that?" he's in hysterics laughing as he's putting in his clubs from his carry-on normal bag and putting in the accessories like balls and tee, I'm still like "no-way bro, are you carrying this?, its bigger than you!" He kept on laughing as he's filling it up, I'm like "Stop! Adding everything into that bag" I wouldn't be hungover for long carrying this bag of his.

As D is lining up his ball kneeling down to putt, he's like "what do you see Pauly?" I said, "aim about a foot outside left downhill slider breaking to the right, go easy it's going to be fast" He's like "Shit! We're in trouble, I thought it broke to the left "I replied "well, close your eyes and hope for the best", getting through the next couple holes was challenging especially when one of the judges called Donnie over to tell him his caddy could get him disqualified for wearing golf shoes, so at our earliest convenience I had to take my spikes out and put tape over the holes, apparently you cannot make extra holes on the golf green or damage the putting surface by dragging your feet.

I attribute most if not all of my successes in golf to Donnie, we worked so hard on practicing not only our goofy challenges at the driving range hitting targets, but our long, long times at the nursery green sometimes for four, five or even six hours at times, just putting, the important putts, because really there are no gimmes, the odd footage putts were the ones we would work on, we would find the line, and chalk it with a chalk line then work on the one, three, five, seven and nine foot putts, we then talked about visualizing the chalk line but that didn't work well, so we started to pace the putt, when you walk to pull the flag out, you're reading the green to the hole and back to your ball, we then discovered if the pace is seven paces you basically pull the putter back to just your big toe on your stance and follow it through, now it Varey's with downhill and uphill lie, in a little while we found a comfortable putting stroke that was reliable.

I really want to express my deep heart gratitude for the time I got to spend with Don, his life was cut way to short and he passed away in June 2022, to everyone that knew Donnie they would attest that he was always a fun-loving positive human and would not hurt anyone or even speak badly about anybody, he would give you not only the shirt off his back he most likely would give you money and give you a ride to where you needed to go. We really tried to connect the past few years, but we could never find the time, lame excuse I know, we both had our work that really got in the way of coming together.

It truly was an honor taking me golfing to so many select courses, and you weren't even embarrassed about my game with other pros that were with us, just would smile and say don't worry Pauly it'll come, just breathe, even now when I go out hitting balls at the range or on the course I always find myself trying to immolate your swing and your putting style old' volks lol, the best days of golf we would follow up with the buffet at Hotel MacDonald, but hey, don't get me wrong we won our share of matches with some big money on the line. Don was also one of my best men on my wedding day, which is soon to be our 25th anniversary on November 15th, 2022.Cheers Donnie, until we meet again, may you rest in peace!

Some of Don's achievements in golf is ridiculous, being ever so humble he would tie many course records without ever saying anything, it was just another ho-hum round and he'd always say "I could've shot better, if I didn't bogey that one hole" I was golfing with D when he broke the record at Pioneer Meadows in Edmonton, I tried calling there, the recording says its permanently closed, D's record I'm sure was 56, he was absolutely on fire, he's had many rounds in the low 60's, I've recently spoke with golf pro Kevin Hogan at Victoria Golf course to ask him of Don's record tying game at the old Vic course.

Kevin was unsure himself because Don being his humble self didn't want to turn in the score card because his other friend and colleague holds the record at the course of a 61 unofficially, there was so many times, when Don was in the zone, not too many golfers could go toe to toe in matching his game, I'm not just saying that I've told him many times having sodas or coffees if he was focused and became a tour player, I'm very certain he would've been successful at it.

There are certain individuals that have come into my life at certain times and we've made a certain impact that has remained has strong as the day we met and started our friendship off with the right foot forward, another one of those friends is Eric Sehn, we hit it off right off the bat, he joined the workforce at the Victoria Golf course and Driving range in the early part of 1991,because of our relationship status with girlfriends we didn't start hanging out until we ditched our baggage and were able to chum around together.

Enter 1992, when we started going to bars it was absolutely nutty, if I wasn't DJing we were at whatever pub, bar or purple onion that was in our way, out of the 150 days of summer we didn't go out for maybe two of them, it was an unbelievable display, I would lay on Erics couch an hour before my shift and guaranteed his roommate always wanted to turn the lamp off, darn it Bill! I'd fall asleep and sure enough would have to race to the golf course to open, speeding down River Valley Road windows all down and going through red lights, crazy days of summer for sure, one of them was the memory that Eric touched on in the Forward he wrote about.

The trip to Vancouver/Victoria also included a jaunt down to Seattle to try and catch a Seahawks game, which by the way I'm not too proud of myself for driving in the condition we were in, we left the bar in Vancouver and had this idea to check out an American football game, I was all over that highway I cannot believe I didn't pass-out and crash. We made it to the border and that guard grilled me for what seemed like forty-five minutes, two long hairs trying to enter the US in the wee hours of the morning, he kept asking me the same questions over and over, at one point I just wanted to say "okay forget it! I don't want to come into your country" but I was thinking that won't look good either, the thing was without having a cell phone or knowledge if there was a football game or not.

When the guard was interrogating me, he kept asking who was playing the football game, I kept saying "I don't even know if they're playing at home this weekend, or if they have a bye or anyway game" it wasn't like the questions were hard, they were just annoying because he kept asking them, I was just so surprised he didn't make me get out of the car and do a sobriety test, he finally cleared us to go through, whew, that was annoying, after making it to Birmingham WA., we got a Hotel and checked in and also to see if the Seahawks were playing at home, it turned out there was no game that weekend. We ended up leaving the next day and went back to Vancouver to go across to the Island and check out Victoria, lots of driving and checking out different venues after getting to the Island even went to the museum and took in some culture.

By the time we drove back to Edmonton and started to settle in and get back into our routine of work and shit, we continued to check out bands that were playing all over the place, from our regular watering holes and all the bars that played live music, plus the Agricom(w/ Black Crowes & Cinderella, and another show w/ George Thorogood), convention Center (w/ Triumph, and also Nazareth), Coliseum(w/

Guns and Roses) and the Stadium shows (w/ Pink Floyd in the rain, and The Rolling Stones on separate bills)we were also checking out places like coffee shops and the Butter dome at U of A, the students union hosted a music fest there, which included a new and upcoming Canadian group called The Tragically Hip along with many other bands, it was pretty lame so we left. Some of the best shows in-which were able to see live, played at the bar called Peoples Pub (Age of Electric, The Headstones, Chocolate Bunnies from Hell, Wild T and the Spirit, Big Sugar and Gowan to name a few), it was attached to the Redford Inn on Whyte (which by the way was bought by some rich American that flattened the Hotel and rebuilt a new one called Varscona with an Irish pub on the sidewalk side).

A handful of us came together at the end of October 1994, just a weekend of hanging out with Erics colleagues from Lac La Biche and an exchange student from Mexico, better yet, we were in our own snow globe for an entire weekend, it was such an incredible experience, it is hard to find in my memory bank such a weekend that is comparable, where nothing from the outside could penetrate our entire existence, yet our ability to move around among the crowds and yet not be part of them at all was just so fascinating, we were like ghosts moving among the living and doing all the things we had desired to do. Hooking up before the weekend festivities got underway, with drinks and an elegant meal and just getting reacquainted having awesome conversation and laughter was special, everything that we did was done in unison, no bickering, dis-agreements or bargain basement trash talk.

We were all staying in the confines of the Commercial Hotel, it really didn't matter where we stayed or hung our hats, we were all good friends and we were in the moment with each other a great within the snow globe, as the weekend drew on, we had tickets to a show at the Jubilee Auditorium, not just a show, a performance unlike any other that was presented to us in that fashion, a flawless angelic harpist and singer Lorena McKenna, what more can you ask for? With a weekend such as this…hang on, we all converge back to the Commercial to watch the live band and basically absorb our time together over the weekend, we only had little time remaining before the exchange student (Laura) from Mexico, has to drive to Calgary and go back home.

In the same time Darwin and I are in synch, and basically, we decided upon the future of Eric and Laura, in our infinite wisdom and in one accord we come up with the notion to get these two married, say what? Yes, once we brought it forward and mentioned it to both of them, it was almost a done deal, they were in agreement, and for the rest of that night and into the early hours we tried to find a justice of the peace to marry them, when the dust had settled, and we couldn't get them married we crashed for the night I went home to get a better sleep (my own bed). When I awoke, I called Eric to see what he was up to, he said "you know what's up," the plan was set, get cleaned up and meet at the JP's home and have a wedding, and so we did and so did they, we went to Peter Schmlars residence (a little wee older gentleman) Eric and Laura were something like Peters 10k married couple.

We all enjoyed a light lunch reception before everyone had to leave out of the snow globe, while the portal was open, Darwin & Canta left for Lac La Biche and Eric and I drove Laura to Calgary for her to fly home to Mexico, Laura had to leave because the student visa was to expire and now they have to fill out separate papers for citizenship and do all the waiting and processing blah blah blah, after all this, they had a reception with Erics parents down in Mexico, then when Laura came back to Canada (Lac La Biche) Erics family had a reception here and now after the smoke is cleared and the i's are dotted and the t's are crossed Eric & Laura Sehn have just celebrated twenty eight years of marriage 11.02.22 congratulations you two, along with two beautiful children.

There are times when something just feels right, and that entire weekend was like no other that I have felt in my lifetime, where five friends could come together and had a tremendous bond for the entire duration and even setting up our good friend for marriage, we can call it a lot of different things like fate or it was meant to be, what if Darwin and I didn't have that conversation to set the wheels in motion, what then? I guess we'll never know.

Blackies essential: necessary, required, needed, integral, vital, critical and imperative must have, must own albums…not in any order, not numbered or lists of any sort…lists are BULLSHIT!!!So is saying this guitarist is better than this one or this musician is better than that one or whatever it is…its garbage, do not buy into that belief…lists are FUCKED and so is the Rolling Stone Mag for publishing a garbage list of the top 500 albums of all-time or any other lists that are made by any publication…MUSIC IS SUBJECTIVE!!!!!!!

My taste in music varies from yours and thousands of others, in fact millions globally.

What I'm merely suggesting are albums for your collection, you may or may not agree, these are albums that I've had the pleasure in owning and re-purchased again, some more than twice, I'm only going to really make one or two selections of a said band or artist, really who needs a dozen records of an individual artist? Unless the value of the records is extremely high, or you enjoy everything that is produced by them…I'll just stick to a couple and see how it goes.

Scars...scabs...and all

Tree of Life

Tree of knowledge of
    Good & evil it's
    Been in the family.
    For 6,000 years
Each one of the members
    Will get their chance.
Give it a shake, try its fruit.
Take some money which do you prefer?
The tree is for everyone, come and dine.
Drink from its wine, it is of course.
Your's and mine. No need to spend a dime.
If you wish to speak to the maker of this fine tree
Choices flow freely, no pressure Just make up your mind...
Will that be one bite of apple?
Or two towers of destruction?

Family Affairs

Diseased by another bottle of red

Dropping tablets to release the pounding.

    In my head

Disposable decades

Getting harder to purchase Easier to throw away.

Eye spy with my little eye…

    Exposed lies, escaping into your ways.

Trying to grasp a mirage of the past.

Clutching the cold stem of a wine glass

Resting on the painted cast, do you think this will last?

Aging quite fast, clinging to labels of freedom, are you set free?

Pour your poison into my wound; take this ache, the heartache

That doesn't vanish and make it numb.

Dealt the cards of a lifetime, what have you Succumb?

    Bluffed your hand all along, caught up in the

Web of pleasure, soon to be consumed by the black widow

Headlines read:

Double dead / suicide

Keep dragging the baggage of our father's lies and

Make their spirit alive, entertainment at the Mirage Hotel:

    Objects in Mirage…

May not be what they appear!

Stone cold love

In our youthful days we danced on clouds

    We surrendered all.

Even dreamt about making vows

The secrets and memories that we once shared.

I can't escape.

    Your scent from my bed

Shedding this callused layer of skin

    That's caused humming and vibrating.

    In my head

I've released this displeasure set from within

    Another 72 hours wasted away…

Crimes of passion

    What else could I say?

A bouquet of dead flowers, blank cards with empty or blurred words

All I wished was for you to stay.

    Now alone, I've paced this town.

With this blank (molded) look staring down

    My fever is running cold.

    With this stone-cold love

No longer to hold.

Across a Clouded Room

When you walk into a room, we are contracted.

Into each other's stare

The glaze of amazement and

Childish smiles (candy apples) All other motion goes:

Unnoticed, uncensored, undetected

As the silenced still frames

Become chiseled on my brain.

(Hard to contain) myself.

The energy remains.

A perfect bond that

Cannot be broke.

Stuck on this distant remote Dancing upon

A sea of smoke

Heaven & earth (when the stars are aligned)

Collide & stop lights.

Make you go blind.

Meet me at Second Cup

Once again, for a little while longer and

Join me for a cup of white hot.

See ya soon,

Across a clouded room

A Salute

A clear blue Alberta sky

Another cold mourning

With no foretold warning

Magnetic frost clinging to the trees.

Soon to be brought to our knees

Frozen into an open trap

As bullets riddled through our Canadian map

Once again…merry go round.

Tear drops coagulating the sands.

As we are handcuffed one more time

A lunatic crippling the laws of the land.

Nobody there to take your hands.

Four RCMP lay dead on the earthen floor.

Ushered out on the third of March 2005 These saints will remain alive.

We know your names as.

Leo, Brock, Peter & Anthony

Thank-you for standing on guard for thee Your spirit soars mightily I salute you!

First Day of School

The only faces that I see are (sad) scared, anguished & defeated.

Trying to escape from the bleak freedom that is being terrorized from them.

The joys of going to school for the day, clutching am old 1920's book and

Smelling the pages of time; a scent in my mind to be in an era were

I was somebody else; a soldier of fortune, a ballet dancer, someone, somewhere!

Wearing a secondhand uniform that is still missing a button.

With a washed away bleached stain. Oh, Mother Russia, Oh Father God

Where have you gone? What kind of men are we? Desensitized with

Contaminated minds. Choking down a muffin and a coffee as we indulge on

the aftermath of the morning news.

My P.O.E.M

Cocooned in black & white metaphors.

    Absorbed, indulged, obsessed.

Soon to break free and spread my wings.

Share to the world and color my graffiti of

What you mean to me

    Over & over painting rainbows of chocolate waves

Throughout the open spaces of wild daises

    Fluttering throughout creation

With my senses a whirl wind of kaleidoscope lollipops

    Seeing, touching, feeling, smelling & tasting your flower

The very essence of divine unity

    Come fly with me my...

Perfect Omniscient Every Moment

Oh Katrina

A maverick set loose

Cascading through open thunder When all elements collide,

    Katrina's power about to put.

    New Orleans under

Early warnings again ignored.

    Americans to proud to leave.

The wind is howling, waves battering upon

    Your shore, destroying all vanities that you adore.

The fragrance of death & disease is everyone's new odor.

    The tides are changing.

New world catastrophes

    Another open grave

Season's greetings

    From all Hurricanes

Daily Scoop

Unveiling pages in every city's newspaper

Forecast, low cloud cover, depressing.

    Dim & bleak with constant rain

Showering through the pain of

    Vexed hearts

Mumbling remains, grumbling graves.

As an old recorder skips through JFK's speech

    …ask not what your country

        Can do for you…

Shadow box strains of human clogged veins

    This just in…

Planet earth is no longer,

    Once a vibrant planet full of life, splendor & wonder

There were approximately 7 billion humans on

This planet that exploded into the universe today

There were no survivors, except those from the reality show.

Survivors 16 – To Mars and Back

    In other news Mars will play host to the next Olympics…

        Has anything changed?

Ctrl-Alt-Delete (Windows 05)

Apparently, there was a window of opportunity
    That existed and without
Hesitation you opened it.
      With a sting of compassion and prayer
        Full of venom
Your opaque style and fleshly desires
    A modern-day hero
Your signet ring pressed against waxed dolls,
    Cellophane wrapped tight.
      Around your brain
Visually impaired for all to see through.
    The pain of your soul

Sixth Sense

Twinkle…twinkle… a little star glazed.

Found your god of Eros.

Tarnished haloes

Polished coats of touch & smell

Pre-occupied your hands of mistrust.

Mouth to mouth prayers of drywall dust

Eyes watering sights of lust

Heard the voices.

Now you plagiarize.

Galaxies above to Sheol below

Found your god with bow & arrow.

(Heartless ego)

Played your eyes.

Caught you starring into hers

Color coated alibis sugar coated.

All but lies.

Tingling pleasures of the

Sixth Sense

$lot Machine

Weaknesses of a brother told to another.

    Held together we cover.

Recognized we've fallen.

    To yet another false idol

How much longer must I wander around this mountain?

Clear that haze that's encompassed my brain.

Standing alone in the midst of my daze

    I left behind.

Where I've wasted so many a wage on…

Scanned another dollar to hear me holler.

Echoing deep within the empty cellar

Processed no images.

    Here in this dark room

Plugged into a vacant picture.

    With no future to

    Hang on my wall.

Just another empty

    $lot Machine

Sweet Soul Sister

Twirling summer dresses
      Spinning round & round
Look at my new sister I have found…
High above the clouds.
      Don't wanna come back down.
Sleepless pajama parties sharing
      Our dreams and screams
            We always laughed so hard and
Peed our panties.
Our shadows became entangled,
      we were inseparable.
High above the clouds.
      Don't wanna come back down.
Running late, missed another mass.
Years gone by and skipped another class.
Holding hands & skimming stones
Jumping rope & stealing smokes
High above the clouds…
We've journeyed a million miles.
      With candy apple smiles
Life was so simple, come here so I can.
Pinch your dimple… one more time.
A Pink Lime Christmas, a penthouse party or
      A concert lest we forget.

Sharing tears at the Tragically Hips

    Farewell show

Storm clouds blew in and still.

    The innocence of the once little girl

    Dancing with her tongue out

    Catching snowflakes & smiling

Like it was her first time…

As I tuck you in and say good night

    We whisper and sing together.

'We had joy, we had fun…we had

    Season's in the sun.'

Until we meet again

    My Sweet Soul Sister

(Dedicated to the memory of Janice R I P 01.22.18)

R I P – Neil Peart (01.07.20)

Travelling through the Limelight…

I find myself in disbelief, just a lad.

My ears in tune when I first heard you.

(Rush) fly by night & 2112

How you could fill the void with multiple beats

    Crashing cymbals, again fast as lightning

    Methodical and in synch

    A conductor at the throne…

Captain Neil Peart, not merely a player

He was a top performer & portrayer.

Lived his Universal Dream

    Was today's Tom Sawyer, Working Man and

New World Man

    Orchestrated and demonstrated too always.

    Be the best…

Never missed a beat.

Over forty years of progressive Canadian Rock success

The iconic drummer

    Whom everyone fashioned them.

    Air drums and became followers after!!!

To one of the best drummers of our time…

What a cold thought

Gov't made agenda.
      Flags no longer wave,
      Created a super virus for
      Yours and my grave
Across a grid locked nation
Keep the masses on their knees.
Stored in self-contained isolation.
      Soon the military will shove.
      There way as they please...
Minions grounded with a
      Summertime curfew
This changes everything, no going back.
Tribal drums beating the earthen floor.
O'er & o'er the distant shore
Can't stop the rhythmic beat
      Shutting all the doors!
Echoing throughout the streets
Tanks rolling on one by one.
Innocence that was out
      Trying to have some fun...
Mirror, mirror on the wall
Our political leaders
      Making this damn judgment call,
Given this day.
      We walk the same game.

Mannequins, robots

    Who's got my strings?

Getting your wires crossed

Our veterans fought to bring us free

Now who? Who can it be?

    Is at the Helm

W.H.O now will bring us down.

    3…2…1…

Can you understand the difference?

Waking up with your face

    Pressed against the clock,

Left without a Tic Tok

    …What a cold thought!

In Dew Time

Slipping away into the Abyss of our thoughts

Our yesterdays, and all of our tomorrows

Trickles of a melted ice cube held in the palm of my hand.

Watching you desperately craving the next desired drip of moisture

That has already soaked through your summer dress.

All that lie beneath the artist, grass-stained canvass from the seventh green.

Of a picture-perfect painting of an innocent young woman

with lightly brushed rouge cheeks

Desired rose petal lips and those inescapable eternal kisses

That makes our mouths tickle and dance inside.

Waltzing along freshly watered fairways,

Moon beams glistening, as we stroll along hand in hand sharing All that we

have, all that we surrender, I'm yours whole-heartedly.

G'night...

I know...
>We watched.
>
>Sun rises & sunsets.
>
>My dream desire was.
>
>Starring at you
>
>Catching those heavenly rays &
>
>Moon beams
>
>Reflecting your beauty
>
>Sparkling champagne eyes

I know...
>We shared laughter & stories.
>
>Even times we had our wrongs.
>
>I hope I played the right.
>
>Country song...
>
>Our Lil' angel
>
>Caught us by surprise.
>
>Let me wipe the teardrops.
>
>From your eyes

I know...
>"I'll see you later tonight."
>
>Driving back was a mystery.
>
>Didn't know this was to be.
>
>My destiny
>
>I held your picture on the phone.
>
>Thought I made it home...
>
>Just fell asleep in your arms and spoke.
>
>"I love you more."
>
>It felt so right and whispered ...
>>G'night.

So Ordinary

Borders between

We crossed paths Endless texts.

Who shares next?

Glory…

Truth, we fall, we laugh.

Lol…

Open heart

Distance apart

With love…the arts

Dreams of life

Dissipating screams

Inner silence of regret

Have we met?

Close our eyes.

Imagine…

That place

With your grace

Dancing along

Shadow dancer

With the night moon

Raindrops shower down.

Wash away the cares

Rising sun

Simple

Gentle warm breeze

Blows the sheer curtains

Brushing the silhouette.

As she lay on the canvass small hairs arise

With a tickle and a smile

Ohhh goddess

The scent of a fresh day

So ordinary

Word up...

As I finish up and conclude on writing this book, I'm reminded of this accident I had outside a city cemetery in 2012 where I worked and a co-worker and myself were waiting for a funeral to arrive so we could usher them in and show them where the burial location was, as we were waiting on the wrong side of the road (it was a dead end road – no pun intended) a truck passed by us as we were talking in the little truck waiting, only minutes passed by and we were nose down in the ditch about eighty feet from where we were waiting, anyway the driver of the said truck that passed by us realized it was a dead end and turned around dropping his cell phone and while reaching for his phone steered his truck into ours crashing into us.

Long story short I was concussed and needed to get checked out in the hospital, going through therapy and the months after getting analyzed by the professionals the brain doctor put into his report that I wasn't educated enough to write poetry or be smart enough to be an artist, that was basically his so-called degree earned opinion, anyway, I laughed and thought instantaneously about not only the movie 'Dead Poets Society' starring the late great Robin Williams as the teacher of the poetry class in Oxford whereas he was teaching the students to be 'free thinkers' and the school was in an uproar over his teaching skills and was frowned upon, and the thousands of musicians and artists who have written many, many lyrics and songs without stepping foot in a school.

What I'm getting at is, you don't need to listen to people's negativity and thoughts of you're not good enough to be doing anything creative or artistic, eliminate those people from your life and continue your own path whatever it may be, passion and desire can always trump any certificate or degree, hell even the 100 rule can help you, eighteen minutes a day at anything you want to learn and practice is all that it takes, if you have the will power to do that 18 minute a day rule for a year, you'll become better than eighty five % of the population, fan-fucking-tactic!!!

So I implore and encourage you if you have grown up and have been stuck in the mentality that this is it, this is what I've been dealt so I'm going to stay here in this situation, you don't have to stay there, you have the ability to move mountains and move beyond your present state. Just like myself, it doesn't matter how long it takes, follow your heart, and don't wait until you come to a crashing halt in the fast lane of life to wake up.

Thank-you to everyone that believed in me and my abilities to finally see this project (Fast Lane in a 97th pool hall) through and a BIG thank-you to everyone at Prime Seven Media for helping me through some obstacles and hic-cups. Hopefully, we can meet and enjoy a conversation with a cup of java.

Printed in the USA
CPSIA information can be obtained
at www.ICGtesting.com
JSHW020746031124
72874JS00001B/3